HARD RIGHT

HARD RIGHT

The New White Power in
South Africa

JOHANN VAN ROOYEN

I.B. TAURIS PUBLISHERS
LONDON · NEW YORK

Published in 1994 by
I.B. Tauris & Co. Ltd
45 Bloomsbury Square
London WC1A 2HY

175 Fifth Avenue
New York
NY 10010

In the United States of America
and Canada distributed by
St Martin's Press
175 Fifth Avenue
New York
NY 10010

A full CIP record for this book is available
from the British Library

Library of Congress Catalog card number: 94–60177

A full CIP record for this book is available
from the Library of Congress

ISBN 1–85043–818–8

Photoset in North Wales by
Derek Doyle & Associates, Mold, Clwyd.
Printed and bound in Great Britain by
WBC Ltd, Bridgend, Mid-Glamorgan.

Contents

List of Abbreviations

AB	Afrikaner Broederbond
AGB	Afrikaanse Gereformeerde Bond
AKB	Afrikanerkultuurbond
ANC	African National Congress
APK	Afrikaanse Protestante Kerk
AV	Afrikaner Volkswag
AVBOB	Afrikaanse Begrafnis Onderneming Beperk [Afrikaans Funeral Undertakers]
AVF	Afrikaner Volksfront [Afrikaner People's Union]
Avstig	Afrikanervryheidstigting [Afrikaner Freedom Foundation]
AVU	Afrikaner Volksunie [Afrikaner People's Front]
AWB	Afrikaner Weerstandsbeweging
AZAPO	Azanian People's Organization
BBB	Blanke Bevrydingsbeweging [White Liberation Movement]
BKA	Boere-Krisisaksie [Boer Crisis Front]
BNB	Blanke Nasionale Beweging [White National Movement]
BRA	Boer Republican Army
BSP	Boerestaat Party
BWB	Boereweerstandsbeweging [Boer Resistance Movement]
CCB	Civil Cooperation Bureau
CNE	Christian National Education
Codesa	Convention for a Democratic South Africa
CoG	'Committee of Generals'

Cosag	Concerned South African Group
COSATU	Congress of South African Trade Unions
CP	Conservative Party
CVO	Christelik Volkseie Onderwys [Christian People's Education]
DP	Democratic Party
DRC	Dutch Reformed Churches
EPG	(Commonwealth) Eminent Persons' Group
ESCOM	Electricity Supply Commission
FAK	Federasie van Afrikaanse Kultuurverenigings [Federation of Afrikaner Cultural Societies]
FOSA	Federation of Parents' Associations
HNP	Herstigte Nasionale Party
IFP	Inkatha Freedom Party
INSA	Institute for Strategic Analysis
KWV	Ko-operatiewe Wijnbouers Vereniging [Cooperative Vintners' Society]
M&M	Market and Opinion Surveys
MI	Military Intelligence
MWU	Mineworkers' Union
NCP	National Conservative Party
NP	National Party
NRP	New Republic Party
OB	Ossewa Brandwag [fascist Afrikaner organization]
OFS	Orange Free State
PAC	Pan African Congress
PBKG	Pretoria Boere Kommando Group
PFP	Progressive Federal Party
PWV	Pretoria–Witwatersrand–Vereeniging
R	Rand [unit of currency]
RSC	Regional Services Councils
Rumosa	Republican Unity Movement of South Africa
SAAF	South African Air Force
SAAU	South African Agricultural Union
SABC	South African Broadcasting Corporation
SABRA	South African Bureau for Racial Affairs
SACOL	South African Confederation of Labour
SACP	South African Communist Party
SADF	South African Defence Force
Sanlam	South African National Life Assurance Company

Santam	South African National Trust and Assurance Company
SAP	South African Party
Spro-cas	Study Project on Christianity in Apartheid Society
SWAPO	South West African People's Organization
TAO	Transvaal Afrikaans Parents' Association
TAU	Transvaal Agricultural Union
TEC	Transitional Executive Council
TG	Toekomsgesprek [lit. Discussion for the Future]
TMA	Transvaal Municipal Association
TPA	Transvaal Provincial Administration
UDF	United Democratic Front
UP	United Party
Vekom	Volkseenheidskomitee [People's Committee for Unity]
WAM	World Apartheid Movement
ZAR	Zuid-Afrikaanse Republiek

List of Tables

Acknowledgements

This book is an edited and updated version of a research project which commenced in 1989 at the Department of Political Studies at the University of Cape Town. My first word of thanks therefore is to Professor David Welsh, under whose supervision and guidance the bulk of the research has been completed, and who has been the single most formative influence on my academic development since my undergraduate years. Professor Welsh was a constant source of encouragement, suggestions, constructive criticism and contacts, all of which proved invaluable for the success of the project. My sincere thanks also to Professor Annette Seegers, Chair of the Department of Political Studies at the UCT, for her help on methodology, and especially to Professor Hermann Giliomee, whose insights on the nature of Afrikaner ethnonationalism have been of great help to me in locating the 'white right wing' within a theoretical matrix, and who kindly agreed to comment on the first draft of this book. I am also indebted to Professor Jack Spence of the Royal Institute of International Affairs in London, who examined the original dissertation and on whose recommendation it was submitted for publication.

My sincere gratitude is also extended to Dr Lester Crook, commissioning editor at I.B. Tauris, for his encouragement, invaluable advice and support throughout, as well as to the editorial staff at I.B. Tauris, namely Sally Crawford, Ruth Thackeray, Helen Simpson and Emma Sinclair-Webb, for their efforts in converting the manuscript into book form. I am also indebted to Gilbert Boehm in Canada, whose computer expertise helped to facilitate this project.

Finally, I would like to extend my sincere gratitude and thanks to my parents, Renier and Alice, for their endless encouragement and financial support, and to my wife and most amicable critic, Janet, for her love and patience.

Preface

This book is an extension of a research project resulting in a doctoral dissertation at the University of Cape Town's Department of Political Studies, on the politics of the white right wing in South Africa. The project commenced in February 1989 and continued for a period of five years, incorporating events up to and including the run-up to South Africa's first non-racial democratic elections scheduled for April 1994. The dramatic political developments which began shortly after this project was launched have altered the political landscape in the country in a most profound and fundamental manner. South African society today, with majority rule imminent, is hardly recognizable as the same country that languished in despair in the grip of the steel-fisted authoritarian rule of the P.W. Botha regime, with all the major pillars of apartheid intact and white domination still firmly entrenched.

Meanwhile, apartheid has been dismantled and most white South Africans have acquiesced in the prospect of a racially integrated society in which they would play only a minor role. This book, however, focuses on that right-wing core group of almost one-and-a-half to two million Afrikaners and other whites, whites who have either failed psychologically to separate themselves from their racist past or are clinging to nationalism as their last link to ethnic distinctiveness and for security in a racially integrated society and a black-dominated government.

This book approaches the right-wing phenomenon from a liberal orientation as a potentially disruptive element during and after the transitional process in South Africa. The premise is that far from being insignificant, the right wing presents a serious challenge and threat not only to the current government and the transitional process, but also to any democratically elected government in the new South Africa. As the growing violence and bloodshed of the early 1990s in South Africa and in divided societies elsewhere in the world have proven, ethnicity has permeative, passionate and tenacious qualities – in its politicized form ethnicity is related to xenophobic nationalism and racism and forms an explosive combination which has led to many instances of genocide, civil war and instability in whole subcontinents. The ideology which guides South Africa's right, although tainted by the racist legacy of its apartheid origins, conforms to all the requirements, and presents all the dangers, of an archetypal ethnonationalist ideology. The book concludes that the right wing is a special case in an already highly divided society, one for which extraordinary constitutional measures would be required, if only for the purpose of minimizing and regulating racial and ethnic conflict in a new South Africa.

South African politics have been in a state of rapid transition ever since F.W. de Klerk crossed his Rubicon on 2 February 1990, and are characterized today by an exceptional degree of volatility. The tragic assassination of Chris Hani in April 1993 is a salient example of how bullets can change history. When the policies and strategies of political parties are in constant flux, this can unleash unforeseeable forces. For this reason it should be stated that a book of this nature can only be up to date at the time of going to press. Nonetheless, the intention is to provide the reader with a framework within which to analyse and evaluate developments in right-wing politics in South Africa as the country enters the final leg of its long journey to a non-racial democracy.

A note on terminology:
The heterogeneity of the South African population and the diverse perceptions of the country's conflicts have long provided political scientists with considerable terminological problems. It is virtually impossible to manoeuvre through this ideological minefield without offending someone, somewhere. The practice in academic discourse on South African politics is generally to use 'race' to delineate differences based on colour, and

'ethnicity' to refer to cultural differences within racial groups. Although this approach is uncomfortably close to the ideology on which apartheid was founded, it is used in this book for the sake of clarity and without the intention of perpetuating any particular ideology. In particular, the term 'black' excludes the coloured and Indian communities, while 'Afrikaner' is equated with Afrikaans-speaking whites, and 'whites' refer to all those of European descent.

Chronology

1652   Jan van Riebeeck arrives at the Cape on behalf of the Dutch East India Company, the beginning of a Dutch colonial settlement which lasts until 1795. Over the next hundred years indigenous Khoisan people are assimilated or exterminated; Dutch settlers move away from Cape Town to make a living as farmers and become known as the Trekboers.

1795   Britain occupies the Cape as caretaker for the Prince of Orange, driven into exile by Napoleon.

1803   Britain turns over the Cape to the Batavian Republic.

1806   After the Batavian Republic sides with France, Britain again occupies the Cape. British forces defeat a small opposing Dutch army in Cape Town; the European population in the Cape now numbers approximately 60,000.

1814   The new British governor of the Cape, Lord Charles Somerset, encourages British settlement in the eastern Cape. In 1820, 4,000 British subjects arrive at Albany.

1815   An Afrikaner farmer, Frederick Bezuidenhout, is killed trying to escape arrest for allegedly maltreating his servants; about 60 colonists rebel against the colonial government (the Slagtersnek Rebellion). The bungled execution of the leaders creates the first Afrikaner martyrs and causes great resentment among Afrikaner farmers against British colonial rule.

1836–40 British frontier policy and resentment of the interference by missionaries lead to the Great Trek, a large-scale Boer migration from the eastern Cape to

the region known as Natal and the interior, opens up
the northern half of South Africa to European settlers
after numerous military confrontations with the many
black tribes who already occupy the territory and their
eventual subjugation.

1838   Defeat of the Zulus at the Blood River, one of the most
decisive events in the history of Afrikaner nationalism.
The Boers make a vow to honour God perpetually
should they be victorious; 16 December celebrated by
Afrikaners ever since as the Day of the Covenant.

1839   Founding of the independent Republic of Natalia.

1843   Britain annexes Natal and a Boer republic is
established in the Transvaal the following year.

1852–54 Britain recognizes the Orange Free State and the
South African Republic (Transvaal) as independent
republics through the Sandrivier and Bloemfontein
Conventions. Both constitutions contain a clause
which stipulates that no equality would be allowed
between white and black, either in church or in state.

1860   The first Indians arrive in South Africa to work as
indentured labourers on Natal sugar plantations.

1866   Diamonds discovered in Kimberley.

1877   Transvaal is annexed by Britain in spite of opposition
by its *Volksraad* (parliament).

1879   Zulus defeat British forces at Isandhlwana, leading
eventually to the destruction of Zulu power at Ulundi
and the annexation of Zululand by Britain.

1881   British forces defeated by the Boers in the Battle of
Majuba (Transvaal); Transvaal independence restored
after what becomes known as the First Boer War/First
War of Freedom.

1886   Gold is discovered on the Witwatersrand in the
Transvaal.

1895   The Jameson raid, an attempt secretly sponsored by
Cecil John Rhodes, the prime minister of the Cape, to
take over the Transvaal by force, fails.

1899–   Second War of Freedom (the Anglo-Boer War) breaks
1902   out; defeat of the two Boer republics, leading to the
Treaty of Vereeniging. Almost 28,000 Boer women
and children, along with almost 14,000 blacks, die of

disease in concentration camps run by the British.

1907   M.K. Gandhi leads a campaign of nonviolent resistance in the Transvaal in response to the oppression of the Indian population.

1910   Union of South Africa formed from the former Boer republics, the Cape Colony and Natal. New constitution virtually ignores black political rights and enshrines racial discrimination.

1912   South African Native National Congress founded with Sol Plaatje as its general secretary; renamed the African National Congress (ANC) in 1923.

1913   Land Act passed, allocating 13 per cent of the country's land to blacks.

1914   National Party founded under leadership of J.B.M. Hertzog.

1918   The Afrikaner Broederbond is founded to promote Afrikaner nationalism – membership is secret and restricted to white Afrikaner males of good financial standing, a restriction that stayed in place until 1993.

1919   Jan Smuts becomes prime minister.

1924   The NP, in coalition with the Labour Party, forms the 'Pact' government with Hertzog as prime minister.

1925   Afrikaans becomes an official language of South Africa.

1927   South Africa receives its own flag alongside the Union Jack.

1931   Statute of Westminster gives the Union parliament complete legislative sovereignty.

1934   United Party (UP) formed under leadership of Hertzog. Many Afrikaner nationalists refuse to support the fusion process and form the 'purified' *Herenigde* National Party (HNP) under leadership of D.F. Malan.

1936   Provisions of the Land Act strengthened and black (property owning) voters disenfranchised.

1938   Centenary anniversary of the Great Trek.

1939   South Africa joins the Allies in the Second World War; large-scale opposition from Afrikaner nationalists. Hertzog resigns and Smuts becomes prime minister.

1941   J.F.J. van Rensburg becomes commandant-general of the Ossewa Brandwag (OB), the most important of the fascist Afrikaner organizations.

1947–48 The Natal and Transvaal Indian Congresses unite with the ANC to fight racial discrimination.

1948 D.F. Malan becomes prime minister and oversees the first purely Afrikaner government. The era of apartheid starts with the introduction of the Mixed Marriages Act (1949), the Immorality Act, Group Areas Act and the Population Registration Act (1950), and the Reservation of Separate amenities Act (1953).

1952 Albert Luthuli becomes president of the ANC; launches a defiance campaign under Nelson Mandela.

1953 The Bantu Education Act ensures the racial segregation of education.

1954 Malan resigns, J.G. Strijdom becomes prime minister.

1955 Freedom Charter, a set of guidelines for a non-racial South Africa, launched.

1956 Arrest of 156 leaders of the ANC for treason; all acquitted over the next four years.

1958 The 'father' of apartheid, H.F. Verwoerd, succeeds Strijdom as prime minister.

1959 The Promotion of Bantu Self-government Act provides for self-government of black homelands; 'Africanist' Pan African Congress of Azania (PAC) founded under leadership of Robert Sobukwe.

1960 Harold Macmillan, in his 'winds of change' speech to the South African parliament, declares that Britain would never support apartheid. Referendum held among whites on transforming South Africa into a republic – won by small majority of about 75,000. In Sharpville 69 black protesters killed during a pass-law protest.

1961 South Africa becomes a republic and leaves the Commonwealth. Luthuli awarded the Nobel Peace Prize.

1962 Mandela arrested in Natal; sentenced to five years in prison for incitement and for leaving the country illegally.

1963 Eight ANC leaders arrested at Rivonia.

1964 Rivonia trialists, together with Mandela, receive life sentences on conviction for sabotage.

1966 Verwoerd assassinated during parliamentary session; succeeded by B.J. Vorster.

1970   The Bantu Homeland Citizenship Act decrees that all blacks, including those outside the homelands, will be a citizen of one of the ten homelands.

1973   Strikes by black workers in Natal lead to the formation of black trade unions throughout the country. The right-wing neo-Nazi Afrikaner Resistance Movement (AWB) founded by Eugene Terre Blanche.

1975   Angola and Mozambique obtain independence from Portugal; South African Defence Force invades Angola.

1976   The Soweto uprisings lead to the death of over 600 blacks.

1977   Black Consciousness leader, Steve Biko, dies after police torture while in custody.

1978   Vorster resigns over the 'Information Scandal'; P.W. Botha narrowly defeats the more right-wing Connie Mulder for the post of prime minister. Andries Treurnicht becomes leader of the NP in the Transvaal.

1980   Zimbabwe gains independence.

1982   In protest at Botha's power-sharing proposals, 22 MPs leave the NP to found the Conservative Party (CP) under leadership of Treurnicht.

1983   The SADF launches pre-emptive counter-insurgency attacks on ANC bases in Angola, Mozambique and Lesotho; the ANC causes great destruction and 19 deaths with the bombing of the Air Force headquarters in the heart of Pretoria. The tricameral power-sharing constitution is approved by 1.36 million white voters, while it is rejected by almost 700,000 voters. The United Democratic Front, an umbrella organization for 600 anti-apartheid organizations, is formed.

1984   Anglican Bishop, Desmond Tutu, receives the Nobel Peace Prize. Massive black protest against tricameral constitution erupts in the Vaal Triangle and spreads to most areas of the country, resulting in soldiers being sent into black townships for the first time to help the police.

1985   The NP accepts in principle equal rights for all. In his hard-line 'Rubicon' speech P.W. Botha rejects foreign interference in South Africa's affairs; he neglects to

announce any new political initiatives, which result in
the collapse of the South African currency, a fleeing of
foreign capital and a refusal of foreign banks to roll
over loans of South Africa.

1986 Pass Laws are abolished, hotels and restaurants opened
to all races, and full property rights are extended to
blacks. Congress of South African Trade Unions
(COSATU) is founded, the country's largest predominantly black labour body.

1987 The first of the Rivonia trialists, Govan Mbeki, is
released from prison on compassionate grounds. In its
first general election, the CP ousts the PFP as the
official opposition in parliament. A delegation of 60
whites, under the leadership of van Zyl Slabbert of
IDASA, meet the ANC in Dakar, Senegal. On their
return they are accused of treachery by the government
and threatened with violence by the right wing.

1988 The ANC publishes its constitutional guidelines. Following an illness, Mandela is transferred from his cell to
a prison warder's house.

1989 After suffering a stroke P.W. Botha resigns as leader of
the NP (and is replaced by F.W. de Klerk) but stays on as
state president. Botha's wish to separate the posts of
party leader and state president leads to a power
struggle which culminates in Botha's resignation. In
Namibia, the liberation organization, SWAPO, wins the
general election.

1990 **February** F.W. de Klerk announces the unbanning of
the ANC and the lifting of restrictions on other
anti-apartheid organizations; Mandela is finally
released after 27 years in jail. **March** Namibia becomes
independent. **May** The first formal meeting between
the government and the ANC and the signing of the
historic 'Groote Schuur Minute', an agreement to
commence with peaceful negotiations. **June** The state
of emergency is lifted after almost four years. **July** The
predominantly Zulu Inkatha organization becomes a
political party, the Inkatha Freedom Party (IFP), and
violence between supporters of the ANC and IFP
spreads from Natal to the Rand. **August** The ANC and

the government meet for the second time, resulting in the Pretoria Minute, the suspension by the ANC of the armed struggle and a commitment by the government to allow ANC exiles to return to the country. **October** NP opens its membership to all races. **December** ANC holds its first legal meeting within South Africa in 30 years.

1991   **February** De Klerk announces the imminent repeal of the Group Areas Act, the Land Acts and the Population Registration Acts, the last pillars of apartheid. **May** The ANC suspends negotiations with the government. Winnie Mandela found guilty of kidnapping and accessory to assault on black children. **July** Nelson Mandela is elected president and Cyril Ramaphosa secretary-general of the ANC. **September** 24 organizations across the political spectrum sign the National Peace Accord. **December** Following the first plenary session of the multiparty Convention for a Democratic South Africa (CODESA), a Declaration of Intent is signed by all parties except the IFP and Bophuthatswana, outlining the basic elements of a post-apartheid constitution.

1992   **February** The NP suffers a major by-election defeat at the hands of the CP in the Potchefstroom constituency; government is forced to call a referendum to reaffirm its mandate to negotiate a new constitution on behalf of whites. **March** The NP/DP's 'Yes' campaign receives an overwhelming majority with 69 per cent of total votes. **June** The ANC launches a campaign of mass action, consisting of strikes, boycotts and protest marches. IFP supporters kill 47 pro-ANC civilians in the Boipatong township, resulting in the ANC's departure from CODESA. **September** 28 ANC protesters are killed by soldiers in the Ciskei, a nominally independent homeland under a black right wing dictator, Oupa Gqozo. The CP, AVU, Vekom, IFP and the governments of Ciskei and Bophuthatswana found a multiracial right-wing alliance, the Concerned South African Group (Cosag), with the aim of opposing bilateral agreements between the ANC and the government. **December** The government retires several senior security force officers and suspends others in response to attempts by elements within the SADF to undermine negotiations and the transition process.

1993 **March** A fully representative multiparty forum, including the IFP, the CP and PAC, begins 'talks about talks'. **April** The secretary-general of the South African Communist Party, Chris Hani, is assassinated by a member of the right wing at his home in Boksburg. Large-scale violence leads to the death of at least 72 people, including several whites. **May** A right-wing alliance, the Afrikaner Volksfront (AVF), is created from 21 right-wing groups under the leadership of General Constand Viljoen, a former chief of the SADF. **June** The multiparty negotiators establish the date for the first democratic non-racial general election as 27 April 1994. **September** The South African parliament approves the establishment of the multiparty overseeing body, the Transitional Executive Council (TEC). In response Mandela requests that the UN lifts sanctions against South Africa. **October** The CP, AVF, Ciskei, Bophuthatswana and IFP form the Freedom Alliance to fight for a federal constitution and greater regional powers. **December** The Freedom Alliance negotiates with the government and the ANC in a final attempt to reach a compromise regarding the interim constitution. On 24 December Parliament approves this, South Africa's first truly democratic constitution. F.W. de Klerk and Nelson Mandela jointly receive the Nobel Peace Prize.

1994 **January** Negotiations between the ANC, NP and Freedom Alliance fail to deliver a compromise agreement on greater regional autonomy, foremost of the right-wing demands. The AVF forms its own interim government with Ferdi Hartzenberg as president and claims Pretoria as capital of the Afrikaner *volkstaat*. **April** South Africa's first non-racial, democratic elections take place.

Introduction

Among the democratic forces in South Africa the tendency for many years has been to reject the right as an irritating but temporary hindrance on the road to a non-racial society, one which would gradually become irrelevant and would eventually disappear as processes of creating a non-racial society and of nation-building gained momentum. This line of argument corresponded with the modernization approach of the 1960s and 1970s which argued that ethnic identities would be replaced by the socio-economic forces inherent to modernization. In addition, some commentators pointed out that, even within the narrow confines of white politics, the right wing represented only about 33 per cent of whites, a proportion which would shrink to a maximum of about 5 per cent of voter support under a new constitution with universal franchise. This being the case, it was argued, why be concerned with an unsophisticated and insignificant group of racist extremists whose feet were firmly planted in the past? This was also the view held by most foreign observers of South African politics, even among those who have been bombarded with sensationalist media images of marauding gangs of right-wing thugs and of heavily armed 'troops' from the extreme right uttering threats of another 'Boer' war.

However, the assassination of the leader of the South African Communist Party, Chris Hani, by members of the right, and the forging of right-wing alliances across racial lines, have finally laid to rest ill-conceived notions that the right wing was irrelevant and that the transition to democracy was going to be peaceful. In the aftermath of the racial violence which erupted

1

following Hani's death in April 1993, the leader of the ANC, Nelson Mandela, warned that white extremists posed the biggest threat to peaceful change in South Africa – it therefore came as no surprise six months later that the leader of South Africa's largest political organization felt compelled to enter into negotiations with a group representing less than 5 per cent of the population, in an attempt to fend off a civil war.

Why, then, should an ostensibly insignificant group such as the white right wing, clinging to a discredited past and propagating seemingly illogical racial and nationalist solutions to South Africa's problems, be regarded as a threat to the prospects for peace in a country on the verge of democracy? To be able to answer this question and to understand the phenomenon of the white right in South Africa, all aspects of its multi-faceted nature need to be considered. Only then is it possible to comprehend the seemingly irrational character of its constitutional policies and to grasp the nuances behind its strategies. In addition to its historical, socio-economic and ethnic roots, one has to focus on the right-wing psyche in order to appreciate the forces which act as a powerful motivation to the right, i.e. racism, nationalism, a fear of losing economic privileges and social status, and the fear of genocide and anarchy.

This book attempts to address these issues by providing an historic overview of the driving force of right-wing politics, namely Afrikaner nationalism, and an objective analysis of interlinking issues such as racism, ethnicity and self-determination. The subject is approached through an examination of two dimensions of conflict: the intra-ethnic conflict between those Afrikaners on the right and those in the centre of the political spectrum over the issue of how the power of the state should be used to promote and protect Afrikaner identity and interests; and the right wing as a component in a racial conflict between right-wing Afrikaner nationalists and black nationalists.

Because of its multi-faceted nature and inherent contradictions, providing a definition of the white right is not a simple task. For the purposes of this study, however, the right wing can be defined as a segment within the white, and in particular Afrikaner, society which adheres to a specific ideology founded on the dual pillars of the separation of the white and black races and on Afrikaner nationalism. On a more theoretical level, the right wing could be analysed in terms of what Horowitz (1985) referred to as the collective drive of an ethnic group or subgroup for social status and power. From a right-wing point of view the only way in which to confirm and protect the status and identity of the Afrikaner and to prevent the group from being dominated by other ethnic groups and races is to exercise power through self-determination in an ethnically homogeneous territory. Horowitz's theory of group entitlement confirms the existence of an ethnic dynamic which places materialistic issues in a subordinate position relative to the striving by ethnic groups for status and power. It also explains why an ethnic group, or in the case of the right wing, a segment of an ethnic group, supports policies which appear incompatible with its own economic and political interests and sometimes contradict rational thought and civilized behaviour. These policies are conceived not in ignorance or wishful thinking, but are often the result of calculated economic and political sacrifices for the sake of ethnic security and status. This theme recurs throughout the book and forms the paradigm within which to understand and to evaluate all aspects of right-wing politics in South Africa.

Chapter 1 deals with the roots of the right wing. It commences with a review of the historic roots of Afrikaner nationalism, which involved a process of ethnic mobilization as enacted originally by the NP in the 1930s, and which was reinvented and perpetuated by the right wing during the 1980s. With Afrikaner nationalism being the driving force of the right wing, as it used to be in the case of the NP, a foundation exists on which to explain the historical origins of the right. As the NP expanded its narrow ethnic origins to incorporate a broader white nationalism in the 1960s and 1970s, and an even broader, territorially based South African nationalism in the late 1980s and early 1990s, it was left to the right wing to take up the cause of Afrikaner nationalism. This resulted in the intra-ethnic struggle over conflicting conceptions of the nature of the Afrikaner identity and the fierce rivalry between the NP and the right wing to capture the support and the loyalty of Afrikanerdom. The *broedertwis* (literally, conflict between brothers) can be divided into several stages, commencing with the Anglo–Boer War and culminating in the election of F.W. de Klerk as state president and the demise of Afrikaner hegemony and white domination in 1994.

The chapter goes on to discuss the economic roots of the right wing and addresses the question of whether the emergence of the right is class-related, in line with the seemingly universal phenomenon of lower socio-economic classes having a propensity towards racism. There is no doubt that the desire to improve the lot of the 'poor whites' played a role in the rise of Afrikaner nationalism in the 1930s, but the correlation between the present-day right and socio-economic issues is less clear. I then discuss the many theoretical attempts to provide evidence for such a correlation, in particular the contention that the founding of the HNP and the CP was a result of the perception among white workers and farmers that the government had forsaken them in favour of big business.

This is followed by an examination of the strength of the ethnic dynamic, i.e. the collective drive of the Afrikaner for social status and power. It also analyses the importance of primordial elements of Afrikaner ethnicity, such as language, religion, culture, and a shared history/mythology, and examines these with reference to how the right wing perceives and interprets its identity. The chapter concludes with a discussion of the concepts of racism and fear, the final elements which assist in the understanding of the roots of the right wing.

Chapter 2 constitutes primarily a description of the numerous organizations and categories of the right wing, with reference to the political orientation, leadership, strength, policies and strategies of the various parties and organizations. Although there are close to two hundred right-wing organizations, each with nominally different objectives and strategies, a unifying factor is their mutual subscription to the overall goal of Afrikaner and/or white self-determination in a separate territory. Although the newly founded Afrikaner Volksfront (AVF) is being perceived as the umbrella body of the right, the CP still represents the heart of the right wing, and the greater part of this chapter deals with this Party and its influence on white politics since 1982.

Chapter 3 deals with the electoral competition between the HNP, CP and the NP up to the suspension of whites-only elections in 1992. This is an important aspect as it provides an insight into the crucial struggle between the two major white parties over a period of ten years, for the support of the white electorate and, ultimately, control of the state. Chapter 4 focuses upon the right wing under the de Klerk administration between 1989 and 1993, and in particular its responses to the dismantling of the pillars of apartheid and the transition towards majority rule. This chapter also provides an analysis of the non-violent strategies of the right to oppose the NP's reforms and its position on violent resistance.

The book concludes with an overview of the prospects of the right wing as the country prepares for the first non-racial general election in its history and for the end of three hundred years of white domination.

1· The Roots of the Right Wing

Historical origins

The origins of Afrikaner Nationalism, 1902–66

As Afrikaners constitute over 60 per cent of the white population of South Africa, a high degree of ethnic political unity has traditionally assured their grip on political power. Hence the almost mystical qualities associated with *volkseenheid* [unity]. As the record shows, however, unity was not the result of some inherent propensity among Afrikaners, who on the contrary have historically always been prone to a factionalism whose roots have lain variously in provincial and regional rivalries, class divisions, ideological differences, conflicts between ambitious rival leaders and in combinations of these sources (Welsh 1988: 2).

The emergence of the contemporary right-wing movement in South Africa can be understood only against the background of the rise of Afrikaner nationalism. As indicated in the above quotation, an inherent characteristic of this particular form of nationalism was that it was never a monolithic movement and was plagued by many ideological, socio-economic and regional differences. Such differences had originated in the defeat suffered by the Boers at the hands of Britain during the Anglo–Boer War of 1899–1902, in the final stages of which deep divisions developed between the *bittereinders* and the *hensoppers* over whether or not to continue with the war. These divisions have continued ever since and provide an explanation of the bitter division among Afrikaners today. It seems sensible, therefore, to start this section by providing a brief overview of the evolution of Afrikaner nationalism and the accompanying tendency towards disunity. We begin with the period following the conclusion of the war in 1902 and focus on historical events which helped to shape Afrikaner nationalism and periodically led to the emergence of Afrikaner nationalist movements to the right of whichever government was in power at a particular time. The unfolding of almost 90 years of *broedertwis* is analysed from an intra-ethnic perspective, i.e. an ideological conflict within the Afrikaner ethnic group principally over how state power should be used to protect the Afrikaner identity and interests.[1] This led to two conflicting conceptions of the Afrikaner identity, with the one side in favour of an exclusive definition of Afrikaner nationalism, while the other promoted a broader white, and in recent years, an inclusive territorially based, non-racial South African nationalism.

The Anglo–Boer War and the disastrous consequences of defeat left the Afrikaners in the conquered Boer Republics a demoralized group of people who seemed destined to be absorbed by British culture, without ever having had a reasonable opportunity of establishing themselves as a distinct and coherent nation. The hopeless position of the Afrikaner at the conclusion of the Anglo–Boer War in 1902 was characterized not only by the destruction of their brief independence and economic prosperity, but also by a loss of confidence in their nationhood, their language, culture and sense of belonging.

As a result of the war, rural Afrikaners suffered extreme poverty, exacerbated by rural dislocation and decline. This led to the rapid urbanization of a people who had never known a form of subsistence other than the land. The poverty problem took on new dimensions in the cities as most of these Afrikaners lacked industrial and vocational education and ended up as unskilled labourers without much hope of promotion. Between 30 and 50 per cent of all Afrikaners were classified as 'poor whites' during the 1920s, amounting to a total of at least 300,000 by 1932, according to the Carnegie Report, a document which later guided the Hertzog government's efforts to uplift poor Afrikaners. Apart from their severe financial difficulties, social and psychological problems were rife due to the seemingly hopeless nature of their plight. In the cities Afrikaners had to contend with the superior status of their recent enemies, the English, whose culture and economic strength seemed overwhelming. In addition the deliberate Anglicization policy followed after 1902 by Alfred Milner, British high commissioner in South Africa, posed a serious threat to the continued existence of the Afrikaner culture and identity.

However, in the face of this adversity and the unfavourable comparison with the English, the stirrings of Afrikaner nationalism reappeared. The notion of being second-class citizens in their own country boosted Afrikaner nationalism and eventually led to 'ethnic mobilization', a process which started in the second decade of the twentieth century and ultimately led to the NP's victory in 1948. Its goal was the mobilization of Afrikaner nationalism in order to grasp political control in South Africa, and it relied on a two-fold strategy: on the one hand, it had materialistic appeal insofar as it offered distinct advantages to the various sections of Afrikanerdom such as farmers, businessmen and semi- or unskilled workers, and on the other, appealed to the status and psychological needs of the Afrikaner (Adam and Giliomee 1979: 61).

Having clearly defined their mission, namely the promotion of the Afrikaans language and literature, the creation of an Afrikaner-dominated republic, and overcoming Afrikaner poverty and inequality with English-speaking whites, the Afrikaners behind the process of ethnic mobilization succeeded in linking their activities through a network of informal voluntary organizations. The end result was a situation in which every institution of the Afrikaner community, including schools, the Dutch Reformed Churches (DRC), local officials, shop-keepers, voluntary societies and cultural organizations, mutually reinforced Afrikaner nationalism and cohesion.

Central to this process was the Broederbond and its role in the three-pronged strategy to promote and establish Afrikaner nationalism and to promote a separate Afrikaner identity by creating a consciousness among Afrikaners based on their language, religion and traditions. The Broederbond was founded in 1918 and its membership was restricted to Protestant Afrikaner males of sound financial standing in the economic, public and professional spheres of life. The organization emphasized the necessity of its secretive and confidential nature, and was divided into a network of cells countrywide, with a membership of 162 in 1925, which eventually increased to 11,190 members in 1978 (Serfontein 1979: 35). Its ideology was founded in the firm conviction in the divinity of its mission and that of the Afrikaner *volk*, as expressed so succinctly by its chairman in 1944: 'The Afrikaner Broederbond was born out of the deep conviction that the Afrikaner *volk* has been planted in this country by the Hand of God, destined to survive as a separate *volk* with its own calling' (cited in Serfontein 1979: 29).

At a cultural level the Broederbond was responsible for the creation in 1929 of the *Federasie van Afrikaanse Kultuurverenigings* (FAK) (Federation of Afrikaner Cultural Societies), which had the task of looking after the cultural interests of the Afrikaner and in particular the Afrikaans language. The revival of the language was a very important part of the process of ethnic mobilization and it played a crucial role especially in the cities where there was an overwhelming English dominance in all spheres of society. The translation of the Bible into Afrikaans (from Dutch) and new Afrikaans literature further stimulated interest in the language, and in 1925 it replaced Dutch as an official language of South Africa under the Pact government (the alliance between the NP and the Labour Party). There was always a close link between the language issue and Afrikaans churches and, as early as 1903, the DRC formed Christian National Education schools to counter the policy of Anglicization (Serfontein 1979: 39).[2]

Attempts by the Broederbond to address the backward economic and financial situation of the Afrikaners also contributed to the process of ethnic mobilization. It founded the *Helpmekaar* organization in 1914, originally to assist Afrikaners involved in the 1914 rebellion. A total of £190,000 was raised within a short period of time and eventually funds were channelled to the establishment of Afrikaner enterprises. These provided employment to Afrikaners and mobilized Afrikaner capital for further expansion, the idea being to establish Afrikaner-controlled businesses financed by the pooling of

Afrikaner capital resources (Adam and Giliomee 1979: 147). O'Meara (1983) described this process as *volkskapitalisme* (people's capitalism), i.e. an economic system whereby the means of production were owned by Afrikaners, who invested in and patronized Afrikaans enterprises, and were structured to employ and care for Afrikaner workers. Large Afrikaner-owned conglomerates such as Nasionale Pers, Santam and Sanlam were founded between 1915 and 1918, and *Federale Volksbeleggings, Ko-operatiewe Wijnbouwers Vereeniging* (KWV) and *Afrikaanse Begrafnis Onderneming Beperk* (AVBOB) came into being during and shortly after the First World War, later followed by Volkskas banking group, the Rembrandt tobacco and liquor group and many others. Their success served to improve the self-confidence and collective wealth of Afrikaners and proved that Afrikaners, too, could be successful in fields other than agriculture.

However, while the process of ethnic mobilization succeeded in lifting the economic and cultural position of the Afrikaner, things were not running as smoothly on the political front. Although the idea of a separate Afrikaner identity survived the Anglo–Boer War, and indeed was strengthened by it, the immediate post-war period was characterized by disunity and *broedertwis* among Afrikaners. The differences between those who wanted unity with their English-speaking compatriots as well as to maintain links with the British empire, and those who were in favour of 'Afrikaner-first' policies, were almost as great as the differences between Afrikaners and English-speakers. The situation has been summarized as follows: 'But while [the English] failed to extinguish the idea of the *volk*, union in one government failed to extinguish the ancient tendency for Afrikaners to split into quarrelsome factions, each governed by a hero, a leader of substance' (de Villiers 1987: 249). The Cape Afrikaners under Jan Hofmeyer had their own party, the *Afrikaner Bond*. In the Free State the *Orangia Unie* party of J.B.M. Hertzog enjoyed the support of most Afrikaners, while the *Het Volk* party of Jan Smuts and Louis Botha was the major party in the Transvaal.

Initially the majority of Afrikaners voiced their opposition to the British occupation and Smuts, Botha and Hertzog refused to serve on Milner's Legislative Council in 1903, insisting on self-government instead (Davenport 1987: 234–6). In spite of this, attempts to reconcile Afrikaners and the English so shortly after the war were relatively successful, and the founding of the Union in 1910 and the South African Party (SAP) under the leadership of former Boer leaders, Smuts and Botha, lessened feelings of hatred and suspicion between the two white groups. The founding of the Union was a compromise between the ideologies of the two white groups, which envisaged the two white language groups flowing into one stream to form a single white nation.

The period of relative tranquillity among Afrikaners which accompanied the founding of the Union did not last very long and was soon interrupted by the reappearance of old political differences. Hertzog was a reluctant member of Botha's cabinet and, contrary to Party policy, he strongly believed in the preservation of the Afrikaner *volk* as a separate entity and that South Africa should be ruled by Afrikaners. He advocated his 'two-stream' policy, whereby the two language groups should develop equally but separately from one another, and propagated a 'South Africa first' policy whereby the country should develop an independent political identity within the British empire. Hertzog's beliefs eventually resulted in his dismissal from the cabinet, and together with D.F. Malan he founded the National Party (NP) in 1914. The NP opposed South African participation in the First World War, but it did not actively get involved with the rebellion of 1914. The rebellion was led by former Boer leaders who opposed South Africa's participation on the side of Britain, and it virtually resulted in an Afrikaner civil war. The suppression of the rebellion by government troops (mostly fellow Afrikaners) caused much bitterness and created further divisions among the *volk*, especially after the death of a number of heroes from the Anglo–Boer War and the execution in 1915 of an army officer, Jopie Fourie, who had joined the rebels without resigning his commission. The rebels accused the SAP of betraying its own people for the sake of the former enemy, an accusation frequently echoed by the right wing some 75 years later during the de Klerk era (see also 'Ethnicity and nationalism', below).

By 1918 the SAP under Smuts and Botha found that many Afrikaners had become supporters of Hertzog's NP. Hertzog realized that he could not defeat the SAP by himself, and was forced to enter into an alliance with the Labour Party (the so-called 'Dirty Alliance' or Pact government). The alliance defeated the SAP in 1924, and the Pact government ruled until 1933, although the NP won the 1929 general election on its own by a clear majority. The significant achievements of Afrikaner nationalism during this period included the official recognition of Afrikaans (as opposed to Dutch), the creation of a single national flag, the introduction of a 'civilized labour policy' and the employment of large numbers of jobless Afrikaners on the railways and other public institutions.

By the early 1930s the country had begun to suffer severe economic strain, which, together with Hertzog's problems with members of his own party, made his government's position increasingly untenable. Hertzog's more benign attitude towards the English-speakers and his attempts to heal the rifts between himself and Smuts resulted in his growing unpopularity within the NP, especially among the hard-line faction under the leadership of the future prime minister, D.F. Malan. The Broederbond also played a role in the growing opposition to Hertzog within the NP – the organization launched a campaign after 1926 to undermine Hertzog's leadership by supporting a Republican Union within the caucus and encouraging a rival leadership faction consisting of men like Malan, J.G. Strijdom and C.R. Swart (Davenport 1987: 321–2). To stave off apparently certain defeat in the next general election scheduled for 1934, Hertzog opted to join the opposition leader, Jan Smuts, in a unity government which included all parties. Initially this cooperation took the form of a coalition government between the NP and the SAP, but later the two joined to form the United Party in 1934, with Hertzog as prime minister and Smuts as his deputy. Malan led the breakaway of a group representing most of the Cape Nationalists, and founded the *Gesuiwerde Nasionale Party* (the Purified Nationalists, today's NP) in 1934. Malan argued that fusion was a betrayal of the Afrikaner *volk*, for the simple reason that it would force Afrikanerdom into a coalition with its arch-opponents, the English and the 'Rand capitalists'.

The Purified NP enjoyed the support of the Broederbond, who helped to consolidate an alliance of the 'Malanites' in the western Cape, the 'Purifieds' in the Transvaal (consisting of civil

servants, small farmers, teachers and the intellectuals of
Potchefstroom), and the management of Nasionale Pers and
Sanlam. The party's goal was total independence for South
Africa and the transformation of Afrikaner culture into the
dominant culture of the country. It also appropriated the
demand for a republic, a demand Hertzog could not pursue as
he could not afford to alienate the monarchist wing of the UP.

From the mid-1930s Afrikaner nationalism became more
aggressive, more ideological and more organized. As would be
the case almost 50 years later between the NP and the CP, an
intense struggle commenced for control of Afrikanerdom at its
grass roots, i.e. party branches, constituency and provincial
committees and candidate selection committees. The Purified
NP, with the aid of the Broederbond, took with it the core of
Hertzog's former party, and succeeded in establishing its
credentials as the champion of the Afrikaner cause by
organizing *Ossewagedenktrek* of 1938, a plan to retrace the path of
the Voortrekkers to commemorate the centenary of the Great
Trek.[3]

When Smuts decided to enter the Second World War in 1939
on the side of Britain, many of the old anti-British and
anti-imperialist sentiments were rekindled, which further
boosted the process of ethnic mobilization as many Afrikaners
once again refused to fight on the side of Britain. Apart from
causing new divisions between those Afrikaners supporting the
UP and those supporting the NP, the war caused further divisions
within the latter group, as the loyalty of Afrikaner nationalists
was divided between the NP on the one hand, and the
paramilitary organizations on the other, chiefly the *Ossewa
Brandwag* (OB) (literally, the ox-wagon sentries). The latter
promoted a local version of National Socialism and attempted to
sabotage South Africa's war effort as the organization believed
that its goal of a South African republic was dependent on a
German victory. The OB enjoyed considerable support among
Afrikaners, with nearly half-a-million members at its peak, in
spite of the fact that it faced determined opposition from Malan
and the future prime minister Hendrik Verwoerd. When
Germany's defeat appeared to be inevitable, its popularity began
to wane, with many of its members (among whom was another
future prime minister, John Vorster) joining the NP or the

Afrikaner Party of N.C. Havenga. By 1943 the Purified NP had become the most important representative of Afrikaner nationalism – it enjoyed the support of most of the Afrikaner intellectuals and had 25 per cent of the seats in parliament.

The Smuts government basked in the glory of South Africa's participation in the Second World War. Its position was temporarily enhanced by the prominence that Smuts enjoyed internationally and by the visit of the British royal family in 1947, a visit which left most Nationalists cold. However, complacency and the perception that the government's immigration scheme was an attempt to 'plough the Afrikaner under' made the UP vulnerable to the NP's determined efforts to dislodge it from power in 1948.[4] The NP further strengthened its electoral position by entering into an election pact with the Afrikaner Party and succeeded in enlisting the support of OB members at constituency level. The election campaign concentrated mainly on racial issues, with the UP being accused of promoting racial integration with its acceptance of the Fagan Report, which recommended that urban blacks be accepted as permanent residents in white areas and declared segregation to be impractical. In 1948 the NP was finally re-elected as the government with a total of 70 seats; nine further seats were won by the Afrikaner Party (later absorbed by the NP), and 65 by the UP opposition.

The NP's victory brought about the realization that the Afrikaners were now in a position to achieve everything they had lost in the Anglo–Boer War. The NP made it a priority to maintain Afrikaner unity and to 'cement the *Volksbeweging*' (people's front), i.e. to bring closer together the party, the government and other Afrikaner organizations like the Broederbond, the Afrikaans press, the Reformed Churches, Afrikaner business and trade unions (Adam and Giliomee 1979: 116). With Malan as prime minister, the NP was projected as the 'mother' of Afrikaner national consciousness and as the protector of rights, privileges and status that came with its new role as government. As the NP's parliamentary majority was fragile its most important task was to consolidate its position.[5] To strengthen its support among Afrikaners it introduced measures aimed at promoting Afrikaner interests, reaffirmed its commitment to the creation of a republic, and actively endevoured to reduce the English-speaking dominance in economic and political spheres. It also implemented stringent new racial laws and laid the foundation of the policy of apartheid with the introduction of the Mixed Marriages Act (1949), the Immorality Act (1950), the Population Registration Act (1950), the Group Areas Act (1950), and the Reservation of Separate Amenities Act (1953).

Despite the best efforts of the NP, however, signs of discord in the *Volksbeweging* were present from the start. The Afrikaans press became a source of disunity because various prime ministers were linked with different newspaper groups. Malan's relationship with the Cape-based *Nasionale Pers* caused a negative reaction among members of the Transvaal NP. Furthermore, Strijdom's and Verwoerd's Transvaal power-base and their association with the Transvaal-based *Perskor*, resulted in Nasionale Pers having to publish its own paper in the Transvaal to reverse its isolation and to spread 'Cape nationalism' in the Transvaal in order to counter the ever-growing dominance of the Transvaal Nationalists (Giliomee 1992: 345). Relations between the *Perskor* group and the NP also became strained in 1968 when Andries Treurnicht, editor of *Hoofstad* (a paper issued in Pretoria), used his publication to spread the 'pure message' of Afrikaner nationalism, thereby contradicting Vorster's new outwardly based foreign policy and reconciliatory approach to English-speakers (Schoeman 1974: 177).

Closely linked to differences between the Cape- and Transvaal-based Afrikaans press was the issue of regional or provincial Party differences, in particular between the Transvaal and the Cape: the NP consisted of four relatively independent provincial parties with their own leaders, bureaucracies and congresses, which led to a natural rivalry between provinces, often corresponding to the location of the power-base of a particular prime minister. To an extent the rivalry was also the result of historical factors, in particular the fact that it was mainly Cape MPs who had founded the *Gesuiwerde* NP in 1934 and who consequently felt that they could lay claim to ideological and logistical superiority over the Transvalers. On the other hand, the Transvaal's greater population, greater number of seats and dominant economic position, resulted in the Transvaal NP regarding itself as the logical power-base of the NP, a situation which placed the leader of the NP in that province in a very powerful position during the election of prime ministers. After Malan's retirement in 1954, most of his successors, Strijdom, Verwoerd, Vorster and de Klerk, were from the Transvaal (the exceptions being Malan and Botha).

With some English-speaking support, Verwoerd managed to win the referendum in 1960 on the creation of a republic. By achieving this long-standing Afrikaner ideal, there was no disputing the fact that Afrikaners had established their dominant position in South African politics. By this time Verwoerd had completed the formulation of the policy of 'grand apartheid', which intended to turn the whites into a majority in South Africa by making all blacks citizens of 'independent' homelands. In 1966 the NP won its largest victory ever (126 seats in parliament and almost 58 per cent of the vote), which indicated that its policies had achieved appeal even among some English-speaking voters. Verwoerd was assassinated in the same year and, with the election of Vorster as prime minister, the uneasy unity in Afrikaner ranks was soon ruptured.

The period 1966–82

The founding of the Herstigte Nasionale Party (HNP) in 1969 was merely the expression of the deeper ideological differences between the *verkramptes* and *verligtes* which had existed within the NP for most of the 1960s and led to the breakup of Afrikaner hegemony. The terms *verlig* and *verkramp* had been coined in 1966 by Willem de Klerk to distinguish between those Afrikaners who resisted any structural changes to apartheid and those who believed that apartheid should adapt to changing circumstances.

The struggle between these two groups for control of the NP had been present, albeit in a muted form, even before Verwoerd's death, but increased in intensity under Vorster. The early *verkramptes* were so caught up in the Verwoerdian slipstream that they felt any modification of his policy to be downright betrayal, a situation which led to severe tension between this faction under the leadership of Albert Hertzog and the relatively more relaxed approach of Vorster (Davenport

1987: 423–4). Shortly after his election as prime minister, Vorster initiated the relaxation of certain petty apartheid laws affecting segregated sport, segregated hotels, separate bus queues, etc. He also dropped previous opposition to admitting foreign black diplomats to South Africa and made approaches and guarantees to English-speakers in an effort to strengthen his electoral base. These developments were symptomatic of a scaling-down of 'Afrikaner-first' policies and resulted in an improvement in Afrikaans–English relations, although English-speakers were still largely excluded from government, with the exceptions of Frank Waring and A.E.G. Trollip in Verwoerd's cabinet.

The changes were seen by the *verkramptes* as the liberalization and subsequent betrayal of Afrikaner nationalism, the dismantling of the Afrikaner nation and the dilution of white supremacy. The *verkrampte* front consisted of three groups: firstly, the Hertzog group, consisting of several MPs and trade union leaders and other activists in all spheres of Afrikaner society, e.g. Albert Hertzog, Gert Beetge, Schalk Botha, Jaap Marais; secondly, those Afrikaners who remained in the background but kept close links with the Hertzog group, e.g. Piet Meyer, chairman of the Broederbond, A.P. Treurnicht, editor of *Hoofstad*, P.F.W. Weiss, chairman of SABRA and J. D. Vorster, brother of the prime minister and actuary of the DRC; thirdly, the so-called 'Purified' Nationalists, consisting of an informal pressure group within the NP and the 'Conservative Study Group' outside the NP, as well as other individuals who had left the NP during the early 1960s (Serfontein 1970: 19). A number of front organizations represented the *verkramptes*, such as *Die Genootskap vir die Handhawing van Afrikaans* (the Society for the Maintenance of Afrikaans), *Die Nasionale Raad teen die Kommunisme* (the National Council against Communism), *Afrikanerverdedigingsfonds* (Afrikaner Defence Fund), the SABC under its chairman Piet Meyer, *Die Kerkbode*, *Die Blanke Bouwerkersvakbond* (White Construction Workers' Union) and Hertzog's Afrikaner Order; among the newspapers representing the *verkramptes* were *Die Vaderland*, *Hoofstad* and the *S.A. Observer*. One of the first open instances of conflict between the *verligte* and *verkrampte* factions within the NP was caused by the *S.A. Observer*, whose editor, S.E.D. Brown, attacked the

'Afrikaner liberalists' (the *verligtes*), for wanting to subjugate 'people's conservatism'.

One of Vorster's biggest opponents turned out to be Piet Meyer, the *verkrampte* chairman of the Broederbond and the SABC, who viewed the government's new policies and the tensions it caused among Afrikaners with great concern. Meyer criticized not only Vorster's policies on sport and wider African issues, but also his personal style of governing, e.g. his passion for golf and his inclination to tell jokes at 'inappropriate occasions'. He made no secret of his desire to get rid of Vorster (Schoeman 1974: 39). Another critic of Vorster's policies was Andries Treurnicht, who used *Hoofstad* to launch his attacks on Vorster and the *verligtes*. In one editorial he disparagingly referred to Vorster's policy of rapprochement with English-speakers: 'There are few things that cause such dismay among Afrikaners as the disavowal of Afrikanerdom for the sake of cooperation with English-speakers' (cited in Schoeman 1974: 183) [translation].

In April 1969 Hertzog delivered a speech dealing with the influence of Calvinism on Afrikaners. According to Hertzog, only Afrikaners with their Calvinistic value-system could survive the 'onslaught against whites in Africa, since liberalism formed an integral part of the English-speaking psyche' (Schoeman 1974: 225–39). It should be noted that at the time the 'accusation' of being a liberal was a major insult in the eyes of an Afrikaner nationalist.[6] Hertzog's speech directly contradicted the official NP policy of rapprochement with the English-speaking whites, and although Treurnicht claimed that he could find no fault with it, Hertzog's speech was repudiated by Vorster. When the leader of the Transvaal NP, Ben Schoeman, described the *verkramptes* as 'little men', matters did not improve.

The final break occurred in September 1969 over the government's decision to allow the New Zealand rugby team to include a Maori in its tour of South Africa. The rebels from the HNP regarded this as a violation of South African sovereignty by 'bowing to foreign dictates' and as contrary to the policy of racially segregated sport. Hertzog and three MPs were expelled from the NP, but Treurnicht, who was expected to join them, backed out at the last minute – he defended his decision on the grounds that leaving the Party was not the right way to fight the

verligte direction of the NP leadership. Treurnicht's decision
soured the personal relationship between him and the HNP
leader Jaap Marais to such an extent that it became one of the
major obstacles in the way of unity between the HNP and CP after
1982.

The split in the NP in 1969 was largely caused by political
differences over segregated sport, immigration, homeland
independence and an outward-looking foreign policy, i.e. over
the purpose of the state and the goals of Afrikaner nationalism.
This is not to deny the fact that the HNP's support was
class-based insofar as it was rooted in the white working class,
impoverished farmers and a few smaller trade unions. However,
contrary to the contention (O'Meara: 1983) that the split was
caused by divergence between the interests of Afrikaner
agricultural capital associated with the petty bourgeoisie and
those of Afrikaner-controlled conglomerates, economic factors
played a secondary role in the events which led to the break-up
of Afrikaner hegemony. The fact is that the privileged position
of the white working class was not seriously affected until the
1970s when the government attempted to free black labour and
to narrow the size of the wage gap between races in the civil
service and in spending on social services. O'Meara's argument
is therefore more relevant to the 1970s when the restrictive
measures on black labour were lifted because of the ever-present
shortage of white manpower in all sections of the economy (see
also 'The socio-economic roots of the right', below).

Apart from the declining numbers of its working-class
support base, the HNP was severely hampered from its birth by
other factors as well. Vorster acted quickly to limit the damage
caused by the break-away and did not hesitate to use the full
force of the Party and the state security apparatus. He called a
general election one year before its scheduled date in an attempt
to deprive the HNP of time to organize itself, which resulted in
the Party losing all four of its MPs. Secondly, a vengeful NP
making a concerted effort to drive the HNP out of all influential
positions in the Afrikaner establishment relegated it to the
fringes of Afrikaner social life. The purging of HNP supporters
from the Broederbond in 1972 became probably the most
symbolic act that of the banishment of HNP members into the
political wilderness (Bekker and Grobbelaar 1987: 71).

Ironically Treurnicht, who was elected chairman of the Broederbond in 1972, did his utmost to purge the organization of HNP sympathizers.[7] Thirdly, the HNP became a victim of its adherence to an outdated ideology. The HNP revealed itself as rigid and sectarian in its appeal and concentrated on a return to stricter application of apartheid, stricter Sunday observance and stricter immigration laws and on propagating Afrikaans as the sole official language. As it tried to draw voters with slogans from a bygone era and an image similar to that of the NP in the 1930s and 1940s, the HNP failed to recognize that most Afrikaners shared in the rapid economic growth of the 1970s, resulting in a new class of Afrikaner with more cosmopolitan ideas and values.[8]

Although the immediate *verkrampte* challenge had been overcome with the decline in the HNP's support during the 1970s, the considerable number of *verkramptes* that remained within the NP, such as Piet Meyer, Koot Vorster and Treurnicht, resulted in a renewed build-up of tension within the party throughout that decade. The extent to which the ideologies of a leading *verkrampte* within the NP, Andries Treurnicht, coincided with those of his sworn enemy, the leader of the HNP, Jaap Marais, even several years after the 1969 split, is striking. For example, both strongly rejected the demand by *verligtes* within the NP to scrap social apartheid: 'Why should we spend all the money and make all the effort to segregate races constitutionally, if we scrap personal and social segregation between the same races?' (Treurnicht 1975: 25–8) [translation]; 'Liberal Nationalists who distinguish between justifiable grand apartheid [black homelands] and unjustifiable petty apartheid [social segregation], are ordinary liberalists who regard apartheid as a transition to racial equality. Apartheid in whatever form, is not a matter of pragmatism, but is a matter of principle' (Jaap Marais, as cited in Shoeman, 1980: 9) [translation].

A survey conducted in the late 1970s found a strong *verkrampte* element within the NP caucus in 1974 and in 1977: 35 per cent of members of the NP approved of job reservation, which coincided with the HNP's official policy; almost half of NP MPs held the same view as the HNP with regard to laws which regulated social relations between race groups; 16 per cent of NP MPs agreed with the HNP's view of the feasibility of a separate homeland for coloureds (Hanf et al 1981: 127–205). The *verkramptes* who remained inside the NP fought a rearguard action against reforms throughout the 1970s, but their influence was slightly curtailed when Treurnicht was replaced as chairman by Gerrit Viljoen in 1974, the latter being an outspoken *verligte*. However, outside the Broederbond, the position of the *verkramptes* was strengthened greatly by the election of Treurnicht as leader of the Transvaal NP in 1978 and his appointment as a member of the cabinet in 1979.

John Vorster's last few years as prime minister until his resignation in 1978 were marked by indecision and paralysis as he was overtaken by events such as the Information Scandal and the increasingly bitter conflict between the two factions within his party.[9] The minister of defence and choice of the *verligtes*, P.W. Botha, became prime minister after narrowly defeating the *verkrampte* candidate, Connie Mulder, by 98 votes to 74. Mulder was the unofficial crown prince tipped to succeed Vorster, but his involvement in the Information Scandal (also known as Muldergate) greatly harmed his stature and threw the *verkramptes* into disarray.

The election of the Cape-based Botha and the defeat of their candidate for the post of prime minister, left the Transvaal-based conservative element of the NP considerably weakened, and greatly intensified the discontent among the *verkrampte* wing. The leading figure of the Information Scandal later described Botha's rise to power as a 'coup d'état' by 'political assassins' (the *verligtes* in the Cape), not only to secure the post of prime minister for their candidate, but also to change the ideology of the NP and remake the Afrikaner, 'even if it meant ripping into his very soul' (Rhoodie 1989: 21–5). Vorster eventually took the post of state president, but was forced to resign a year later in response to the findings of the Erasmus Commission which reflected badly on his role in the Information Scandal. Mulder was also forced to resign as a member of the cabinet, as MP, and as member of the NP. He later founded his own party, the National Conservative Party (NCP).

The demise of Mulder's political career inside the NP paved the way for Treurnicht to become leader of the NP in the Transvaal in 1978. From then on most *verkrampte* discontent inside the NP would originate with Treurnicht, whose election could be construed as an act of revenge by the *verkramptes* for the defeat of their candidate for the post of prime minister. Treurnicht acted as a counterweight to Botha's reforms and fought his obstructionist battle against the reformist initiatives with the moral support of several right-wing movements which had sprung up in the late 1970s and early 1980s. These included Mulder's NCP, a revitalized HNP, the Afrikaner Weer-standsbeweging (AWB), the *Kappiekommando* and *Aksie-Eie-Toekoms* (the Front for a Separate Future).

Treurnicht's style of obstructing reform was characterized by his ideological conservatism, relentless criticism of perceived deviations from what he regarded as the official NP policy, and subtle efforts to replace Botha supporters with his own in influential positions of the Transvaal NP (Ries and Dommisse 1983: 75–107). Botha's election as prime minister did not reflect the true power balance between *verligtes* and *verkramptes* in the NP, as was evident from the difficulty he had in imposing his authority on the party, the caucus and the bureaucracy.

The *verkrampte* position was further strengthened over the next four years as a result of Botha's reforms. Botha's official position was that apartheid was a recipe for 'permanent conflict', and in his 'adapt or die' speech in 1979 he attempted to instil into many sceptical whites the urgency of political reform and warned them to expect a decline in the level of their privileges due to the socio-economic advancement of the black population. This speech became the official NP reformist slogan for the next couple of years. In 1979 he announced a 12-point plan which made provision for power-sharing between whites, coloureds and Indians and committed his party to the dismantling of racial discrimination. From 1976 onwards the government faced an increasingly hostile attitude from abroad in the form of sanctions and boycotts; every reform measure was seen as a concession to foreign pressure. An issue which further alienated the *verkramptes* was Botha's authoritarian personality and his management style, by which he centralized decision-making and transferred more power to technocrats and securocrats. This resulted in a deterioration in the grass-roots party organization and gave rise to the perception that the Party was losing its democratic mass base (Bekker and Grobbelaar 1987: 72).

Several other incidents events during the late 1970s and early

1980s brought the long-expected split between *verligte* and *verkrampte* closer to reality. In 1979 Treurnicht and a *verligte* Transvaal National Party MP, Louis Nel, became involved in a public argument over Nel's criticism of a joke told by Treurnicht at an NP function. On the insistence of the *verkrampte* wing of the NP Nel was expelled from the party because he refused to apologize to Treurnicht. Nel was allowed back into the party only after interventions on his behalf from *verligtes* in the Party, the prime minister himself and newspapers like *Beeld* (Ries and Dommisse 1983: 75–117). Treurnicht became involved in another controversy shortly after his appointment to the cabinet, this time for criticizing Piet Koornhof's 'Apartheid is dead' speech as not representative of party policy. In September 1979 Botha struck back by warning the NP leadership in the Transvaal 'to get their house in order', following a series of Transvaal by-elections in which serious inroads had been made in the NP majorities. He also defended his policy of rapprochement towards the coloured community and again warned Treurnicht indirectly that 'ministers should comply with the policies of the party and government or else resign' (Ries and Dommisse 1983: 75–117).

Treurnicht ignored Botha's admonition and soon became involved in another controversy, this time over the participation of a coloured schoolboy team in the Craven Week rugby tournament in 1980. When Treurnicht intervened on the side of the Transvaal Teaching Association's decision to prevent the coloured team from participating, Botha publicly repudiated Treurnicht's stance by insisting that 'attitudes which sour relations between coloureds and whites should be dropped without further ado'. Botha launched a further attack on Treurnicht a few days later when he emphasized that there could be only one leader in the country, no doubt referring to the fact that Treurnicht had taken it upon himself to interpret and determine government policy.

In response to what he regarded as unfair treatment of his provincial leader, another member of the cabinet, Ferdi Hartzenberg, handed in his resignation. He withdrew it only after lengthy negotiations in March 1982, when a provisional 'peace accord' was reached through the intervention of cabinet ministers F.W. de Klerk and Ben Schoeman. The result was that

Treurnicht, Hartzenberg and Koos van der Merwe pledged their allegiance to the party and committed themselves fully to support the leadership of P.W. Botha. Although the Craven Week tournament was completed with the participation of the coloured team, Treurnicht never changed his stance, and in fact, insisted a few weeks later that 'nothing has changed' (Ries and Dommisse 1983: 89–90). The uneasy truce was soon shattered by the contentious issue of power-sharing, a concept which referred to the proposed inclusion of Indians and coloureds in the parliament, albeit in separate chambers. These proposals had been formulated in 1977, and according to Treurnicht, they referred to three separate parliaments linked through a multiracial but white-dominated council of cabinets (Lemon 1987: 109–10). Treurnicht's interpretation differed from the 'healthy power-sharing' implied by P.W. Botha, according to whom there would be one parliament, for whites, coloureds and Asians. Differently put, Botha's view implied a form of power-sharing, while Treurnicht envisaged a division of power, and was convinced that this was what had been agreed to by the NP in 1977. Treurnicht had expressed his distaste of one system of government for all as far back as 1975: 'The change of direction demanded by certain Afrikaners, which implies ... one political dispensation for whites, coloureds, Indians and urban blacks, is not a change of direction but a reversal of direction, which would lead to political and social friction' (Treurnicht 1975: 74) [translation].

The bickering within the NP became unbearable, and in February 1982 the NP leadership decided to force a showdown with the Treurnicht group. During a caucus meeting a motion of 'full confidence and unqualified support for the prime minister, his leadership and his interpretation of NP policy' was introduced by a Botha supporter, Fanie Botha (Davenport 1987: 452). Twenty-two members refused to support this motion on the grounds that the concept of power-sharing was utterly foreign to Nationalist philosophy, that it diluted white and Afrikaner exclusivity, and that it would have a negative effect on the interests and survival prospects of the Afrikaner nation. To this Treurnicht added that he would support nobody 'unconditionally' except for God.

Although their resignation would have been the logical step

the Treurnicht group refused to resign from the NP, arguing that they, and not P.W. Botha and his *verligte* followers, represented the official NP policy. To break the deadlock, Treurnicht called a meeting in Pretoria of the Transvaal Head Committee of the NP, with the goal of obtaining the support of the NP's most powerful provincial branch. As part of a pre-arranged strategy to counter Treurnicht's challenge, Botha himself (who 'happened' to be in Pretoria at the time), although not part of the Transvaal Head Committee, was invited to attend the meeting. Botha's formidable presence helped to persuade the majority of the members not to back Treurnicht, and a motion of full confidence in Botha and his interpretation of the power-sharing proposals was carried by an overwhelming majority of 172 votes to 36 (Ries and Dommisse 1983: 153).

The events at the Transvaal NP meeting indicated that the scope of the rebellion was limited, and it signalled the end of the Treurnicht group as part of the NP. Treurnicht and Hartzenberg resigned from the cabinet, and they and 14 other MPs were expelled from the party, later to be followed by two more resignations. In March 1982 the Conservative Party (CP) was formed in Pretoria before a crowd of 8000 people, including delegates from 99 constituencies, members of the AWB, the Kappiekommando and the NCP of Connie Mulder; among well-known individuals were the former minister of justice, Jimmy Kruger, and the widow of the former prime minister, Betsie Verwoerd.[10] The CP took with it large parts of the organization of the NP, including almost one-quarter of the Transvaal district and branch committee members and an estimated 40 per cent of Afrikaner support (Charney 1984: 273–75; Lipton 1986: 319). The new party founded its own newspaper, *Patriot*, and initially enjoyed relatively sympathetic coverage from two Pretoria-based newspapers, *Oggendblad* and *Hoofstad*, belonging to the NP-supporting newspaper group, Perskor (Ries and Dommisse 1983: 195).

Elements within the leadership of the Broederbond, such as its chairman Carel Boshoff, were supportive of the Treurnicht group, even though Boshoff indicated in March 1982 that the Broederbond would not take sides in the conflict. Boshoff resigned shortly afterwards, but remained chairman of a Broederbond front organization, SABRA (the South African

Bureau of Racial Affairs – see Chapter 2), from which he attacked the implementation of power-sharing. Unlike SABRA, the FAK remained loyal to the NP, which resulted in the right wing having to found a separate cultural organization, the Afrikaner Volkswag (People's Guard), also under Boshoff's leadership.

Apart from divisions within the churches, educational and cultural bodies, the split in Afrikanerdom also reverberated in the business world in the form of clashes between *verligte* and *verkrampte* Afrikaner interests within companies and between companies. The Cape-based Sanlam and Nasionale Pers were solidly behind the *verligtes*, while in the Transvaal, Volkskas Bank and Perskor initially were more sympathetic towards the CP, as these firms had stronger ties with civil servants, farmers and the Afrikaner working class as a whole. Strong support for the CP was also found in the lower sectors of the civil service, whose members felt anxious about increasing competition from blacks. In the agricultural sector support for the two parties depended on two factors: firstly, the size of the particular farming enterprise – the NP was seen as favouring the big farmer over the smaller one; secondly, on regional differences – the northern farmers saw the Botha government as favouring the Cape and Natal export-orientated farmers over the Transvaal, Free State and Northern Cape food producers (Charney 1984: 275–76).

The socio-economic roots of the right

It is universally evident that lower-class people are more conservatively orientated towards changes in conventional behaviour patterns than people in the higher professional, income and educational strata are. Ignorance and faulty insights into the ways in which society functions and changes, coupled with a tendency to cling to any custom or system that protects survival-related interests, influence lower-class people to oppose radical social change to a greater degree than higher class persons (Rhoodie et al 1985: 327).

The argument put forward by Rhoodie et al corresponds to the findings of researchers elsewhere, for example, Simpson and Yinger (1985), who found strong evidence of a link between class differentials and prejudice; Westie and Westie, writing in

1957, found that lower-class whites in the USA expressed the greatest feelings of social distance from blacks; in 1955 Stouffer found that intolerance went up as position on the status ladder went down; and the National Opinion Research Centre in the USA (1972–80), found that attitudes of whites on racial intermarriage, school desegregation, interracial socializing, neighbourhood integration, became more tolerant as they achieved higher socio-economic status as measured by income or education (cited in Simpson and Yinger, 1985: 67).

One of the most distinctive features of South African society is the overlapping of race and class, with whites traditionally having among the highest incomes per capita in the world, while almost one-half of blacks live below the bread-line. With such strong differences between the economic positions of black and white, class-based theories concerning the correlation between capital and apartheid form a considerable part of the literature dealing with the causes of racial antagonism in South Africa. In this tradition, F.A. Johnstone has argued in the mid-1970s that white domination was a product of the system of production of which it formed a part; in 1973 Wolpe had argued that apartheid was a conspiracy between the Afrikaner capitalist class and Afrikaner workers to maintain African labour power as cheap labour through political repression, which increased the profits of the capitalists and guaranteed the position of the white worker in the labour aristocracy; and O'Meara (1983) explained the emergence of Afrikaner nationalism as a 'historically specific, flexible and differentiated response of various identifiable and changing class forces – in alliance to the contradictions and struggles generated by the developments of capitalism'. Although these class-based perspectives form an important part of the debate on the origins of apartheid, a critical discussion of them falls beyond the scope of this book, and it will suffice to say that class-based explanations tend to underestimate the important role of ethnicity and identity issues as forces in their own right, forces which cannot merely be reduced to or made subservient to class.

As indicated earlier, class differences among whites initially coincided with the divisions between the two language groups during the early part of the twentieth century, when Afrikaners, due to historical and structural factors, had occupied the lower end of the socio-economic stratum. Following the ethnic mobilization and the economic upliftment of the Afrikaner such class differences between the white language groups gradually disappeared and were replaced with class differences among Afrikaners within the *volksbeweging*. Although the HNP's breakaway in 1969 was largely the result of the growing disaffection among *verkrampte* Afrikaners with the political direction of the NP, the early signs of unhappiness among the Afrikaner working class, attested to by the largely working-class component of the HNP's support, were the precursor to the growing alienation of the white working class during the 1970s. Although this topic was briefly touched upon in the previous section of this chapter, a more thorough analysis is necessary to explain how the rift between the Afrikaner establishment and the Afrikaner working class developed and why the latter was so reluctant to form an alliance with the black working class (its supposed 'natural ally' according to Marxist theory) against capital.

Throughout most of the twentieth century a close relationship existed between white labour and apartheid. White workers actively promoted many apartheid policies, as preferential labour policies ensured their high wages and a very secure position. The efforts by white labour to exclude blacks from certain jobs were further boosted by segregationist policies implemented by the NP government after 1948 (even though white labour had benefited from racially exclusivist legislation ever since 1911). Preferential labour policies provided substantial benefits to white labour by putting whites at the head of the job queue, helping to solve the 'poor white' problem and protecting white wages from black competition. These policies were so effective that by 1970 the ratio between white and black wages was 21:1 in mining and 6:1 in manufacturing (Lipton 1985: 183–226). From the point of view of white labour, apartheid remained beneficial in that it provided an effective closed shop, avoiding competition from and undercutting by black workers, as well as providing preferential access to benefits such as housing, welfare, education, social status and access to the highest echelons of political power in order to protect these privileges.

However, by the mid-1960s rapid economic growth and the

widening gap between black and white wages encouraged capital
to attempt to reduce its costs by substituting black labour for
white. The ensuing struggle between white labour, capital and
the government over the elimination of the policies which
protected the privileged position of white labour, was fuelled by
a divergence of Afrikaner class interests due to the changing
socio-economic circumstances of its members. By 1970 the
Afrikaners' socio-economic composition had been transformed
from a group consisting mainly of farmers, workers and
lower-echelon bureaucrats, to a highly urbanized people, mostly
employed as white-collar workers. In the early 1970s only 15 per
cent of Afrikaners were involved in either agriculture or
blue-collar work, while 65 per cent were employed in
white-collar positions. The Afrikaner class structure then began
to coincide with that of English-speakers, and this expedited the
decline in their support for racist policies.

Between 1970 and 1987 the government's policies followed
and in some cases led to the socio-economic changes which
accompanied the changing power balance in the Afrikaner class
structure. According to Giliomee (1989: 118–25) these
socio-economic changes were a result of: firstly, a declining
white demographic base which led to a shortage of white
manpower in the public and private sectors and forced the
government to alleviate this shortage by implementing labour
reforms to open the reservoir of black labour; secondly, the
removal of restrictions on the training of black labour and
the setting up of a common industrial relations system changed
the racial profile of the labour market; and thirdly, economic
stagnation and efforts by the public and private sectors to
redistribute wages in favour of blacks led to a decline in the
white share of total personal income. The decline of apartheid
and white privilege began, according to Giliomee, when the
government began relaxing some of the restrictions on black
labour during the 1970s e.g. the scrapping of statutory job
reservation, the attempts to narrow racially based wage
differentials and the racial gap in the civil service, and to
equalize spending on white and black social services.

A combination of declining income, high inflation and a
growing tax burden resulted in a sharp white political backlash
against the redistributive policies of the government. The right

wing claimed that the government was selling out lower-level white civil servants in order to improve the living standards of blacks. A large section of the lower-echelon white workers saw socio-economic reforms and black advancement as a direct threat to their position. They were totally unprepared for it, having been under state protection for so long, and attempted to obstruct these reforms on every level.

The declining power of white agriculture and white labour and the strengthening position of Afrikaner urban capital, bureaucracy and political establishment were manifested in labour and subsidization policies which adversely affected these previously protected sectors. While there was a marked improvement in the relations between the government and urban and mining capital, the relationship between white mineworkers and the government deteriorated, as the former defied laws which were intended to relax the job bar in homeland mines. A further breach with white labour occurred with the implementation of the Riekert Report of 1979 (implying greater mobility for urban blacks), the Wiehahn Commission report of 1979 (abolishing statutory job reservation, the opening of apprenticeships to blacks, and the registering of black trade unions) and the de Lange Report of 1981 (equal quality of education for all races). The intent was to close the skills gap and to increase demand by incorporating organized black workers into the labour aristocracy, but many white workers saw the new labour system as a direct threat to their own economic security. White workers resented the desegregation of facilities and the possibility of having to work under blacks and feared the possibility of being replaced or having their wages undercut by the competition from cheaper black labour. The ranks of a resentful white working class were increased by civil servants at the lower end of the scale who feared black competition and by some teachers and clergy who had a vested interest in continued Afrikaner hegemony (Lipton 1986: 308). The plight of the white working class was eased by generous financial and other compensation, but it did not prevent the decline of their industrial and political power, which was exacerbated by the decline in their numbers: white-only registered trade unions saw a decline in membership from 240,000 in 1980 to below 100,000 in 1989, while the numbers of white workers employed in blue-collar and agricultural occupations declined from 72 per cent in 1936 to 35 per cent in 1977 (Giliomee 1989: 118–25).

The split in the NP and the founding of the CP in 1982 also had roots in the process of a class realignment whereby a new Afrikaner middle class emerged whose view on socio-economic and political issues differed substantially from that of the old ethnic alliance which brought the NP to power in 1948. The remnants of the white working class and the lower echelons of the civil service supported the CP, as did the maize farmers in the northern provinces who relied heavily on labour-repressive policies (Charney 1984: 278). For this reason the CP concentrated upon economic issues during election campaigns by blaming the government for the continuing impoverishment of the whites, and as a result won many constituencies in blue-collar areas and received strong support from struggling maize farmers in the rural Transvaal and Free State districts during elections. However, unlike the HNP, the CP managed to achieve a level of respectability among various classes of whites – the party's complex support-base consisted of not only working-class whites and farmers, but also of clergy, academics, teachers, doctors, other professionals and, in all, a considerable cross-section of the Afrikaner establishment.

Surveys relating to the right's class roots
The findings of a number of studies further substantiate the argument that the modern-day right, although not solely a class phenomenon, has strong support among whites on the lower socio-economic strata. Although these findings have weaknesses insofar as variables such as income, education and occupation, cannot, in isolation, be equated with class, they tend to confirm the hypothesis formulated by Rhoodie et al (1985) which suggests that lower-class people are more conservatively orientated towards changes in conventional behaviour patterns.

The findings cited by Charney (1984), derived from a *Star Retail Data Library Survey*, provided useful data on the relationship between class and racism among Johannesburg whites in 1982. The views of whites at the higher end of the socio-economic scale to the possible opening of government schools and public transport to all races, differed considerably from those in the lower supervisory, clerical, artisan and unskilled worker categories. Afrikaners and English-speakers in the middle-class job categories reacted favourably to the prospects of racial integration, while those in the working class in both language groups reacted unfavourably. With regard to the repeal of one particular apartheid measure, the survey found that only 25 per cent of Afrikaners and 20 per cent of English-speakers in the middle to upper job category rejected the racial integration of public transport, as opposed to the 82 per cent of Afrikaners and 44 per cent of English-speakers in the lower category who held the same view.

The survey conducted by Rhoodie, de Kock and Couper (Rhoodie et al, 1985) confirmed the existence of a positive correlation between the politically conservative ideology and white voters at the lower end of the socio-economic spectrum in South Africa. The respondents were questioned on their support for social and 'grand' apartheid measures which existed at the time or were in the process of being scrapped. Their findings indicated the existence of very definite differences in the perception which respondents had of socio-political change, depending on their levels of personal income and education. In each category of apartheid legislation a considerable majority of respondents in the lower educational strata supported the retention of those laws, compared to those respondents who had a higher level of education. While 28 per cent of respondents without school-leaving qualifications wanted all 21 apartheid measures to remain, only 13 per cent of those in the higher education bracket were in favour of the retention of all these measures; 68 per cent of those with lower educational qualifications supported the retention of the Immorality Act, against the 56 per cent in the higher education bracket. Similarly, 67 per cent of those in the lower income group were in favour of retaining the Act, against 56 per cent in the higher income group.

The survey conducted by Gagiano (1990) highlighted the variable of education as a component of class. The research dealt with the impact of political reforms on the attitudes of white students of both language groups. The results of Gagiano's survey placed students as a category to the left of the political spectrum. Only 14 per cent of white students and 24 per cent of Afrikaner students supported the right-wing parties, which suggested that the support among white students for the right wing was less than half of the national average of almost 30 per cent.[11]

The survey by Manzo and McGowan (1989) focused on the political sentiments of Afrikaner élites in fields such as politics, civil service, business, religion, universities and the media. Of the test sample 81 per cent received above average incomes and 96 per cent had received some form of post-secondary education. The findings indicated only 11 per cent support for right-wing parties, i.e. about one-third of the national average at the time.

The previously unpublished data of the national opinion poll firm, Market and Opinion Surveys (M&M, 1989), established a correlation between income and ideology in white politics, as illustrated, for example, by the DP (Democratic Party) support among Afrikaners, which increased from 7 per cent in the lowest income category to 17 per cent in the highest. The CP's support declined almost proportionally with the increase in income per category: among Afrikaners it declined from 39 per cent in the lowest income category to 23 per cent in the highest.

In conclusion: the emergence of the modern-day right wing had some roots in the breakup of the Afrikaner class alliance and class issues continued to play a considerable role in the growth of support for apartheid and for the right wing. The beneficial relationship between the white working class and apartheid partly explains why the NP lost increasing numbers of its supporters to the right in the 1970s and 1980s. The government's policies aimed at the socio-economic upliftment of blacks through increased spending on education, housing and welfare services, eroded the remaining socio-economic privileges associated with being white in South Africa, and led to a decline in the rate of white incomes in real terms by almost 10 per cent between 1975 and 1979. The whites at the lower end of the economic scale were affected the most severely, and have supported the right-wing parties because of a firm conviction that their policies, if implemented, would ensure a return to the subsidies and privileges guaranteed by an Afrikaner-dominated government.

However, as only about 40 per cent of the CP's support is

located in the lower to middle income group, the above
proposition does not explain why so many Afrikaners from
higher income and educational groups support the CP, nor why
they would support a party whose policies are guaranteed to
destroy the economy utterly, or why some right-wing supporters
would be prepared to endure considerable economic hardships
to create a white homeland in an economic desert, and without
the help of black labour. The explanation for this seemingly
irrational political behaviour lies with the 'ethnic dynamic'
suggested by Horowitz (1985), i.e. the collective drive by ethnic
groups for power and status in which socio-economic issues play
virtually no role. I now go on to discuss the powerful forces
associated with Afrikaner ethnicity and nationalism.

Ethnicity and nationalism

As I have suggested, Afrikaner political behaviour over the
centuries was underpinned by two motivating and
justifying forces: nationalist aspiration and racial ideology
(Horowitz 1991: 13).

In this section I hope to address the nationalist aspirations of
the right as the vehicle with which to obtain political power and
to protect Afrikaner status and identity. However, as Horowitz
has indicated, these aspirations are partly founded in
ethnocentrism and racism, which in turn are rooted in anxiety
and the fear of group domination and genocide. The result is
that Afrikaner nationalism became associated with racism,
apartheid and white supremacy.
    Although the issues of nationalism, racism and fear are dis-
cussed separately below, they are strongly interrelated. Horowitz
explained that group self-esteem, anxiety and prejudice are
interrelated insofar as prejudice allows for a discharge of hostility, thereby reducing anxiety, while the degree of group self-
esteem determines the degree of hostility towards other groups
(1985: 179). These three issues are crucial to understanding the
'ethnic dynamic' which, according to Horowitz, is the driving
force behind an ethnic group's quest for the power which would
entitle it to dominate other groups or to avoid being dominated
itself. Horowitz's argument that 'Power may be desired, not only

for the lesser things it can gain, but for the greater things it
reflects and prevents' (1985: 187) applies also to Afrikaner
nationalism and its attempts to protect the status of the
Afrikaner and maintain its grip on power.

In response to the challenge to the status and legitimacy of the
Afrikaner as the dominant force in South Africa for more than
40 years, Afrikaner nationalists have followed a two-pronged
strategy to protect their hold on power: on the one hand the NP
fought to maintain a grip on power through power-sharing
arrangements, while the right wing struggled to keep the state
exclusively in the hands of the Afrikaner, if not in the entire
country, then at least in an Afrikaner homeland. As South
African society went through a process of transformation
during the early 1990s, the NP attempted to broaden its
support-base by moving away from ethnic Afrikaner nationalist
symbolism, by formulating a non-racial, non-ethnic, territorial
definition of South African nationalism. However, this allowed
the right wing to capitalize on the primordial issues which were
associated with Afrikaner ethnicity and its accompanying
symbols which the NP had previously used to mobilize
Afrikanerdom.

The concept of nationalism basically refers to the political
expression of a shared ethnic consciousness by people normally
sharing a common territory, descent, language, religion, history
and customs. However, often these common denominators are
perceived by a people in an emotional and chauvinistic way,
giving way to ethnocentrism, a term coined by W.G. Sumner in
1906, which denotes attitudes supposing the superiority of one's
own ethnic or racial group. While ethnocentrism by itself does
not necessarily imply hostility towards other groups, it does
contain a predisposition to regard other groups as different,
which in turn may lead to the view that these groups are inferior
(van Zyl Slabbert and Welsh 1979: 12).

In Afrikaner nationalist terminology the common ethnic
attributes are the Afrikaans language, Reformed religion and
Afrikaner history with its claim to the fatherland; shared views
on these issues confirm the status of the Afrikaner as a distinct
nation entitled to self-determination within a specific territory.
However, ethnocentrism has long been part of Afrikaner
nationalism and has also become the trademark of the white

right wing. Its ethnocentric interpretation of nationalism has combined the more positive aspects of nationalism, such as the desire to protect and promote the Afrikaner language and culture, with ethnocentric notions of the 'superiority' of the Afrikaner people and the white race over 'inferior' black peoples, as well as a self-serving interpretation of history. As was the case with the NP after 1948, the right wing attempted to interpret the elements of Afrikaner nationalism in a way that would serve its ideology of self-determination and racially based territorial and social segregation. It appropriated the elements and symbols of Afrikaner nationalism and combined these with historical myths to give substance to its version of Afrikaner history and to explain the current political and socio-economic realities in South Africa.

Language
According to Horowitz (1985: 217–22) language is a powerful symbol of domination because its status denotes the status of the group that speaks it. In South Africa, Afrikaans was a major tool in the process of ethnic mobilization during the 1930s and 1940s, and its promotion later as an official language confirmed the 'special status' of the Afrikaner people. The Afrikaans language is therefore regarded as one of the major justifications for the Afrikaner nationalists' belief that it constitutes a distinct and separate *volk* (people) with a legitimate right to self-determination.

Some right-wing organizations view the primacy of the Afrikaans language with more fervour than others. Not to alienate its many English-speaking supporters, the CP regards its constituency as the 'white nation', i.e. Afrikaners, English-speakers and those of European stock who share right-wing sentiments. The HNP emphasizes that it speaks only on behalf of the Afrikaans-speaking whites; the Afrikaner Volksunie (AVU) regards all Afrikaans-speakers irrespective of race as part of its constituency, while the AWB and the Boerestaat Party reject the term 'Afrikaner' in favour of 'Boer' and claim that only the descendants of the Voortrekkers can be regarded as Boers – the leader of the Boerestaat Party, Robert van Tonder, refers to Afrikaans spoken in the Transvaal and OFS as *Boeretaal* or *Boeraans* (van Tonder 1990: 65).

Religion

Since early on the Afrikaans churches have regarded it as their duty to emphasize the link between religion and the nationalist and apartheid ideologies. Their collective philosophy was also based on the belief that the Afrikaners were a distinct people elected and sent by God to spread Christianity among the black nations of South Africa, while at the same time keeping a separate identity and racial purity. As Moodie observed in his description of the 'Afrikaner civil religion':

> The divine agent of the Afrikaner civil faith is Christian and Calvinist – an active sovereign God, who calls the elect, who promises and punishes, who brings forth life from death in the course of history. The object of His saving activity – the Afrikaner People – is not a church, [or] a community of the saved, [but] a whole nation with its distinct language and culture, its own history and destiny (1975: xvii).

A distinct religious element in the early Afrikaner nationalist mythology was the 'Israelite myth', i.e. references to the Afrikaners as a 'chosen people' and to South Africa as the 'promised land'. Loubser (cited in Ridge 1987) argued that the Calvinist distinction between the elect and the damned led to a natural classification of the 'heathen' blacks as the damned, and therefore that it justified hostile acts committed by the frontiersmen. Although the Voortrekkers did not literally identify themselves with the history of Israel, evidence of Israelite analogies permeates Afrikaner history, e.g. references to Natal as the 'promised land', to the Voortrekkers entering the wilderness without a 'Moses and Aaron', and Paul Kruger's use of the words 'God's people' to describe the Boers. The majority of historians believe that early Afrikaners did not see themselves as a 'chosen people' in any dogmatic way, but rather used a cluster of Israelite metaphors to give some tentative form to their own view of themselves.

Although all but the most extremist right-wing organizations today deny that they regard the Afrikaners as a 'chosen people' destined to rule others because of a divinely ordained superiority, most right-wing supporters believe that the

Afrikaner nationhood enjoys divine sanction (Zille 1988: 66). While most adhere to the traditional Afrikaner nationalist religion, Calvinist Protestantism, a few have formed white supremacist sects such as the Israelites (see also Chapter 3).

The role of history and mythology

> Forgetting history, or even getting history wrong, is an essential factor in the formation of a nation (Ernest Renan, cited by Eric Hobsbawm in *New Statesman and Society*, 24 April 1992).

A crucial factor in the process of ethnic mobilization of the Afrikaner in the 1930s and 1940s was the formulation of an Afrikaner nationalist mythology, i.e. appropriating events with historical and religious significance to the Afrikaner. Events which were founded in historical facts were presented or interpreted in such a way as to justify the Afrikaner nationalist ideology. The Afrikaner nationalist mythology was perpetuated by means of the Christian National Education (CNE) network, whereby Afrikaner youth was indoctrinated with the fundamentals of Afrikaner nationalism and Calvinistic Christianity. CNE educated young Afrikaners to believe in the superiority of their religion and their people, and the network became an integral part of Afrikaner and other white education.

CNE played an important part in the ideological indoctrination of most of today's Afrikaners and undoubtedly had a profound effect on those who continue to support the right wing. Concurring, H.J. van Daalden, a professor at the predominantly black University of Fort Hare, argued that researchers aiming at a better understanding of the Barend Strydom syndrome (Strydom killed eight blacks in Pretoria in 1988 because he believed blacks were inferior people – pages 50–51) should focus their research on the junior-school history curriculum (*Rapport*, 21 July 1991). In a similar vein a communication analyst, J.M. du Preez (1986), identified certain 'master symbols' which appeared in the prescribed history, geography and literature books of Afrikaner schoolchildren, and were intended to impress onto children the 'God-given superiority' and 'special' status of whites and Afrikaners in South Africa. Du Preez argued that the system of symbols adopted by Afrikaners had serious shortcomings insofar as it lacked objectivity and was out of touch with modern industrial society, and was the reason why so many Afrikaners have been unable to adapt to political and social changes since the 1970s, an observation confirmed by Thompson: 'Nevertheless, most Afrikaners of the younger as well as the older generations retain from their schooling a generalized assumption that racial and ethnic categories are fundamental, a strong sense of identity as Afrikaners and as white South Africans and, indeed, a belief in the master symbols' (1985: 237).

The shared historical experiences of the Afrikaner during three hundred years of settlement in South Africa played a major role in the shaping of Afrikaner nationalism. Afrikaner nationalism, which forms the basis of the right-wing movement, is in itself a product of the centuries-old conflict between an embattled minority of Afrikaners and a number of adversaries, which ranged from indigenous black opponents, the British empire and mass poverty to the perceived threats from the Roman Catholic Church and from black- and communist-inspired 'total onslaught' propaganda (the *Roomse, Swart* and *Rooi Gevaar*).

The virtual hijacking of Afrikaner history by the right was most clearly illustrated during the commemorative celebrations of the 150th anniversary of the Great Trek in 1988, when right-wing cultural organizations not only secured for its celebrations the Voortrekker Monument (in Pretoria), a shrine of Afrikaner nationalists, but also attracted vastly greater numbers of Afrikaners than the official government-sponsored assemblage. The absorption of historical events of this nature had helped to shape the Afrikaner psyche and to awaken its national consciousness, some of which have been appropriated by the right and are used in a symbolic way to prove that the right wing, and not the NP, is the true representative of Afrikanerdom.

Historical events
Apart from the border wars against the Xhosa and the constant interference by the distant British colonial government in Cape Town, it was the Slagtersnek Rebellion of 1815 that left the deepest mark on the consciousness of the colonists in the Eastern Cape. Their subjugation and the bungled execution of

five rebels led to a belief among the colonists of divine intervention, and the lack of compassion from the authorities resulted in
great bitterness. Slagtersnek later became a beacon to activate
colonial resistance to British cultural and political imperialism.

Of greater significance was the Great Trek, a mass migration
of Afrikaner colonists in the eastern Cape because of
interference in their affairs by the colonial government in Cape
Town. Much of the dissatisfaction originated in the emancipa-
tion of slaves and the issue of legal equalization of a local tribe,
the Khoikhoi, a move regarded by the white colonists as being in
conflict with biblical prescriptions and with natural distinctions
of origin and belief (Leatt et al 1986: 71). These beliefs
accompanied the Voortrekkers during the Great Trek of the
1830s and were reinforced after the series of battles with black
groups in the interior. The Trek was used by Afrikaner
historians and ideologues as a milestone in the development of
conscious Afrikaner nationalism, and it became the central event
in the evolution of the Afrikaner mystique (Davenport 1987:
53). Thompson concurred: 'The Great Trek became the central
theme in the Afrikaner nationalist mythology that came to
maturity in the first half of the twentieth century ... and at the
core of the story was the Covenant' (1985: 180). It was during
the Great Trek that the covenant was entered into; Voortrekker
leaders such as Piet Retief, Andries Pretorius and Sarel Cilliers
became heroic figures, and events such as the battles and
massacres at places like Blaauwkrantz and Blood River were
later commemorated in the form of the 'sacred' Voortrekker
Monument.

Having appropriated most symbols of Afrikaner nationalism,
the 'sacred history' of the Great Trek also became a dominant
part of the mythology of the latter-day right wing. The battle of
Blood River, where the Voortrekkers defeated the Zulu and
entered into a covenant with God, is of particular importance to
the right wing. Whereas the government has tried to scale down
the racial undertones of the Day of the Vow in recent years, the
right wing regards it with extreme reverence and as proof that
the Afrikaner does have divine blessing for his 'mission' in South
Africa. Andries Treurnicht described the CP's view of the
covenant as 'the day when Afrikaners thank God for our
deliverance and commemorate a particular historical battle in

which our people survived and which brought us to safety' (cited in Thompson 1985: 226).

Another event of great consequence in the Afrikaner and right-wing mythology is the Anglo–Boer War. The courageous manner in which the outnumbered Republican Boers conducted the war, the tremendous suffering of non-combatants in British concentration camps, the aggressive post-war anglicization policy, and the loss of prosperity and ultimately freedom, left an indelible mark on the national consciousness of the Afrikaner. Apart from the fact that the Afrikaners in the Boer Republics lost their independence, Boer homes and farms were destroyed and their families placed in concentration camps, eventually leading to the death of almost 28,000 women and children because of poor medical conditions and disease. Recollections of sufferings in the concentration camps remain deeply ingrained in the Afrikaner psyche, and the deaths are still poignantly cited by the right as a reason for demanding self-determination. This helps us to understand the emotionality behind the creed of Afrikaner nationalists 'never to lose sovereignty again'.[12] The leader of the Boerestaat Party, Robert van Tonder, describes the 'genocidal' aspect of the war as follows: 'These were the first concentration camps in the world, in which the British deliberately killed 27,000 defenceless people' (van Tonder 1990: 26) [translation].

The guerrilla war which the Boers fought with considerable success created heroes such as Piet Cronje, Koos de la Rey and Christiaan de Wet. Also Paul Kruger enjoys reverential admiration: his statue on Church Square in Pretoria and his grave in Heroes' Acre in a cemetery in Pretoria are seen by the right wing as part of its heritage. The monument at Paardekraal, which commemorates the declaration of war on Britain in 1899, also became a right-wing shrine and a venue for AWB rallies.

The distinction drawn between the *bittereinders* (those who wanted to keep on fighting) and the *hensoppers* (those who preferred peace above further conflict) has its roots in the final phases of the Anglo–Boer War, but it is an emotionally charged issue which is still used by the right today to describe the NP's 'capitulation' to the ANC. This distinction persisted throughout the twentieth century, albeit in different guises, e.g. the *broedertwis* between *verligte* and *verkampte* Afrikaners and between right-wing and more liberal-minded Afrikaners. According to *Patriot* the *hensopper* tradition reappeared during the 1914 rebellion and again during the *Ossewa Brandwag* era of the 1940s, and is represented today by the so-called 'realists' (the NP) who believe that there is no sense in further opposing black majority government.

A related theme derived from the war is that of *veraad* (treachery), a term used in this context to describe the behaviour of any member of the Afrikaner people who was deemed to have turned his back on his people. During the Anglo–Boer War many *hensoppers* joined the British army in the fight to subjugate the remaining Boer forces. The issue also reappeared during South African participation in the two world wars, when some Afrikaners who fought in government forces on the side of Britain were described as traitors to the Afrikaner people. Van Tonder described the suppression of the 1914 rebellion by the government (under leadership of the former Boer commanders Smuts and Botha) as 'the action of two former anglicized Boer leaders who turned against their own people' (1990: 28). The theme of treachery again became prominent in speeches by members of the right following February 1989 and the new era of reforms by the de Klerk administration: 'The members of the NP have become a lot of traitors' (Koos van der Merwe, cited in *Hansard*, 6 February 1990); 'The NP is committing acts of treason against its own people' (CP MP, Moolman Mentz, quoted in *Patriot*: 7 June 1991); 'If one disregards the land of one's own people, it is akin to treachery' (Andries Treurnicht, *Patriot*: 7 June 1991) [translations].

The Anglo–Boer War has also become the historical *raison d'être* for the claims made by the extreme right organizations such as the AWB and the Boerestaat Party, both of which are demanding the restoration of the Boer Republics. Their claim is based on the territory which was occupied by the Boers in the Transvaal, Free State and Vryheid, and which enjoyed internationally recognized independence until 1902.

Evidence of the emotional links between the war and the right wing occasionally surfaces, for example, the shots fired at the British Embassy in Pretoria in 1990 and a bomb attack on Melrose House, scene of the Boer surrender in 1902. The analogy between the 'pending' *Derde Vryheidsoorlog* (the third war of freedom) and the previous two such wars in 1880–81 and in 1899–1902 have been an important element of the CP's rhetoric. Other symbols carried over from the Anglo–Boer War and used in particular by the Boerestaat Party and the AWB include the *Vierkleur* (the four-colour flag) of the former *Zuid-Afrikaanse Republiek* (Transvaal) and its former anthem *Ken u die volk* (literally, Do you know the people).[13]

Another event of great symbolic significance to the right wing is the 1914 Rebellion, which occurred in response to the decision of the South African government to join the First World War on the side of Britain. It was inconceivable to many Afrikaners to join forces with their former British enemy which had humiliated them 12 years previously, and in addition, the supposed enemy, Germany, had been sympathetic to the Boer cause during the Anglo–Boer War. Many existing Boer heroes like de Wet, Christiaan Beyers, Jan Kemp and Manie Maritz became involved in the rebellion but because of a lack of a coherent plan and efficient organization, the rebellion was easily suppressed by the Smuts–Botha government, using only Afrikaner troops. According to *Patriot* (3 August 1990), the rebellion imprinted a 'great truth' into the consciousness of the Afrikaner, namely that the 'nation's honour is often saved by small groups of men and women who face the greatest odds against them' – this was undoubtedly a reference to the right wing's 'heroic struggle' against the overwhelming tide of non-racialism and democracy. The rebellion's contribution to Afrikaner nationalism was considerable, as it added new faces to the Afrikaner hall of fame and produced more legends and martyrs to inspire a new nationalist movement in the 1930s (Davenport 1977: 272).

The outbreak of the Second World War in 1939 created new opportunities for elements within Afrikaner nationalism to create myths and symbols, some of which have remained important to this day among such organizations as the AWB. The decision of the government to participate in the Second World War on the side of Britain led many Afrikaners actively to resist such a move, leading to the formation of the *Ossewa Brandwag* (OB) during the war. The OB was initially a cultural organization founded with the ideal of promoting Afrikaner patriotism and values derived from the Great Trek, and organized cultural events intended to revive Afrikaner nationalism, e.g. public festivals, wreath-layings, target-shoots, *jukskei* matches (played with ox-yoke pins), camps, lectures on folk history and folk literature (Davenport 1977: 333). Later its espousal of national socialism became more pronounced, especially with regard to its belief in the primacy of the nation and in the superiority of the white race. During the Second World War the OB developed a more militant character under the leadership of Hans van Rensburg, and succeeded in attracting several hundred thousand supporters. It generally did not commit acts of violence or sabotage until 1942 when its alter ego, the *Stormjaers* (stormtroopers), attempted to sabotage the war effort by blowing up railway lines and vital installations.

The real significance of the fascist movements of the 1940s lies in the fact that, to a large extent, they became the spiritual forefather of the present AWB and other right-wing splinter groups such as the Afrikaner National Socialists.[14] Similarities between the fascist organizations of the 1940s and those of today are especially visible in their approaches to violence, their obsession with the primacy of the *volk*, the cult of a strong leader, anti-Semitism, and in their flags and emblems.

In addition to their mutual belief in the concept of racial superiority, the OB's belief that a state can represent only one nation, and that the individual can subsist only within the sphere of the nation, is also present in the AWB philosophy. The AWB's threats of violence and accusations of treachery are also strongly reminiscent of behaviour of the OB and Greyshirts in the 1940s. The claim by the OB that the supporters of the Union government were traitors is comparable to the AWB's and the CP's accusations of the treachery committed by the de Klerk administration.

Both the fascist organizations in the 1940s and the right wing today propagated some form of anti-Semitism, a phenomenon that was fairly widespread throughout the Afrikaner society during the 1940s, e.g. D.F. Malan initiated an NP proposal in parliament demanding that Jewish immigration to the country should be stopped and that Jews be refused entry to certain occupations, and Verwoerd demanded that a quota system be introduced to prevent Jews from entering businesses and the professions (Moodie 1975: 166–7). However, the most virulent form of anti-Semitism was propagated by the Greyshirts under L.T. Weichardt, whose views on this topic were not that different from those of Eugene Terre Blanche: 'True to the methods of the anti-Christ, which resides in International Judaism, this anti-Christ has carefully stretched its tentacles around the resources of the fatherland' (Kemp 1990: 19). Terre Blanche also suggested that South African Jews should not be allowed to vote, and in 1987 he joined with the Afrikaner National Socialists in commemorating the death of Hitler's former deputy, Rudolph Hess (Kemp 1990: 78–154).

Other similarities between the right-wing AWB and the fascism of the 1940s can be found in their negative perception of the democratic institutions of government. Both the 1940s fascists and AWB disclaimed parliamentary politics, e.g. the Greyshirts' intention to rule by a dictatorship similar to that of Hitler, corresponded to the idea of a dictatorship in the AWB's original Programme of Principles (Kemp 1990: 19).

Parallels also exist between the struggle within Afrikanerdom during the 1940s and the *broedertwis* of the 1960s and 1970s, in particular with reference to the continuity of the actions of Piet Meyer. Meyer, who supported the OB during the 1940s in its rivalry with the NP of Malan, aligned himself on the side of the *verkramptes* during the 1960s and led the campaign to undermine the leadership of John Vorster.[15]

Similarities can also be found in the symbols and emblems of the 1940s fascist organizations and the AWB. The flag of the former Zuid-Afrikaanse Republiek was the flag used at OB meetings during the 1940s, and is one of the two flags used today at AWB meetings. The AWB's flag comprises three sevens arranged in a pattern strongly reminiscent of the Nazi swastika, the use of black for the motifs with red and white for the background colours also being similar. Also the AWB's choice of the eagle as an emblem appears to have Nazi origins, although there have been claims that it was derived from the Bible and from the coat-of-arms of the former Boer Republics (Kemp 1990: 151).

Finally, according to an article by Hans Strydom (*Sunday Times*, 29 April 1990), both organizations found strong support among the police, e.g. a former Springbok heavyweight boxer Robey Leibbrandt, a Nazi agent who returned to South Africa to organize anti-government resistance in 1941, had so much support among the police that some refused to help with the investigation against him or even to put up a 'wanted' poster of Leibbrandt in their police stations. Similarly, the investigators who were trying to apprehend one-time right-wing fugitive, Piet Rudolph, complained that they could not trust anyone in the police.

The significance of territory

> Territory is, at the least, a critical factor in maintaining group separateness. Without it a nationality has difficulty becoming a nation and a nation cannot become a state (Isaacs 1975: 45).

Historical evidence of the link between a distinct and separate territory and the Afrikaner people is fundamental to the demand of the right wing for self-determination in an Afrikaner fatherland. As in the case of other historical myths appropriated by the right wing, the issue of white and Afrikaner claims to land is prone to subjective interpretations and mythology. A foremost part of the right-wing philosophy, until recently, was the conviction that the whole territory of South Africa, with the exception of the 13 per cent which makes up the black homelands, belonged to the whites. Most Afrikaners grew up with this myth, which had a religious dimension: the analogy between the Promised Land given to Israel by God and the Boer victory at the battle of Blood River forms a prominent part of the belief that God wanted the land to belong to the Afrikaner and to white civilization.

Another Afrikaner nationalist myth which features prominently in right-wing claims is the myth of 'vacant land', which rests on three contentious assumptions: firstly that black tribes arrived in South Africa at virtually the same time as the white settlers and therefore had no prior claims to the land; secondly that the large-scale genocide (Difaqane) and inter-ethnic warfare between black tribes left the whole interior depopulated; and thirdly that the Boers traded and bought land from the remaining black tribes on a totally honest and justified basis. Although the myth of vacant land has been proven false by

historical evidence, it has never succeeded in changing the
perceptions of the right-wing supporters who had been
indoctrinated since their early school years:

> It is of extreme importance to realize that at no stage did
> the Trekkers take land away from blacks who were
> occupying it at the time of the Trekkers' arrival. The black
> people presently residing in the original Boer Republics of
> the Transvaal, OFS and Northern Natal came to the area in
> search of food and work after it had been settled by whites
> (AWB pamphlet, cited by Kemp 1990: 109) [translation].

> We lay no claim to the land of other nations. We obtained
> our land through legal occupation of unoccupied areas,
> through agreements, cession, trade and to a lesser extent,
> justifiable conquest (Treurnicht, as cited in *Vrye Weekblad*,
> 22 March 1991) [translation].

Until its conversion to the idea of a smaller white homeland in
1992, the CP argued that historically based ethnic and racial
settlement patterns confirmed the validity of its policy of partition. Ferdi Hartzenberg, deputy leader of the party at the time,
based his party's claim to an exclusive white territory on religious
grounds: 'Our fatherland is a gift from God and we won't ask
Mandela if we can live here or have any rights' (*Cape Times*, 16
August 1990). Although no more realistic, Treurnicht at least
recognized that the uneven distribution of land was a source of
concern for others: 'We own land, which we didn't steal. There
are various ways in which land becomes the property of the
people. Actually, that is something that people blame us for. We
have 87 per cent of the land' (*Time*, 13 August 1990).
    What stands out from all these quotes is the firm conviction of
the right wing that they can lay claim to a historically separate
and distinct territory, a belief rooted in distorted perceptions of
reality and a self-serving interpretation of religious, historical
and political events. Such distorted beliefs or myths formed the
crux of their strong opposition to the repeal of the Land Acts of
1913 and 1936 and the Group Areas Act, as the repeal of these
laws was deemed to remove their claim to a concept of their
own fatherland: 'An own territory is one of the foundation
stones of political power. The government's intention to repeal

[the Land Acts] is a flagrant attack on our right to self-determination on our own territory.... The government's decision forces us to engage in a freedom struggle' (CP press release, *Vrye Weekblad*, 22 March 1991) [translation].

Roots in racism

I am quite frank in saying that I am race conscious. I am aware of the fact that I am a white man. I don't think that's racism. I would say racism, in the negative sense of the word, would mean not only being conscious of the fact that you belong to a certain racial group, but denying other people certain rights and discriminating in the negative sense of the word against people (Treurnicht, cited in *Time*, 13 August 1990).

The concept of racism is closely related to that of ethnocentrism and white supremacy and denotes a belief in the superiority of a particular race, which, by implication, provides grounds for the justification of racial discrimination. A complete analysis of racism would ideally also include a discussion of individual personality aberrations, innate prejudice and discrimination as examined by social psychological theories. These, however, fall outside the scope of this book, and are therefore referred to only superficially.

Racism implies a belief that such racial differences provide adequate grounds for differential treatment, in particular for granting rights and privileges to members of one race and withholding them from members of another (Scruton 1982: 390). According to Pierre van den Berghe, racism denotes 'any set of beliefs that organic, genetically transmitted differences (whether real or imagined) between human groups are intrinsically associated with the presence or absence of certain socially relevant abilities or characteristics, hence that such differences are a legitimate basis of invidious distinctions between groups socially defined as races' (1978: 11).

Psychological theorists use the individual personality as the basis of an explanation for racism and purport to show that racism is ultimately reducible to a set of attitudes which are socially derived but become part of the individual personality. The two theories which are particularly relevant seek to explain frustration–aggression and the authoritarian personality.

According to the frustration–aggression theory, every person is a cluster of forces which often block goal-directed behaviour, which in turn creates hostile impulses in the individual. This frustration cannot always be directed towards the source of frustration because the source may be too powerful or unknown. It leads to free-floating, undirected frustrations which are then displaced or targeted to an unrelated victim or scapegoat, which cannot realistically be shown to be the cause of the difficulties. This aggression is accompanied by some emotional and intellectual strains because of the irrationality and injustice of such action, which in turn leads to the aggressor looking for justification for his behaviour. Then follows a 'discovery' or fabrication of evidence of undesirable traits proving that the victim deserved the treatment meted out by the aggressor. When the choice of victims becomes culturally stabilized on members of a certain group, racial or ethnic prejudice will result (van den Berghe 1978: 19; Simpson and Yinger 1985: 73).

Studies of the authoritarian personality suggest that some people are psychologically predisposed to be prejudiced against members of other racial and ethnic groups. Prejudice in this case is a manifestation of a basically insecure person who represses many of his own impulses, perceives life as capricious and threatening and sees all human relationships in competitive power terms.

Although it is beyond the scope of this book, it would be interesting to match the personality profiles of racist mass-murderers like the self-proclaimed White Wolf Barend Strydom or AWB member Eugene Marais, with the character traits suggested by the two personality theories: for example, would Marais' attempt to justify the murder of several innocent black people on grounds that 'blacks are animals' fit the description of the frustration–aggression personality, which appears to match the argument of Marais that blacks were nothing but animals and that it therefore was not a sin to kill them. On his release from prison in 1992 after serving only four years of several life sentences for his murder of eight black civilians, Strydom had no remorse and maintained that he had done nothing wrong, for his victims were 'enemies of the Afrikaner people and were justifiably killed'.

Other theories deal with historical, structural and sociological issues, collectively referred to by Pierre van den Berghe as 'social determinism'. In societies where racism is constantly rewarded in terms of power, prestige, approval and wealth, racial tolerance, 'deviant behaviour' such as liberalism and colour-blindness are severely punished (van den Berghe 1978: 20). Similarly, the social approach explains racism as the product of the socialization of the individual into a specific culture, leaving him with an array of learned racial responses: 'We are taught to be prejudiced against certain groups just as we are taught to dislike certain foods that people in other societies consider great delicacies ... individuals may be equipped with a number of culturally learned responses to minority groups ... that are part of the standard cultural equipment' (Simpson and Yinger 1985: 91). Rather than viewing racism as an innate antipathy towards other racial or ethnic groups, racism is viewed as a learned response. In this regard certain aspects of language may contribute to the learning of the traditions of prejudice – some things are 'white and clean' and others are 'black and dirty'.

This is relevant to the South African context from two perspectives. Firstly, the socialization of generation upon generation of whites into a society obsessed with racial superiority imprinted racist beliefs into the psyche of individual whites, and helps to explain the tenacity of racism among whites; secondly, the long-held perception among whites that 'blackness' has negative connotations (ugly, sin and dirt), might explain the introduction of social apartheid. The latter, in essence, was not crucial to the grand apartheid ideals of the NP (the creation of a homogeneous white South Africa), and was in reality an attempt to 'shield' whites from day-to-day contact with the 'impure' black population. Such interracial contact was forbidden in most social spheres, e.g. in sexual relations and marriage; in public amenities (sports facilities, parks, pools, the sea, lavatories) and in restaurants, hotels and Afrikaans churches.

Although the right wing is the sole propagator of a racist philosophy in South Africa today, racism has been an integral part of the white psyche ever since 1652 when the first settlers arrived at the Cape with preconceived ideas of blacks as barbarians and heathens. During the subsequent decades racial attitudes hardened at the eastern Cape frontier where whites developed a strong sense of superiority because of the master–slave relationship and the violent clashes with indigenous blacks (MacCrone 1957; Adam and Giliomee 1979; Elphick and Giliomee 1979). The NP institutionalized racism through its apartheid policy after 1948, but towards the end of the 1960s the party began slowly moving away from its rigid racial ideology and eventually to non-racialism under F.W. de Klerk. Having appropriated, with a few minor modifications, all of the NP's former policies, it stands to reason that racism is an intrinsic part of the right wing and everything it stands for.

Overt expressions of racism vary from organization to organization although accusations of racism are strongly rejected by all but the most extreme right-wing organizations. Evidence cited below, however, substantiates the perception that racism is an inherent part of the right-wing psyche. Most of the extra-parliamentary groups are more overtly racist than the more subtle approach of the CP. In the case of organizations like the AWB, the former *Blanke Bevrydingsbeweging* (BBB), *Orde Boerevolk* and the World Apartheid Movement (WAM), blatant racism is evident in practice and theory. Johan Schabort of the BBB explained the nature of 'white superiority' as follows: 'We believe in the genetic superiority of the white race, and we believe it is the duty of the white race to stop the natural increase and the decadence of the black races from destroying this planet' (cited in Zille 1988: 61). Schabort further argued that 'interbreeding' of races leads to inferiority and that whites obtain the highest scores in IQ tests due to their superior intelligence (*The Argus*, 12 November 1989).

Some AWB followers have used even cruder language to describe their racial sentiments. During a right-wing rally in Pretoria in 1989, blacks were targeted with expressions such as 'Let the kaffirs kill themselves', 'go away baboons', 'World apartheid movement – solution for AIDS' (*Sunday Star*, 24 September 1989). At a public meeting in Germiston in 1990, Terre Blanche described the state president as *meidagtig* (a discredited racist Afrikaans word literally translated as 'like a maidservant' and generally used to mean coward), and referred to Mandela as 'that damned Xhosa' (*Vrye Weekblad*, 27 July

1990). The coarse racist sentiments uttered by an AWB supporter in Port Elizabeth to indicate her opposition to the repeal of the Group Areas Act are probably representative of the typical extreme right wing: 'My husband is also AWB – he hates kaffirs.... We don't want scum to move into our neighbourhood' (*Vrye Weekblad*, 1 February 1991) [translation].

In February 1991 a CP city councillor in Port Elizabeth, Chris Meyer, indicated in slightly less overt racist tones that black homeowners were not welcome in his ward: 'It does not matter if [a black person] is a doctor, policeman, or priest – the issue is the protection of our own identity and the protection of the character of our suburb – if you allow one black, where do you draw the line?' This line of reasoning is typical of the CP, which rejects racism 'in the sense of negative discrimination regarding others' but sees nothing wrong with 'positive discrimination regarding their own members' (Bekker et al 1989: 13). Treurnicht argued that the CP was not racist, because racism implies 'denying other people certain rights', which, he claimed, was not part of the CP's policy (*Time*, 13 August 1990). Other CP members were less concerned with hiding their racism behind terms such as 'constructive or positive discrimination'. At the CP's 1990 Natal Congress, delegates voiced their racism in the most blatant terms: some were concerned over the 'sexual dangers which white girls will face from black boys in integrated schools', and over 'the existence of cultural differences which will result in white scholars being drawn down to the level of blacks'. Other comments included that 'blacks should be sent to industrial schools to be taught to work with their hands, as they cannot benefit from subjects like history and geography', 'that separate white and black blood banks should be introduced at hospitals because of the danger of AIDS in the blood of blacks', and that blacks should be 'culled like seals' to control their numbers (*Rapport*, 5 August 1990; *Cape Times*, 6 August 1990).

The CP refusal to budge from its position on a 'white' homeland is the most damning evidence of its racist orientation. The CP's only criterion for membership is pigmentation, and it defines the term Afrikaner broadly enough to include whites from European stock but not coloureds who speak Afrikaans, a clear indication that its philosophy is founded in race rather than in ethnicity. However, since 1990 the pragmatic wing of the

CP has strongly advocated a total rejection of such racist sentiments and negative conduct, and when the split occurred within the CP in 1992, the AVU insisted that it would represent Afrikaners rather than whites, which could include Afrikaans-speakers from the coloured community.

Roots in fear

> Fear is the driving force of white politics – that is why the right wing will keep growing (Z.B. du Toit, former editor of *Patriot*, cited in Zille 1988: 76).

> [Right-wing fears] may be baseless, but nevertheless are genuine. It is therefore the task of the ANC to address these fears realistically and seriously (Nelson Mandela, at a UN press conference, 24 September 1993).

The final ingredient of the right-wing psyche, an element of great importance in understanding not only right-wing behaviour but also that of many other whites, be they Afrikaners or not, concerns the fears they have regarding their collective security, their personal safety and the preservation of their culture and way of life. Of these the most important is the question of survival, i.e. physical safety of individuals and of the people. These fears should be analysed against the background of several cases of mass-genocide of nations during the twentieth century, and examples of instability and lawlessness which often accompany periods of great structural change. The element of fear is associated with expressions of both nationalism and racism – the fear that ethnic groups have of losing their identity through assimilation into larger 'alien' groups – evokes nationalist sentiment among members of that group. But the scope of such group-based fear is much more extensive than the fear of losing an identity, and in the case of the right wing the fear for the survival of the Afrikaner identity is supplemented by the fear for physical survival. This section will highlight how the fear of genocide, of expulsion, of anarchy and of revenge has become rooted into the psyche of the right wing and whites in general, and how it acts as a powerful motivational force to maintain a grip on power and access to security structures.

The fears of whites traditionally are directly related to their political, economic and social position under a future majority government, i.e. what Horowitz refers to as the fear of ethnic domination and suppression which is a motivating force for the acquisition of power as an end in itself (1985: 187). Much of the apprehension among whites of black rule has its roots in the incidents of violence and anarchy, often targeted against whites, which accompanied the decolonization of Africa. Such negative perceptions received further impetus from the anti-ANC and anti-communist propaganda devised by the NP during the years of the era of the 'total onslaught',[16] and was fuelled by real and imagined 'horror' stories from white 'refugees' from black rule elsewhere in Africa.

In their comparative study on the evolution of the ethnic conflict in Northern Ireland and Lebanon, Crighton and MacIver came to the conclusion that protracted conflicts are identity-driven and the result of an underlying fear of extinction that grows out of the experience of being a vulnerable ethnic group living with memories of persecution and massacre. According to these authors, the experiences of settler communities (the Maronites in Lebanon and the Protestants in Northern Ireland) have led to the common perception of threat and fear of annihilation, which made survival their most salient goal. Deep-seated fears of antagonistic majorities and group insecurity led to the establishment of policies and political institutions which guaranteed their political dominance (1991: 127–37). Crighton's and MacIver's comments about these communities are also applicable to the Afrikaners, who had similar experiences during their settler era and who followed similar undemocratic policies to prevent domination by the black majority. The centuries-old fear of being dominated, a fear heightened by periods of subjugation to British colonial rule, provided the impetus for the obsession of Afrikaner nationalists never again to be subjected to 'alien' (including black) rule in their 'fatherland'. This fear forms the basis for the demand of the right wing for Afrikaner self-determination, either as a sovereign state (the CP and AWB) or at least as an autonomous region within a federal South Africa (the AVU, and possibly the AVF).

White fears with regard to black rule have two dimensions.

The first are fears of non-violent threats, concerning reverse discrimination, the loss of privileges, possessions, cultural identity (among Afrikaners) and a lowering of living standards and quality of life. The second dimension of fear concerns the physical survival of whites and includes the fear of genocide, mass expulsion, anarchy, violence and crime (Hugo 1988: 5). These fears are discernible among whites of all language groups and political persuasions, the extent of which is clearly visible from the two-and-a-half million firearms in the possession of white civilians, i.e. a ratio of one firearm per white adult (*Cape Times*, 23 July 1990).

Africa's poor record on democracy, human and minority rights was always a source of great anxiety to South African whites. Living on the 'dark' continent and with the fear of blacks etched on their consciousness, white South Africans have always been easy targets for the *swart gevaar* (the black threat) propaganda with which the NP succeeded in scaring generations of whites into supporting it, a fact on which the right wing has capitalized. The right wing focused upon the political upheavals in Africa during and after decolonization to justify its policies and to scare white voters away from the 'threat' posed by reformist policies: 'If I were living in Europe or the United States where there is a respect for democracy then I would be prepared to take the risk [of majority rule], but not in Africa.... Look at the rest of Africa. No capitalism. No moderates. No multiparty governments' (CP MP Pieter Mulder, cited in *Patriot*, 22 June 1990). The experiences of whites in African states with similar racial configurations to that of South Africa, namely Algeria, Angola and Mozambique, Kenya, Zimbabwe and Namibia, featured prominently in the right-wing campaign.

Algeria was one of the worst cases of racial conflicts in Africa. During its liberation struggle (1954–62) French military units and the *pieds noirs* (the French settlers comprising about 12 per cent of the population) were pitched against the Algerian Arabs. Although both sides committed atrocities, the decision by the Arab National Liberation Front to adopt a deliberate policy to kill French settlers without distinction of age or sex, was held forth as a typical example of African savagery. The aspect of the Algerian war which stuck most strongly in the minds of most white South Africans was the mass flight of almost two million white Algerians to France. For the right wing, the parallels are clear: Afrikaners have no 'France' to flee to:

> No white community in Africa has so far been able to tolerate [being a powerless minority under a revolutionary black government]: most of them have fled, thousands to our country. Our people, on the other hand, have no boat waiting in the harbour. We cannot flee, nor will we flee. We will not submit ourselves to this type of domination (CP response to the White Paper on Land Reform, March 1991).

The Portuguese colonies, Angola and Mozambique, won their independence in the mid-1970s after a lengthy military confrontation with the Portuguese authorities. The transfer of power occurred reasonably peacefully, although 300,000 Portuguese had to be airlifted out of Angola in 1975. Many of them settled in South Africa and joined right-wing parties. In Kenya, the Mau Mau rebellion which commenced in the 1950s led to the death of only 32 of the 70,000 whites, but it had a considerable impact on South African whites because of the presence of 2000 Afrikaans-speaking whites in Kenya. This rebellion had an enduring impact on the white South African psyche: 'The term "Mau Mau" evokes images of isolated farms, lonely little groups of whites ... being crept up on by black figures. There are probably no two words which have greater power to arouse in white people every conceivable racially based fear' (Maughan-Brown, cited in Hugo 1988: 10).

Zimbabwe is frequently cited by the right as analogous with South Africa under majority rule. By focusing on the negative elements of Zimbabwean politics and economy and by using slogans such as 'Rhodesia Reformed and Surrendered' and 'For her sake, don't repeat Rhodesia', the CP had won over many supporters from the NP in subsequent elections during the 1980s. By presenting Zimbabwe as another example of the forlorn struggle by white settler societies against the 'hordes' of Africa and that any form of concession or change would result in a slow form of suicide, the right sent out a clear message: 'Fight, don't compromise' (Berger and Godsell 1988: 269). The independence of Namibia in 1990 had strong symbolic meaning for the right wing, firstly, because certain right-wing organizations still regard part of that country as part of South Africa, and also because of the considerable right-wing support among Namibian whites. By the time Namibia had achieved independence its white population had declined from over 100,000 to about 30,000, although those who left did so voluntarily. Namibia's president, Sam Nujoma, has stressed national reconciliation at every opportunity and has appointed whites in several senior government positions. In spite of this, the right wing saw the Namibian issue very differently: 'In the final analysis, Namibia simply could not be any different from the rest of Africa. The same anti-white mentality which controls Africa is now running Namibia' (*Patriot*, 22 June 1990).

While the experiences of colonial whites in Africa may in some cases confirm the worst suspicions of the right wing, it must be stressed that these suspicions are to a great extent supported by preconceived perceptions inherent in the right wing's racist philosophy. This is also evident from the themes which dominate right-wing fears. Apart from the fear of losing their economically privileged position and its manifestations, e.g. jobs, houses, cars, savings, they also fear the loss of their way of life, the lowering of standards, the loss of the Afrikaner culture and identity. Also prevalent is a fear not only of communism, anarchy, violence and crime but ultimately a fear of the complete extinction of the whites as a viable community in South Africa. All these are discernible in excerpts from pronouncements made by right-wing leaders – often tinged by racist, crude and violent language and, in most cases, founded in right-wing mythology and racial and ideological preconceptions rather than in fact. The following quotes are a small sample, but representative of the more general fears and anxieties of the right wing:

> You can't give them local government rights and offer them national power-sharing and expect it to all end there. It's bound to result in black majority rule and the extinction of the white man in Africa (CP-MP, R. de Ville, cited in Leach 1989: 81).

It becomes clear that African states never succeeded in

constitutionally protecting minorities. They all inherited multiparty democratic systems from the colonial powers and some even had a Bill of Rights. Unfortunately this Bill of Rights did not prevent millions of Biafrians in Nigeria from being exterminated (Pieter Mulder, *Patriot*, 1 June 1990).

The ANC still has plans for a 'Nuremberg'-style trial to punish people for crimes against humanity, such 'crimes' including measures taken to separate races (*Patriot*, 11 May 1990).

What will Mr de Klerk do in a few years' time when a black government introduces a one-party state, introduces mass-nationalization and press censorship? (*Patriot*, 11 May 1990).

Survey findings on the fears of whites in general
Evidence of right-wing fears in isolation is rare, but it can safely be assumed that the following surveys, which deal with white and Afrikaner fears in general, are wholly applicable to members of the right wing, whose fears of black rule are even higher than those of the white population in general.

An M&M survey of February 1990 found that approximately one-third of whites in the survey opposed the release of long-term security prisoners, the repeal of the Separate Amenities Act and the unbanning of black liberation organizations. Almost half of all Afrikaners and more than three-quarters of CP supporters opposed these developments. These reforms were perceived as a direct threat to their way of life after 40 years of security offered by the NP. It is also obvious that the greatest anxiety was centred around the unbanning of black resistance movements, indicating a fear of the unknown and proof of the efficiency of the NP's propaganda and indoctrination in keeping the vast majority of whites in the dark about the true purpose of these liberation organizations.

The survey by Manzo and McGowan (1989) dealt with the fears of 'élite' Afrikaners and found that over 95 per cent of prominent Afrikaners regarded every aspect of black resistance to apartheid as a threat. As was to be expected, violence and terror aimed at whites in urban areas are regarded as the most serious threat by the respondents, while violence in black areas came a close second, most probably because of the fear that it might spread to white areas at some stage. It is quite surprising that the SACP was regarded by only 38 per cent of respondents as a serious threat, in spite of the fact that the party at this stage still possessed much of its mystique as it was still banned and the demise of communism worldwide was not yet as frank and obvious as it was to become. A further 66 per cent of respondents feared that economic growth, free enterprise, white employment and white prosperity would be adversely affected by black rule, 83 per cent expected that a majority government would be inept, 87 per cent feared a deterioration in their quality of life, and 80 per cent feared that democracy and minority rights would suffer.

The survey by Hugo (1988; Table 1) on white attitudes to black majority rule in South Africa corresponds closely to the findings of both the M&M and Manzo and McGowan surveys.

Table 1
White perceptions of the prospect of majority rule – Hugo, 1988

Perceived threat	Afrikaners (%)	English-speakers (%)
Physical safety would be threatened	78.5	70.1
Language and culture won't be protected	88.5	75.2
Income and living standards would suffer	82.4	78.9
Law and order won't be upheld	84.0	73.3
Blacks would discriminate against whites	91.4	78.2
White women would be molested by blacks	85.3	60.1
Communist policies would be implemented	88.3	67.9
White possessions would not be safe	87.5	69.5

From these figures it appears that the vast majority of whites from both language groups was distinctly nervous of a black government. Apart from serious doubts about the inability of such a government to maintain law and order, more than three-quarters of Afrikaner respondents feared that under a black government their physical safety, possessions and culture would be threatened. In addition, they were convinced that such a government would be of communist origin and would permit reverse discrimination. The majority of English-speakers had similar fears, which is a clear indication that such fears are deeply ingrained in the white psyche, which is not surprising as these surveys indicate that between 78 and 86 per cent of whites believe that their physical safety would be threatened by majority rule.

The findings tend to confirm Z.B. du Toit's contention (above) that 'fear is the driving force of white politics', and the implication is that these fears, whether founded in fact or fiction, are a very real part of the Afrikaner and white psyche, and will strongly influence their approach to future political developments. Fears of suppression, domination and genocide, which are inherent in most minority groups, serve as a powerful motivating force for the acquisition of power by such groups. This is also the case in South Africa, where the core of the conflict lies in the fact that Afrikaners and whites insist upon clinging to power in order to prevent 'black domination'. While the NP hides its intention under the guise of power-sharing, and the CP expresses it as the demand for self-determination, the ultimate goal is the same: to prevent control of the state slipping from Afrikaner and white hands. Loss of such control, in their view, would leave whites and Afrikaners vulnerable to domination by the majority, and would put at risk the status and endanger the identity of the Afrikaner.

2· Dimensions of the Right Wing

As mentioned earlier, Afrikaner nationalism has never been a monolithic phenomenon, and its history is interspersed with incidents of internal conflict and dissension. As Afrikaner nationalism is also the guiding principle of the right wing, it is therefore not surprising that differences also exist within the right wing. This chapter deals with the dimensions of right-wing politics and with the issues, policies and strategies which cause divisions among the various categories and organizations. It should be emphasized that these differences are not fundamental in nature, but rather refer to different expressions of the demand for Afrikaner self-determination and to the different strategies followed by various groups. Apart from the distinctions between the various categories within the right wing and the numerous organizations identified as right wing, it has become common practice further to classify right-wing organizations according to their positions on the ideological 'left–right' spectrum. Distinctions are now made between, firstly, those on the 'left' of the right wing, referred to as the 'moderate', 'new' or 'pragmatic right', i.e. those who are in favour of at least considering the possibility of an autonomous, non-racial Afrikaner region within a united but federal South Africa (the AVU and AVF); secondly, those at the centre of the right wing, also called the 'traditional right', i.e. the CP, which until recently wanted to re-implement apartheid but now demands a sovereign white homeland loosely linked to a South African confederation – it also avoids blatant racism, and would be prepared to use violence as a final resort; thirdly, those on the right of the right wing, also referred to as the 'radical' or 'extreme right', who operate mostly outside the confines of institutional politics, openly propagate racism and white supremacy, frequently break the law, and have no misgivings about using violence or threats of violence (e.g. the AWB). Generically they are termed the white right wing because of their collective identification with the aspirations of Afrikaner nationalism. In spite of this even the very definition of Afrikanerdom varies from organization to organization: it can be broad enough to include all Afrikaans-speakers (including Afrikaans-speaking coloureds), or narrower to incorporate only Afrikaners and other whites of European stock who support the right-wing cause. In some cases, it incorporates only those Boer Afrikaans-speakers living in the two northern provinces who can trace their ancestry back to the Voortrekkers and the Anglo–Boer War.

It should be clear that the above is little more than a description of the issues which hold together and divide the right wing, without giving a proper definition that would stand up to closer scrutiny. The right wing clearly does not represent an ethnic group *per se*, as its support is limited to only about half of all Afrikaners. Nor is its support limited to Afrikaners only, as it enjoys considerable support among English-speaking conservatives as well. These observations indicate that the white right wing might be defined as a segment within the white racial group driven by the forces of Afrikaner nationalism, with the goal of self-determination and racial exclusiveness, and with a distinct ideological leaning towards political conservatism.

In spite of the diversity of the right wing, one organization, the CP, stands out as pivotal and as the chief parliamentary representative of the right-wing movement. With the exception of other parties, membership of the CP does not exclude membership of any of the other right-wing organizations: many CP supporters would also belong to one or more of the many right-wing cultural, religious or paramilitary organizations.

Political parties
The Conservative Party
Although the CP is part of the right-wing front for unity, the Afrikaner Volksfront (AVF), the Party has been the pivotal axis of the right wing since its founding in 1982. As discussed in the

preceding chapter, the CP was founded by Treurnicht and other MPs who had left the NP over the issue of power-sharing and the tricameral constitution. The CP received a total of 673,079 votes (31 per cent) and 39 seats in the last whites-only general election in 1989. Since then it has gained a further three seats during ensuing by-elections, and lost seven seats due to the expulsion of two MPs and the defection of five more in 1992 to found the Afrikaner Volksunie (AVU). Although 875,619 people supported the CP-led No campaign during the 1992 referendum (an increase of 202,540 since 1989), the right's share of the total vote remained constant at 31 per cent (due to a higher voter turn-out than in 1989). From the referendum results it appeared that the CP had reached its electoral ceiling of approximately one-third of white voters, with further defections from the NP to the right ending up with the Inkatha Freedom Party (IFP), which, according to one recent poll,[1] was supported by 27 per cent of whites in the Witwatersrand. Should the CP decide to participate in the first non-racial election in 1994, its white support (at 1992 levels) would translate roughly into 5 per cent of the total electorate.

In 1993 the CP chose a new leader, Ferdi Hartzenberg, following the death of Treurnicht who had led the party since 1982. Whereas Treurnicht was pragmatic and his views located in the ideological centre of the party, Hartzenberg is known for his ideological rigidity and Verwoerdian mentality. However, the choice of Hartzenberg was hardly an inspiration to disillusioned CP supporters, who wanted a long-awaited 'saviour' who could lead the right out of its post-referendum lows and who would provide a new impetus to the quest for Afrikaner self-determination. This was obvious from the lack of enthusiasm which met Hartzenberg's appointment in May 1993 and by the overwhelmingly positive response to the founding of the AVF under the leadership of Constand Viljoen, former head of the South African Defence Force (SADF).

From its founding the CP's support-base had a distinct regional trend. All but one of the MPs who left the NP in 1982 to found the CP were from the Transvaal. Ironically, when the Purified Nationalists broke with Hertzog in 1934, which, it can be argued, was also a split to the right, his caucus consisted mostly of Cape Nationalists.[2] The Transvaal character of the CP was reaffirmed during the 1987 general election when all 22 of its seats were located in that province. In the 1989 general election the party finally broke out of its narrow provincial base, and won eight of its 39 seats in the Cape and Free State provinces. In that election the CP also expanded its reach into urban and peri-urban seats, although these were still predominantly Afrikaner and working-class constituencies, e.g. Brakpan, Carletonville, Randfontein, Roodepoort and Uitenhage. After 1989, however, the CP experienced rapid growth outside its traditional support-base, as was evident from the swing towards the party among English-speaking voters (e.g. in Umlazi), among middle-class urban voters (e.g. in Randburg), and in NP heartland in the western Cape (e.g. in Ceres, Vasco and Maitland).

The evolution of the CP's constitutional policies can be divided into two distinct phases: the first phase covers the period stretching from the founding of the party in 1982 to approximately 1990, when the official party policy became known as 'partition' (see below), which largely implied a return to Verwoerdian apartheid. The second phase covers the years 1990 to 1993, when the CP's policies, under pressure from moderates within the party and changing political circumstances, began moving away from traditional Verwoerdian apartheid closer to the concept of Afrikaner self-determination in a smaller white homeland. The transformation of the CP's policies is discussed at length in Chapter 4 as part of the right wing in the de Klerk era.

Partition is generally defined as the division of a territory of a state into two or more geopolitical units or regions which subsequently function as separate political entities or states. The rationale behind partition can be found, according to Deutsch (1984: 134), in the quest for a reduction in collision and conflict opportunities among different groups, but the practical implication of partition is the reduction of friction between ethnic groups by creating more homogeneous political units and by spatially separating antagonists (Horowitz 1985: 589).

Over the years, various models of partition have been implemented in South Africa, the most notorious being Verwoerd's brainchild, referred to as 'grand apartheid' or homeland partition. Homeland partition rested on the assumption that the whole of South Africa belonged to the whites, except for the 13 per cent of the country that had been set aside for the various black 'nations', all of which had their own designated national territory (with borders drawn by whites) and in which their citizens could exercise their political rights. This policy eventually led to the formation of ten black national states: Transkei, Ciskei, Bophuthatswana, Venda, Lebowa, KwaZulu, Qwa Qwa, Kangwane, KwaNdebele and Gazankulu. Only the first four achieved 'statehood' by being granted 'independence' by the South African government. The policy of 'grand apartheid' was never a viable one, for the simple reason that blacks, who constitute 70 per cent of the population, were allotted 13 per cent of the land area, while 16 per cent of the population ruled over the remainder. In addition, the majority of blacks lived outside the homelands in the urban areas of South Africa, and had no intention of either moving back to these homelands or allowing themselves to be forced to exert their political rights there.

Apart from homeland partition, proposals for 'radical partition' also attracted a great deal of attention throughout the 1970s and early 1980s, and were intended to improve on homeland partition by providing a more equitable division of land between black and white. Most of these proposals were based on the plan of the former secretary of native affairs, Werner Eiselen, who in 1955 proposed the demarcation of the country into two halves (Tiryakian 1967; Blenck and von der Ropp 1976; Maasdorp 1980). The Eiselen Line, as it became known, divided the country in a predominantly black northern half, and a southern half which was supposed to be reserved as a predominantly white and coloured area.[3]

In spite of the fact that it had already proved to be unrealizable, with a few modifications the CP basically took over the NP's policy of separate development and of classical apartheid as implemented by Verwoerd during the 1960s. The CP's policy of partition, in its purest form, implied a return to Verwoerdian homeland apartheid, based on the 'right to self-determination of every nation in South Africa, in particular the Afrikaner and all those who identify with the Afrikaner's struggle for freedom' (CP Election Manifesto, 1989). The 'white homeland' would consist of all land occupied by whites after the borders of black homelands had been consolidated in line with the 1936 Land Act, and in this territory blacks would have no political rights. 'Black nations' were to be given independence in their own homelands on 13 per cent of South African territory with political boundaries that would correspond with the existing ethnic and racial divisions. As the existing group definitions and the political boundaries have been determined solely by the NP and the Afrikaner establishment since the 1950s, it is not surprising that CP policy stipulated that whites would be entitled to the largest part of the country. Blacks residing within the borders of white South Africa were regarded as temporary migrant workers with no political rights and would eventually be repatriated to the homelands, involving mass forced removals. In addition partition made provision for the creation of coloured and Indian homelands and black 'city states' e.g. Soweto, where those blacks who have become permanently urbanized would have been granted their 'independence' (CP Election Manifesto, 1989). The policies envisaged by the CP to keep blacks out of 'white' South Africa were an exact duplicate of the NP strategies in the heyday of apartheid – these included forced removals, decentralization to border industries, influx control and limiting black urbanization to black homelands or bordering areas. As in the case of the NP's former policies, only whites could own land or be citizens of South Africa; blacks would have to exercise their political rights inside their own states irrespective of where they were born or were living (CP Election News, July 1989).

In line with the other tenets of apartheid which it inherited from the NP, the CP rejected all forms of racial integration on social and political levels. The CP's policy of complete racial segregation was based on the notion of racial exclusivity i.e. that the white community should have access to separate social institutions such as schools, housing, churches, medical services, recreational facilities, beaches, central business districts, etc. Until their repeal by the NP in 1990–91, the Group Areas and Separate Amenities Acts were of particular importance to the CP, as these were regarded as the key to white exclusivity and to the survival of the white nation: 'Only through the rigid enforcement of separate residential areas can separate schools, an own community life, own voters rolls and own political representation, be guaranteed' (Treurnicht, cited in the *Sunday Times*, 3 September 1989).

The CP's economic policy indicated a preference for a strong state presence in the economy. Although the CP supports a free market system, it is not unconditionally committed to capitalism and free markets, since its partition policy by itself implies considerable central government intervention in the economy, e.g. enforcing influx control and closing of central business districts to non-white traders. Its position on foreign investment is one of curbing the influence of large monopolies and multinational corporations, and ironically, in respect of monopoly capital, the CP's approach differed little from that of the ANC: 'We shall protect the consumer, small businessman and entrepreneur against monopolies which abuse the concept of free enterprise' (CP election pamphlet in the Maitland by-election, February 1991).

The CP was especially critical of the NP over what it perceived as a redistribution of wealth from white to black: 'The government not only shares its political power, but also its economic resources.... At the tempo with which this is occurring, there will be little left to do for the ANC with regard to redistribution, as the government would have done it all' (*Patriot*, 8 March 1991) [translation]. Part of its argument was that the NP's commitment to creating a welfare state for blacks, and using white taxes to subsidize black administrations, education, housing, transport and pensions, had contributed to the economic decline of whites and the indebtedness of the state (Zille 1988: 84). To substantiate this allegation, the CP claimed that government debt had increased from about R18 billion in 1983, when the tricameral constitution was implemented, to R55 billion in 1989, and that the purchasing power of the rand had declined from 100 cents in 1970 to 7 cents in 1991 (*Patriot*, 7 June 1991). The CP also accused the NP of wasting money as a result of poor administration, misdirected state spending and corruption. Particular allegations included the fact that senior bureaucrats and ministers who had to resign still received large pensions; that NP propaganda was paid for with state funds; and that there had been exorbitant renovations on ministerial housing (e.g. the R2 million spent on Pik Botha's private home). Massive corruption was exposed in the findings of no fewer than six commissions which had investigated financial irregularities within government departments, leading to the resignation of two MPs, one cabinet minister and two director-generals (CP Election News, 1989).

White unemployment has also been used as ammunition for the CP's attacks on the government. The party claimed that the increase in white unemployment of 113 per cent between 1990 and 1991 was a direct result of inept government policies such as privatization and less spending on defence corporations such as Armscor (Armaments Development and Production Corporation) and Atlas. In addition, the poverty among some whites has forced them to find jobs as domestic servants or petrol-station attendants, i.e. jobs which are regarded by racist whites as demeaning and normally reserved for blacks (*Patriot*, 17 May 1991). The reappearance over the past few years of the 'poor white' problem of the 1930s is further evidence, according to the CP, of the government's uncaring attitude towards lower-class whites, which led to 'unprecedented misery and poverty which today exist among thousands of whites' (*Patriot*, 21 June 1991) [translation]. The CP soon realized that it was better placed than the government to champion the cause of the latter-day 'poor whites': in 1991 the CP, in conjunction with other right-wing organizations, launched a charity campaign called *Aksie Helpmekaar* (The Front for Helping Fellow Citizens) and later *Volkshulp 2000* (People's Assistance), which were similar to the *Reddingsdaadbond* of the 1940s – its goal being the formation of a labour bureau and providing the basic necessities for poor whites. A similar organization, *Boere Krisisaksie* (Farmers' Crisis Front), was founded by right-wing farmers to provide aid and drought relief to needy farmers who opposed the government's land reforms. Its labour policy is designed to grant the white workers the special privileges to which they were accustomed before the 1970s, e.g. by restoring job reservation and influx control, and by banning black trade unions. The CP accused the NP of 'betraying the white worker' by taking away state protection against black competition, and claimed that its policy would provide for the preference of white workers in white areas.

The CP takes a hard-line approach to security issues. In the Botha era it fully supported cross-border raids into neighbouring countries, the presence of the Defence Force in townships and a strong, politicized police force. The party's views on crime and violence underline its hard-line approach to security issues in general. Throughout the many by-elections and the three general elections of the 1980s and early 1990s, the right wing had repeatedly used the theme of the growing black self-assertiveness, of unrest, violence and crime to draw whites into its *laager*. In this aspect the right had to compete with the NP, who used similar tactics during the same period in order to entice voters away from the liberal opposition. It blamed the government's more 'sensitive' approach to squatting, the repeal of influx control laws, and the relaxing of the Group Areas Act for the rise in crime. But the party also saw a more sinister aspect of crime, one which held that blacks regarded any form of violation against whites not as crime but as acts of revenge against the white population. In response to the rise in crime in white suburbs, the CP requested that the government should introduce a nightly curfew in white suburbs which would 'prevent unemployed blacks from entering white suburbs' (*Patriot*, 5 October 1990). It also strongly criticized the lifting of the state of emergency in June 1990, as this was done in spite of the 'highest murder, unrest and violence statistics in ten years' (*Patriot*, 15 June 1990).

The CP's pre-1992 foreign policy was firmly based on the rejection of foreign interference in South Africa's domestic affairs, which was regarded as motivated by blatant self-interest rather than as an outrage against apartheid (Zille 1988: 79). The party believed that it would have been able to normalize relations with the outside world once its policy of partition had solved the 'national' question of South Africa. The CP emphasized that it would not ask for the lifting of sanctions if it meant the capitulation of the whites (Patriot, 6 July 1990). The party has a particularly negative perception of the USA, on the grounds of its 'imperialistic' nature and its 'self-serving interference' in South Africa's affairs. Its strongly anti-American stance resulted in the party denouncing the USA's role in the Gulf war and it criticized the NP government for offering its moral support to the USA during that war without demanding that the superpower first scrapped sanctions against South Africa. The CP also took strong exception to the unilateral destruction of South Africa's nuclear arsenal by the de Klerk administration after 1989, which Hartzenberg regarded as the 'worst crime that any one individual had ever committed against the South African people' (*Patriot*, 9 April 1993).

A brief mention of the developments within the CP during the early 1990s must suffice here (for further details see Chapter 4). The new political realities of the reforms under F.W. de Klerk led to the emergence of a sizeable pragmatic wing within the CP who wanted the party to change direction from adherence to racist philosophies (on which the policies of apartheid and partition had been founded) to Afrikaner self-determination. The conflict between the *volkstaters* (as they became known) and the apartheid-traditionalists within the CP lasted for nearly three years, and eventually led to the breakaway of a core group of the former to found their own party, the AVU. During this period, however, the CP eventually embraced certain of the *volkstaat* principles, including the acceptance in principle that a white homeland would be limited in size, and even briefly joined multiparty negotiations in 1993. However, the CP maintained its untenable position on obtaining complete sovereignty for the proposed racially based white *volkstaat*.

Until 1992 the CP's goal of resisting reforms and obstructing the transitional process was aimed at forcing the NP government through extra-parliamentary pressure to call a whites-only general election or referendum on a new constitution. Following its crushing defeat in the March 1992 referendum, the CP shifted its focus away from winning control of the South African state through the ballot box to a less ambitious goal, the attainment of Afrikaner self-determination in a sovereign white homeland.

In an effort to revitalize its relevancy after the referendum defeat and the defection of the AVU, the CP succeeded in forging two alliances during this period. In September 1992 it founded the Concerned South African Group (Cosag) in conjunction with the AVU, Vekom and three conservative black homeland leaders, Mangosuthu Buthelezi of KwaZulu, Lucas Mangope of Bophuthatswana and Oupa Gqozo of the Ciskei. As a non-racial right-wing alliance, Cosag aimed at countering bilateral negotiations and agreements between the ANC and NP, and promoting the idea of a South African confederacy. In May 1993 the CP came together with 20 other white right-wing groups to form the Afrikaner Volksfront (AVF), with the goal of promoting right-wing unity and the realization of an Afrikaner *volkstaat*. Although its leader General Constand Viljoen is not a member of the CP, most of the AVF's executive council consists of CP MPs.

The Afrikaner Volksunie (AVU) (Afrikaner People's Union)

The AVU was founded in August 1992 when the three-year-long struggle within the CP between its moderate wing and the apartheid-traditionalists had reached breaking point. Following the referendum defeat in March 1992 the *volkstaters* intensified their demand for changes to the CP's policies – in particular that the term 'white' be replaced with 'Afrikaner', that the CP enter into negotiations with all parties, and that the policies of partition and apartheid be replaced with self-determination in a *volkstaat*. The rejection by the CP executive of the proposal submitted by the group led by Andries Beyers led to the resignation of five CP MPs, which was surprising as the strength of the *volkstaat* faction was estimated at about one-third of the CP's caucus, i.e. about 12 to 25 MPs. Beyers claimed at the time that his rebels had the support of at least 12 more MPs in the CP caucus who were adopting a 'wait-and-see attitude' (*Rapport*, 16 August 1992). Along with their departure many ordinary members of the party and executive members at constituency level resigned as well, while the editor and four senior staff members of *Patriot* were fired from their jobs (ibid). The two prominent *volkstaat*-supporting MPs expelled earlier, Koos van der Merwe and Koos Botha, were initially not invited to join the party because they were deemed ideologically too close to the NP, but Botha later became a member.

The major policy differences between the AVU and the CP concerned the new party's emphasis on a territorially less ambitious homeland, a demand for self-determination (not apartheid), an emphasis on the Afrikaner ethnic group (not the white racial group), and negotiations with all parties (not just with conservative homeland leaders). On the latter issue Beyers was adamant: 'We want to discuss our idea with everybody across the political spectrum. We want to bring it across that the Afrikaner is not selfish and that we are interested in peace and harmony' (*Sunday Times*, 16 August 1992). With regard to the Party's support for a non-racial definition of Afrikanerdom,

Beyers said: 'We are bargaining on behalf of the Afrikaans-speaking South Africans. If we are bargaining on behalf of a race we would be accused of racism and we are not doing that' (*Patriot*, 5 March 1993).

By 1993 the ideological distance between the two parties became even greater as the AVU began displaying even greater pragmatism on the issues of autonomy, citizenship rights and the location of the *volkstaat*. While the CP still insisted on complete independence for a white state, the AVU indicated that it would accept an autonomous region within a federally structured non-racial South Africa; unlike the CP, the AVU indicated that everyone in that territory, irrespective of race, would enjoy full citizenship rights; unlike the CP, the AVU was able to submit detailed plans of the proposed location and exact boundaries of its proposed *volkstaat* to the multiparty negotiation forum.

The relative enthusiasm with which the ANC and NP welcomed the AVU's pragmatism instilled a fear in the CP that the AVU might steal its supporters and could assume the role of the official representative of Afrikanerdom. This resulted in considerable hostility towards the AVU from the CP leadership, illustrated by Hartzenberg's accusation that the AVU's proposals were 'worse than those of President de Klerk' (*Sunday Times*, 16 August 1992). Other CP MPs accused Beyers of being a *draadsitter* (a fence-sitter), and of stabbing the CP in the back (*Patriot*, 9 April 1993; 26 May 1993). Relations between the two parties improved only marginally as a result of their joint participation in Cosag and with their involvement in the founding of the AVF in May 1993. Beyers drew heavy criticism from the CP when he refused unconditionally to sign the founding acts of the AVF because of a citizenship clause which would discriminate against other races in the proposed *volkstaat*. Although the CP suggested that the Beyers Party should be expelled from the AVF, a compromise was reached whereby the AVU signed the founding act but not the contentious clause (*Die Burger*, 21 May 1993).

In spite of its involvement with other right-wing organizations and its leading role in the founding of the AVF, the AVU has generally attempted to play a constructive role in the negotiation process. As indicated earlier, the AVU was prepared to alter its position as part of the negotiation process, serving on the committees appointed by the negotiating forum to deal with various constitutional aspects. Beyers had a meeting with Mandela early in 1993, and his party's position was sympathetically considered by both the NP and the ANC.

However, even the AVU succumbed to the Afrikaner tradition of *broedertwis*. In August 1993 two of its MPs resigned from the AVU and suggested that they might join the AVF. Their reason for leaving was over the party's continued participation at the negotiation table following the withdrawal of its Cosag partners, the CP and IFP. Beyers admitted at the time that he expected more resignations[4] and that it would probably lead to the dissolution of his Party, but insisted that he would remain with the Party until the last (*Rapport*, 26 September 1993). In September 1993, Beyers, joined by the remainder of the AVU's caucus, left the AVU to become an Independent MP. In October 1993 Beyers completed the circle by returning to the NP. His move occurred 11 years after he left the NP to join the CP and less than two years after he won the decisive Potchefstroom by-election for the CP, a victory which forced the NP into calling a referendum and which, in turn, for ever destroyed the CP's claim to be a government-in-waiting. The AVU's representatives at the multiparty negotiating forum, led by Corlia Kruger and her husband, continued their attempts to negotiate some form of Afrikaner federal state under the AVU banner. However, lacking any political clout or power base whatsoever, they were not particularly successful, apart from causing intense frustration among the other delegates for their time-consuming objections and long-winded speeches to the forum.

The Herstigte Nasionale Party (HNP) (Reconstituted National Party)
The HNP was founded in 1969 under the leadership of Albert Hertzog, who left the NP with Jaap Marais and two other disaffected MPs over the political direction of the NP under Vorster. The HNP's poor electoral performance throughout its existence is probably its single most notable characteristic: it received 53,000 votes in 1970 and 34,000 in 1977; there was a short-lived boost in 1981 with 192,304 votes but no seats in parliament. After the birth of the CP the HNP's support continued to decline from 61,456 votes in 1987 (3.1 per cent of

the vote) to 5,531 votes in 1989 (0.25 per cent). The HNP was effectively finished as a political entity of any relevance after 1989, but the persistence (some would say foolhardiness) of its second leader, Jaap Marais, had kept it going at least nominally by early 1994. The Party even organized a march (with 37 people) on parliament in November 1993, to protest the passing into legislation of the transitional executive council.

The HNP's apartheid-based policies have not evolved much over the years from the Verwoerdian model on which they were founded. The HNP believed that the whole of South Africa apart from the homeland areas belonged to whites and that blacks working in 'white' South Africa are there only on a temporary basis. However, the HNP does not envisage an Indian homeland and proposes that all Indians should be repatriated to India.[5] The HNP's definition of the *volk* excludes English-speakers; unlike the CP, the party argues that Afrikaans should be the sole official language of the country. The HNP's economic policy is socialist by nature and conforms to *volkskapitalisme* (O'Meara 1983), i.e. the creation of jobs and businesses for Afrikaners with the help of the state. The HNP remains close to its working-class origins and used to maintain close ties with certain white right-wing trade unions, in particular the Mineworkers' Union (MWU) and the White Building Workers' Union.

However, for most of its existence the HNP remained isolated, both through its own volition and because of the actions of its opponents. In 1981 the Party refused to enter into a short-lived right-wing front called *Aksie Red Blank Suid-Afrika* (the Front for Saving White South Africa). Ever since the founding of the CP in 1982, the personal strife between Marais and Treurnicht prevented the two parties from amalgamating. Marais was of the opinion that Treurnicht had forsaken him in 1969 by remaining within the NP, and furthermore, while he (Marais) had been fighting the right-wing battle for two decades, Treurnicht had a hand in formulating the NP's reforms. In addition, Marais regarded his party's survival as an independent entity as beneficial to the right-wing cause: 'We [the HNP] must continue to pressure the CP from the right to ensure that the latter does not shift towards the left too much in its efforts to draw support away from the NP' (*Rapport*, 10 May 1987).

Against all the odds the HNP still exists as a political party and continues to publish its mouthpiece, *Die Afrikaner*, on a weekly basis. Marais was occasionally interviewed by the SABC until 1992. Although the HNP had reservations about the role of the generals in the newly created AVF and over its interpretation of self-determination, Jaap Marais was elected to its executive council in May 1993.

The Boerestaat Party (BSP)

The BSP was founded in 1988 by Robert van Tonder. Its founding congress was attended by fewer than 120 people and the party has never participated in any election. Van Tonder had resigned from the NP in 1961 because of his opposition to Verwoerd's plan to encourage British immigration to South Africa, and he subsequently founded the Conservative Study Group. The publication of his book *Die Stryd Duur Voort* (The Struggle Continues) in 1966, was he claimed (1990: 89), a direct cause of the founding of the HNP in 1969, as it spelled out the right-wing alternative to the NP's direction. It was on van Tonder's insistence that the HNP viewed Afrikaans as the only official language, and his efforts to promote Afrikaans and to fight discrimination against the language in shops and elsewhere, earned him the nickname, 'Taalbul' (literally: language bull).

The political philosophy of the BSP assumes that South Africa consists of 15 separate nations, each with its own language, culture and territory, e.g. the Boer, Xhosa, Zulu and other 'nationalities'. For this reason, van Tonder (interview, 10 April 1991) denies that a uniform South African language or culture exists and he takes great pleasure in inviting anyone to speak 'South African' to him. He also believes that the 'citizens' of the former Boer Republics constitute a 'nation' by themselves, and do not belong to the 'so-called' Afrikaner nation, even though they happen to speak the same language. Only those Afrikaners of Voortrekker descent and whose forefathers fought in the Anglo–Boer War are regarded as Boer, which excludes the Afrikaners in the Cape and Natal who are referred to as 'Cape Dutch' and 'Afrikaner liberals'.

Van Tonder argues that the sovereign Boer Republics were robbed of their independence by the British Empire during the Anglo–Boer War of 1899–1902, a fact which he wants to contest at the UN. The Boerestaat Party's policy is to restore the independence of the ZAR (Transvaal), the Orange Free State and Vryheid, by way of secession from the remaining part of South Africa (van Tonder 1990: 43–86).

There are close links between the BSP and the *Boereweerstandsbeweging* (BWB) of Andrew Ford. The BWB is often regarded as the military wing of the party, but its newsletters refer to an alliance of two separate organizations (newsletter, March 1990).

The BSP publishes a regular newsletter to propagate its nationalist and racist ideology. The newsletters frequently refer to events of historic value to Afrikaners, and have on occasion urged the destruction of Melrose House, the venue in Pretoria where the Treaty of Vereeniging was signed in 1902. Other items that have appeared in the newsletters (March 1990; January 1991) dealt with the 'heroic struggle' of Piet Rudolph while on the run from the police, sympathetic and admiring articles on the Nazi war effort, disparaging references to the liaison of de Klerk's son with a girl of colour, and the 'treachery' of the state president (who in BSP circles is known as 'Pienk Frikkie' in allusion to his supposed 'communist' leanings).

Other parties

The *Blanke Party* (White Party) of Johan Schabort, was founded in 1985 (Bekker et al 1989). It was overtly racist and propagated a secessionist version of partition. By 1989 the *Blanke Party* was supported by few more than the immediate family of its founder and was disbanded shortly afterwards. Johan Schabort became a member of the CP in 1990.

Although existing in name for a few years previously, the AWB's *Blanke Volkstaat Party* was never launched in an organizational sense even by 1989 (Bekker et al 1989: 39–40). Its leader, Eugene Terre Blanche, tried to become involved in parliamentary politics during the 1989 general election but the CP refused to accede to his demand to contest the Krugersdorp constituency on behalf of the right wing (Kemp 1990: 130).

The National Conservative Party (NCP) was founded in 1979 by Connie Mulder, the former NP minister of information. Mulder, the *verkrampte* candidate, was defeated by the *verligte* choice, P.W. Botha, for the post of prime minister in 1978.

The NCP participated in the 1981 general election in an informal alliance with the HNP and received 19,249 votes (1.4 per cent of the total), but no seats in parliament. The party was incorporated into the CP in 1982; two of Mulder's sons became CP MPs.

Intellectual and cultural organizations

The South African Bureau of Racial Affairs (SABRA)
SABRA was formed in 1948 as part of an attempt by Afrikaner nationalists to counter the 'liberalism' of the South African Institute of Race Relations. The organization was funded by the Broederbond and charged with constructing the philosophical pillars of apartheid, becoming the 'perfect ideological assembly line for the Nationalist government' (Leach 1989: 168). The intellectual foundation of SABRA consisted largely of academics from the University of Stellenbosch, who sought to provide a moral and scientific rationale for apartheid after 1950. Occasionally, however, the academics at SABRA proved themselves to be too liberal for the NP's liking, e.g. when they clashed with Verwoerd over the report of the 1956 Tomlinson Commission over aspects of the homeland policy. He strongly objected to the criticism of his homeland policies voiced by SABRA and managed to eject the dissident academics from the organization (Schoeman 1973: 230).

After that SABRA consistently maintained a conservative stance on most policy matters, and even became biased in favour of the *verkrampte* wing of the NP. One of its chairmen, P.D.F. Weis, had supported the Hertzog group, while another conservative, Carel Boshoff, was elected to the post in 1972. Understandably, the organization was not supportive of the NP's new direction under Vorster and the divisions between SABRA and the NP gradually widened during the 1970s after the government had rejected the policy of racial segregation in the spheres of labour, public amenities and services.

The differences between the NP and SABRA became irreconcilable under P.W. Botha as SABRA rejected the government's new racial policies, in particular the 1984 tricameral constitution. Remaining ties between the NP and SABRA were broken after the founding of the CP in 1982, whereafter SABRA became an integral part of right-wing politics. In April 1984 SABRA, now reflecting the CP's point of view, explained why it rejected power-sharing with coloureds and Indians: '[Power-sharing] ignores the conflict potential which exists between these groups by nature of differences in their lifestyles, numbers and physical types' (*Journal of Racial Affairs*, xxxv/2, 1984).

Between 1982 and 1985 SABRA had provided the right-wing movement with some of the ideological foundations for its constitutional proposals and carried out research on models of partition under the guidance of Carel Boshoff, Hercules Booysen and others. The organization claimed to do scientific research on racial issues and to suggest solutions within the context of separate development and racial segregation, in contrast to such 'integrationist' organizations as the South African Institute of International Affairs, the South African Institute of Race Relations and the Study Project on Christianity in Apartheid Society (Spro-cas). In 1985 SABRA reaffirmed its opposition to the tricameral constitution, on the grounds that it was unacceptable to the majority of blacks and large sections of the white community, and because it ignored the 'existence of nations' in South Africa. SABRA's suggestion that a *volkstaat* be created for each nation in South Africa was in line with its traditional philosophy but, in a surprising development, it broke ranks with the CP's apartheid model by rejecting a return to the pre-1983 era, as 'those bridges had been burned' (SABRA, 1985).

SABRA's new doctrine was noticeable in 1986 when the organization suggested that an Afrikaner *volkstaat* be founded in the 'white' parts of the country. A similar Declaration of Intent, issued in 1987, spelled out the requirement for the creation of a viable *volkstaat*, namely that it should constitute a continuous, uninterrupted geographical area which takes cognizance of Afrikaner history and which could be defended by military means. By 1990 the idea of an Afrikaner *volkstaat* had became an integral part of SABRA's philosophy, and the organization argued that Afrikaners would have to get involved in the process of negotiations in order to put forward its 'legitimate' case for self-determination. It also accepted that South Africa would eventually be ruled by a black majority and proposed therefore that a *volkstaat* would have to obtain sovereignty through a negotiated secession from a non-racial South Africa (*Journal of Racial Affairs*, xli/3, 1990). Boshoff rejected the CP's policies as unworkable and morally indefensible and claimed that the answer lay in a smaller Afrikaner state, whose independence could be achieved by secession from a larger black-dominated South Africa.

By 1991 SABRA further increased the distance between itself and other right-wing organizations by suggesting the possibility of a 'Federal Afrikaner Republic' which could be part of the greater, non-racial South Africa (*Die Burger*, 29 August 1990). This proposal, suggested by SABRA's executive director, A.J. de Beer, represented a sharp deviation from the organization's previous position that the Afrikaner should accept nothing less than complete independence, and interestingly enough, was the forerunner of the AVU's proposal two years later for a federal Afrikaner region within a greater South Africa.

Afrikanervryheidstigting (Avstig) (Afrikaner Freedom Foundation)
Without sacrificing his position as chairman of SABRA, Boshoff decided to promote his vision of an Afrikaner *volkstaat* more actively through the founding of Avstig in 1988. The founding principles of the organization were based on the belief that since black majority rule was unavoidable and white minority rule morally unjustifiable, Afrikaners would have to form their own *volkstaat* in a smaller part of South Africa (*Sunday Times*, 10 June 1988; 19 June 1988). Avstig argued that the logical and morally correct solution to the Afrikaner's fear of black domination was the secession of an Afrikaner state from the rest of South Africa, in conjunction with an internal settlement whereby the rest of the country would have to be transferred to black majority rule.

In February 1989 Boshoff released detailed plans for the creation of an exclusive Afrikaner nation state. Boshoff's plans for an Afrikaner state envisaged a much smaller territory than that suggested earlier by SABRA, and excluded the traditional Afrikaner/Boer areas in the Transvaal and Free State. The boundaries of this proposed state were to incorporate the north-western Cape and southern Namibia. This area is economically underdeveloped and located mostly in a semi-desert environment, but has some potential for economic growth because of the presence of part of the Orange River, the three harbours of Saldanha Bay, Luderitz and Lamberts Bay, and a variety of minerals such as diamonds, copper and iron. It also has an international airport at Upington and a railway line catering in particular for the transport of iron ore from Sishen to Saldanha. Its GDP was about R4 billion in 1989, which represented 2 per cent of South Africa's total GDP in that year (*Finansies en Tegniek*, 31 August 1990).[6]

Avstig took some practical steps to achieve its goal for a *volkstaat* actively encouraging Afrikaners to migrate to the north-western Cape. Towards the end of 1990 about 92 Afrikaner families, largely from the Transvaal, arrived as permanent settlers in the area of the proposed *volkstaat*, especially in Olifantshoek. These migrations of Afrikaners from various parts of the country were referred to as 'Treks', e.g. the Meyerton Trek, the Valhalla Trek and the Tzaneen Trek (*Sunday Times*, 21 October 1990). According to the Orandee Development Corporation which assisted with the migration, over 12,000 people had signed a petition in 1990 whereby they undertook to move to Boshoff's *volkstaat* (*Die Burger*, 17 October 1990). In February 1991 the Afrikaner Volkswag bought the town of Orania from the Department of Water Affairs for R1 million. The town had 90 existing houses and covered an area of 400 hectares. According to Boshoff, Orania was intended to be the basis of the *volkstaat*, which would come into existence only once Afrikaners physically occupied Orania and other such growth points (*Vrye Weekblad*, 15 February 1991). By March 1991 Orania offered potential Afrikaner investors a timeshare holiday resort, a home for senior citizens, a farming cooperative, various businesses, a private hospital ('be nursed by your own people') and Afrikaner 'people's schools' (*Rapport*, 31 March 1991).

Boshoff's ability to adapt his proposals according to the changing political situation, his willingness to negotiate, and the relative modesty of his territorial claims, gave him a sympathetic ear among the ANC leadership. In 1990 Nelson Mandela indicated that the ANC would be prepared to listen to Boshoff's proposals: 'We welcome the expressed willingness of Dr Carel Boshoff and his colleagues to engage in the national dialogue about the future of our country despite our vastly differing perspectives of what that future should be'.[7] After Avstig made some further fundamental policy changes early in 1993, in which it stated that it no longer insisted on complete independence as a pre-condition for negotiations and that all residents in its proposed *volkstaat* would enjoy full political rights, the organization had a successful meeting with Mandela in March 1993 (*Cape Times*, 9 July 1993). Although nothing definite emerged from the meeting, it was significant that one of the ANC's earlier proposals (March 1993) dealing with federal regions contained references to a region (Namaqualand/lower Orange River) of which the boundaries partially corresponded with those of Avstig's *volkstaat*. Similarly, the proposals of the delimitation commission of the negotiation forum, presented in August 1993, made provision for a federal region referred to as 'Northern Cape', which is virtually identical with the proposals Avstig made in 1989 for a *volkstaat* (*Rapport*, 8 August 1993).

Toekomsgesprek (TG)

This right-wing think-tank, whose name translates literally as 'Discussion of the Future', was founded in 1983 and is the CP's alternative to the Broederbond. The organization has attempted to infiltrate and gain control of civic organizations, school committees and agricultural cooperatives with the objective of spreading the right-wing ideology. In 1991 the strength of TG was about 3000, consisting of prominent academics and people in leading positions in Afrikaner society, including almost all CP MPs (*Die Burger*, 25 January 1991; *Insig*, April 1990).

In spite of the fact that TG urged the CP in 1991 to form a people's army, the organization's ideological position always appeared slightly to the left of the CP and it often considered policies which were radically different from those of the CP. The organization was thought to be the driving force behind the Koos document (*Hansard*, 29 April 1991), which described the CP's policies as impractical and out of touch with reality (see page 160 for more information). Details of another document compiled by TG's executive council again contradicted existing CP policies (*Rapport*, 18 July 1993). The document suggested that the term 'white nation' should be rejected in favour of an ethnic definition of Afrikanerdom, that the CP had to indicate the precise borders of its proposed *volkstaat*, and that a military

take-over of the government by the right wing was not a viable
option because of the moral and religious background of the
Afrikaner.

Vereniging van Oranjewerkers
This organization was founded in 1980 and was led by H.
Booysen and H.F. Verwoerd (the latter is the son of the 'father'
of apartheid). It had only 17 founding members, but
membership had grown to an estimated 2,500 by 1986 (Bekker
et al 1989: 42). It published a quarterly journal, *Oranje
Perspektief*, and has published a number of brochures and books
under the imprint *Oranjewerkers Promosies*. The organization
received financial support from the *Genootskap van Oranje-
Sakekringe* (the Society of Orange Business Associations).

Its primary goal was to identify and develop certain
growth-points ('heartlands') which were to facilitate the creation
of the future homeland. The organization held the view that the
Afrikaner had no moral right to the largest part of South Africa,
and proposed to buy up land for exclusive Afrikaner settlement.
It regarded a *volkstaat* as the only solution to the Afrikaner's
quest for freedom in a country with many different 'nations' and
argued that its goal could be justified on biblical grounds, with
reference to the book of Genesis in which today's 'chaos' can be
ascribed to the attempts at Babel to 'create a world citizenship'
(Bruwer et al 1990: 19).

The Oranjewerkers' desire for self-sufficiency and exclusive
white labour was put to the test in the areas which it has set aside
for development as growth-points for a future white homeland.
The first of these growth-points was located in Morgenzon in
the eastern Transvaal, where about 32 members of the
movement had settled by 1988. Members of the organization
who settled in Morgenzon refused to serve blacks in shops, and
were consequently exposed to black consumer boycotts.

Although Verwoerd insisted that his followers were prepared
to make short-term sacrifices to enjoy long-term freedom,
'irreversible political realities' resulted in Verwoerd's resignation
in 1991. Shortly afterwards the organization indicated that it was
going to change its name and move its headquarters back to
Pretoria (*Rapport*, 4 August 1991).

Volkseenheidskomitee (Vekom) (People's Committee for Unity)

In his capacity as chief of military intelligence, the founder of Vekom, General Tienie Groenewald, was one of P.W. Botha's chief security advisers for many years. Unhappy with the NP under a 'visionless' F.W. de Klerk, Groenewald retired in 1990 and decided to use his extensive security experience for the benefit of the right wing. To market himself, he formed the Institute for Strategic Analysis (INSA), and later allegedly also offered his services to the military dictator of the Ciskei, Oupa Gqozo, through a front company called Multi Media Services (*Rapport*, 7 March 1993). Vekom, officially launched in early 1992, was formed initially with the goal of facilitating unity in the right wing, but also became involved in the promotion of the Afrikaner *volkstaat* in parts of the Transvaal and Free State. The area proposed by Vekom covers only 16 per cent of South Africa, but contains 70 per cent (two million) of all Afrikaners. Although 2.1 million blacks reside in the proposed territory, Groenewald argued that economic realities rather than racial discrimination would entice them to leave the *volkstaat*, thereby allowing a majority occupation by Afrikaners (*Rapport*, 7 March 1993).

Groenewald turned out to be a popular speaker and his high profile in the media helped Vekom rapidly to increase its organizational structure throughout the country (*The Argus*, 8 May 1993). Groenewald has received international attention with his exaggerated claims concerning the right's 'defensive' capabilities: in May 1993 he claimed that the right could mobilize 500,000 whites to fight on behalf of a secessionist Afrikaner state (*The Economist*, 15 May 1993). Although Vekom's application to participate at the multiparty planning conference was rejected, the organization became a fully fledged member of the multiracial right-wing alliance, Cosag, and Groenewald, as part of the 'Committee of Generals', was instrumental in the formation of the right-wing unity front, the AVF, in May 1993.

The Afrikaner Volkswag (AV)

The Afrikaner Volkswag was founded in 1984 by Carel Boshoff, shortly after he resigned from the Broederbond. This was the fifth right-wing organization with which he became affiliated after leaving the fold of the NP, the other four being the CP,

SABRA, the NG Bond and Avstig. Boshoff originally founded the AV to counter the FAK (the cultural arm of the NP-supporting Broederbond). The AV had a membership of between 35,000 and 50,000 members (Zille 1988: 58; Bekker et al 1989: 41).

The organization's goals were to facilitate Afrikaner unity and to coordinate the cultural activities of the right wing. Its membership traversed divisions within the right, illustrated by the fact that Treurnicht, Marais and Terre Blanche were all members (Welsh 1988: 4). It promoted Afrikaner nationalism through the use of Afrikaner symbols such as the ox wagon, the Voortrekker dress and traditional cultural events. The AV's most resounding success to date has been its organization of the alternative celebrations of the 150th anniversary of the Great Trek in 1988, which in its sheer scope (almost 25,000 people attended the final day of the AV gathering in Pretoria[8]) overshadowed the 'official' celebrations held under the aegis of the FAK. The latter was a low-key affair and attracted little interest, even though it culminated with a speech at the Voortrekker monument by the then state president, P.W. Botha. The government was deeply distressed by the hijacking of this symbolic event and refused to provide any financial assistance to the Volkswag's celebrations. As a result the organization was still saddled with debts three years later and put out a request that towns and cities 'sympathetic' to the right-wing cause should help to shoulder the burden of debt.

In October 1990 a new cultural body, the Afrikaner *Kultuurbond* (AKB), later known as the Afrikaner *Kultuurraad*, was founded. The AKB did not intend to compete with the AV, but merely served as an umbrella federation for all Afrikaner cultural organizations (*Patriot*, 16 November 1990).

Religious organizations

Dutch Reformed Churches (DRC)
Even before the NP came to power in 1948, the three Afrikaans Reformed Churches, known as the *Susterkerke* (sister churches), all became actively involved in the moral justification of apartheid ideology by providing it with a scriptural basis. Their contribution to promoting Afrikaner nationalism resulted in a continued and close association with the NP and its policies after

1948. By 1961 unity within and among the *Susterkerke* became strained after a group of Dutch Reformed theologians refuted apartheid on biblical and moral grounds in a document entitled *Vertraagde Aksie* ('Delayed Action'). These strains were exacerbated in 1966 when a special commission of the DRC published a report entitled *Studiestukke*, in which the position of the DRC as a people's church was questioned (Moodie 1975: 290).

The tension among the three Afrikaans Reformed Churches was exacerbated by the split in the NP in 1982. The political divisions among Afrikaners were also reflected in the churches: The *Hervormde Kerk* leaned towards the right insofar as it maintained racial exclusivity: no blacks were allowed to become members of the Church and common worship was prohibited. The *Gereformeerde Kerk* also showed a bias to the right after the conservatives in the Church had gained control ever since 1982, as was evident from the increasing dominance of conservatives at the unofficial headquarters of the Church at Potchefstroom and from the resignation of the liberal principal of Potchefstroom University. However, in 1991 the all-white synod of the Church rejected apartheid explicitly and under much internal criticism said it could not be justified on biblical grounds (*Vrye Weekblad*, 25 November 1991).

The DRC experienced tension between its conservative and more liberal members as early as 1960 and especially after 1982. The rejection of the basic tenets of apartheid by the World Council of Churches at the Cottesloe conference in 1960 was supported by several delegates from the Transvaal and Cape synods of the DRC. In response to pressure from Verwoerd, who regarded the DRC as crucial to Afrikaner unity, the Church leaders and synods rejected the Cottesloe consultation. The split in the NP in 1982 had a profound effect on the DRC, which was by far the largest Afrikaans Church. According to Nico Smith, a liberal theologian, the DRC was poised to pledge its support to the CP after the split in 1982, but due to the frantic efforts by the Broederbond, and as a result of the election of the relatively liberal Johan Heyns as moderator, the DRC's direction turned away from the CP (cited in Leach 1989: 127).

The tension within the DRC reached its peak in 1986 when the Church endorsed a document entitled 'Church and Society', in which the DRC finally distanced itself from apartheid. The document refuted the biblical foundations of apartheid and clearly stated that race no longer could be the denominator by which people were separated, that racism was a sin, and that the Church should distance itself from the NP government. This evoked a tremendous response from the right led by conservative members of the DRC such as Carel Boshoff (a former professor of theology) and Treurnicht (a former minister in the Church). The dissidents tried to force the Church to reject its commitment to open church membership and mixed marriages and even published their own report ('Faith and Protest') in which it was argued that the separate existence and development of nations was in accordance with scripture and that the DRC had lost its moral foundation. Boshoff, Treurnicht and others decided to remain part of the Church as well as to form a conservative grouping, the NG Bond, which had the aim of opposing the liberal direction of the Church from within. These fifth columnists were a constant source of criticism of reform and especially of the de Klerk administration, and drew condemnation from the mouthpiece of the DRC, *Die Kerkbode*, for sowing discord within the Church and for 'becoming a church within a church' (*Patriot*, 22 March 1991). Other DRC members whose sympathies were allied to the right wing formed their own church, the *Afrikaanse Protestante Kerk*.

The Afrikaanse Protestante Kerk (APK)
The APK was founded in 1987 under the leadership of Willie Lubbe. Within three months after its founding the new Church had a membership of about 15,000 and 60 parishes, which increased to about 30,000 members and 150 congregations after its first year (*Sunday Times*, 5 March 1989). The APK restricts membership to Afrikaners and believes that each nation will be represented separately in heaven, and that the mission of the Afrikaner *volk* is to 'gather treasures on earth to prepare itself for a separate existence in heaven' (*Vrye Weekblad*, 23 November 1990).

The NG (Nederduits Gereformeerde) Bond
The NG Bond is an informal right-wing grouping within the DRC

and was founded in 1986 under the leadership of Carel Boshoff, in response to the acceptance by the DRC of *Kerk en Samelewing*, the 'Church and Society' document. The goal of this group is to 'preserve the historical character' of the DRC and to fend off 'challenges' that the Church faces in the form of 'liberalism, an open society and the social revolution which will be brought about by the new South Africa' (*Vrye Weekblad*, 23 November 1990).

Fundamentalist religious organizations
Of these only the activities of the Israel Vision Church/*Gemeente van die Verbondsvolk* (lit. the Congregation of People of the Covenant) have any real significance. This sect propagates racial exclusivity and claims that only whites can go to heaven, since only they are descendants of the 'chosen people', the Israelites (Bekker et al 1989: 39). Two AWB members, convicted for the murder of seven blacks, based their defence during their trials on indoctrination by the sect. One of them, Eugene Marais, explained his actions as follows: 'All those people who were not Israelites had not been made by God, but by Satan. Blacks were animals of the field, animals that looked like people ... it was therefore not a sin to kill blacks' (*Die Burger*, 14 March 1991). The sect has about 10,000 followers and its spokesman is Gert Steenkamp.

Civic institutions
The right wing attempted to resist government policy within local government and civic institutions by infiltrating agricultural cooperatives, school committees, regional services councils (RSCs) and trade unions. The CP perceived the contest between itself and the NP at extra-parliamentary level as more of a level playing field than that in parliament itself, where its role as official opposition could not prevent the government from repealing apartheid laws. However, at local government level and in other 'civic' spheres the CP was in a more powerful position, e.g. it controlled the majority of local authorities in the Transvaal where its right-wing policies could actually be implemented without too much central government interference.

Local government
In the municipal elections of 1988 the CP won 101 out of a possible 150 of all the local councils in the Transvaal, and about

22 per cent of all local authorities countrywide (Bekker et al 1989: 16–34). After subsequent municipal by-elections the CP had the support of 66 city councils in the Transvaal, 12 in the Free State and nine in the Cape. The strong presence of the CP in the Transvaal gave it control of the powerful Transvaal Municipal Association (TMA). Following the 1988 elections many of the CP-controlled councils implemented a deliberate policy of obstructing and reversing the NP efforts aimed at reducing and later eliminating racial discrimination in public facilities, residential areas and central business districts. In July 1993 the TMA vowed to resist with non-compliance or violence the government's plans to integrate the local government structures countrywide which were scheduled for September 1993, a step which was intended to destroy the CP's control of the councils under its banner (see also Chapter 4).

Regional services councils (RSCs)
RSCs were the multiracial bodies which replaced provincial councils that had been dominated by white local authorities. Because the RSCs were run on the principle of power-sharing they were initially rejected by the CP. This decision to boycott them was later reversed when the party realized that its stance would result in those local authorities under its control finding themselves at a serious disadvantage; furthermore, it would deprive the CP of the opportunity to undermine the RSCs from within. By 1988 the CP exerted a strong influence over nine of the 12 RSCs in the Transvaal, and it attempted to obstruct reforms and to deprive black areas of RSC funds, if such funding was not deemed to be beneficial to participating white local governments (Bekker et al 1989: 17).

Agricultural institutions
The right wing made a determined effort to infiltrate and control agricultural cooperatives and provincial agricultural unions, and gained control of several, including the Transvaal Agricultural Union (TAU) and its counterpart in the Free State, the Free State Agricultural Union. The TAU had 14,000 members in 1993 and was under the chairmanship of CP MP, Dries Bruwer. The relationship between the CP and the agricultural unions did not always run smoothly. In April 1991

the CP expressed its dismay over the slow response of the unions to register their protest over the intended repeal of the Land Acts before the Joint Committee on Land Reform Legislation. At the time, only the TAU and a few district agricultural unions had bothered to testify. CP MP Pieter Gouws questioned the non-involvement of the agricultural unions and refused to accept that they represented the views of the farmers (*Pretoria News*, 11 April 1991).

In 1991 a breach developed between the more conservative agricultural unions in the northern part of the country and the more liberal ones in the south, with the South African Agricultural Union caught in the middle. Apart from the fact that the Cape farmers were always regarded as less conservative than their Transvaal counterparts, they were in the process of winning back their traditional fruit and wine export markets in Europe, and they feared that the bad publicity of the Ventersdorp incident in May 1991 would hamper their efforts.[9]

Schools

Since 1982 the right wing has been extending its influence to all levels of white, and especially Afrikaner, education. In a typical Transvaal town of Bethal, 75 per cent of the local school committees were run by right wingers by the late 1980s (Bekker et al 1989: 43). Parents' associations were especially targeted by the right. After the government had allowed schools in 1990 to decide for themselves whether or not to open their doors to all races, the CP made a concerted effort to convince the parents to vote against what was called 'model B' (which allowed open schools), or preferably, not to vote at all, i.e. to ignore the new opening legislation completely. The party had some success, as the parents' associations of the Cape and the majority of white parents in the Transvaal rejected racially integrated education. In contrast the Transvaal Parents' Association (TAO) itself approved the proposals, but after severe pressure was exerted by the CP, the TAO, together with the Cape and Northern Cape Parents' Associations and the supreme Federation of Parents' Associations (FOSA), rejected open schools (*Rapport*, 7 October 1990; *Patriot*, 2 November 1990). Nonetheless, by 1993 most formerly white schools were in the process of being opened to all races.

Trade unions
The White Mineworkers' Union (MWU), the largest and best-known of the white trade unions, was an early supporter of the right-wing cause. It was linked to the HNP when that party broke with the NP in 1966 and later with the CP. It is led by Peet Ungerer and has 50,000 members (*Vrye Weekblad*, 8 July 1993). Other major trade unions that were deemed to be sympathetic to the right-wing cause included the White Construction Workers' Union, the Transvaal Municipal Workers' Union, the Transnet Union and the South African Iron and Steel Workers' Union with 41,000 members in 1990 (*The Argus*, 24 July 1990). Seven white trade unions were affiliated to the South African Confederation of Labour (SACOL), a body which had 85,000 members. Of the total of 212 registered trade unions in 1991, 32 were exclusively white (*Vrye Weekblad*, 1 March 1991).

White workers generally felt threatened by the political changes following February 1990 and were enthusiastic supporters of the CP's efforts to mobilize the unions around right-wing political issues and to form an umbrella organization for all white trade unions. The MWU, Transnet Union, Transvaal Municipal Workers' Union and the South African Iron and Steel Workers' Union became members of the Afrikaner Volksfront in 1993. As part of the right-wing resistance to a transitional government, the MWU threatened to use its support among white workers in key positions in the mining industry, in ESCOM (the Electricity Supply Commission), the chemical and nuclear-power industries, and the Rand Waterboard (*Vrye Weekblad*, 8 July 1993).

Paramilitary organizations
There were over 20 paramilitary groups with a combined membership of over 18,000, and a further 30 fundamentalist organizations in South Africa in 1990 (Booyse 1990: 7). However, since then their numbers have grown to almost 200 (*Time*, 3 May 1993). As new paramilitary and fundamentalist groups spring up virtually overnight and others disappear with equal regularity, it remains difficult to keep a complete record. Some of the more notorious include: The Afrikaner Weer-standsbeweging (AWB), Boere Krisisaksie (BKA), the Boere Weer-standsbeweging (BWB), Kommandoleer, Brandwag Volksleer,

Pretoria Boere Kommando Group (PBKG), White Front, Aquila Defence Unit, Stormvalke, Magsaksie Afrikaner Nasionalisme, White Security, National Manpower Action, Action Self-Defence, White Wolves, Flamingoes, Order of Death, Cape Rebels, White National Movement, White Resistance Movement, Patriotic Front, Boer Army, White Commando, Orde Boere-volk, Purified Afrikaner Weerstandsbeweging and the Transvaal Separatists. Of these only the largest ones require further mention.

The Afrikaner Weerstandsbeweging (AWB) (Afrikaner Resistance Movement)

Following the HNP's poor performances at the polls, the AWB was founded in 1973 by Eugene Terre Blanche to protest against the direction of Vorster's government and the 'deficiency' of the Westminster system of government. The organization's early militancy was illustrated by its plans to infest the Sun City hotel complex in Bophuthatswana with syphilis germs and to blow up several racially desegregated hotels early in the 1980s, and by the discovery by the police of an arms cache belonging to the AWB on a Transvaal farm (Kemp 1990: 47). Terre Blanche and eight AWB members were arrested for the possession of arms, ammunition and explosives in 1982; two of them were sentenced to 15 years' imprisonment, but Terre Blanche himself received only a suspended sentence. An incident in 1979 gave the AWB instant notoriety when Terre Blanche and others physically assaulted (with tar and feathers) a Pretoria academic, Floors van Jaarsveld, when the latter questioned the Afrikaners' interpretation of the Day of the Covenant. According to Terre Blanche, the court case and his conviction following the assault were a victory for all Afrikaner nationalists: 'I have no remorse about the incident. I am very proud of it. It effectively warded off the onslaught on our Day of the Covenant' (*Pretoria News*, 23 June 1988).

The ideology of the AWB is based on the belief that whites are superior to blacks and that the Boer culture and nation are sacred. Although Terre Blanche denies that his organization is racist, racism is an integral part of its philosophy: 'We will govern ourselves with our own superior white genes' (Terre Blanche, as quoted by Leach 1989: 100). It is also evident from frequently used AWB racial terminology such as *koelies, verkaffering, meid* and *basters*.

The AWB demands the restoration of the Boer Republics and northern Natal. The philosophy behind these territorial claims is that the former Boer Republics were deprived of their internationally acknowledged independence by the British after the Anglo–Boer War, and that the descendants of these Boers were legally entitled to the reconstitution of these republics (Zille 1988: 73; *Vrye Weekblad*, 21 September 1990). The AWB wants to organize the Boer state along Christian Nationalist lines with Afrikaans as the language and the *Vierkleur* (Four Colours) as the flag, with citizenship available to members of the *Boerevolk* and English-speakers who are prepared to be assimilated and who support the concept of an independent Boer state. Later he added the condition of Christianity, i.e. excluding Jews (Kemp 1990: 111).

Following the successful disruption of meetings held by members of the NP during the 1980s, hence also increased press coverage, the membership of the AWB soared. In 1988 its strength was estimated at between 5000 and 9000 signed-up members, 150,000 supporters and about 500,000 tacit sympathizers (Zille 1988: 59). Terre Blanche estimated the AWB's strength at 20,000 in 1993, but police sources claimed it was not more than 15,000 (*The Sunday Times*, 25 April 1993).

The AWB's support grew rapidly between 1987 and 1988, which could be largely ascribed to the right wing's show of strength during the 1987 election when the CP became the official opposition. In response the NP's reforms came to a virtual halt and it provided no clear indication of its future plans, creating a vacuum in which the AWB flourished. In addition, the powerful demagogic oratory of Terre Blanche attracted greater numbers of supporters. By openly challenging and threatening the authority of the government, he ensured prominent media coverage for himself and the AWB. In March 1988 the organization held a mass meeting in Pretoria attended by between 6000 and 10,000 supporters, which attracted considerable numbers of representatives from the international press (Kotze and Beyers 1988: 92). In the same year the AWB registered its political wing, the *Blanke Volkstaat Party*. Its reputation was boosted when Albert Hertzog, founder of the

HNP and leader until 1979, threw his support behind the organization and provided it with financial assistance (Kemp 1990: 8).

However, after reaching its peak in 1988 the organization experienced a series of setbacks, starting with Terre Blanche's arrest on charges of malicious damage to property and *crimen injuria*. Although he was acquitted, he subsequently had to deal with persistent rumours of his alleged womanizing and alcoholism, while newspaper reports linked him to a scandal involving a former *Sunday Times* journalist, Jani Allan. In a newspaper interview with Terre Blanche Allan had described him in glowing terms: 'I'm impaled on the blue flames of his blow-torch eyes' (*The Sunday Times*, 9 August 1992). This made such an impression on the AWB leader that he allegedly agreed to cooperate with her in writing a book on the AWB, but the working relationship eventually turned into a personal one. Terre Blanche's affair with Allan was eventually revealed in lurid detail in a British court in 1992, during which the journalist described her former lover as a 'pig in a safari suit' (*The Sunday Times* [UK], 9 August 1992).

In the aftermath of the Allan affair the AWB's membership declined rapidly, as many of its members realized that the negative publicity and their leader's buffoonery had made the AWB a laughing stock. Militant AWB members left the organization because they realized that their leader's revolutionary zeal extended little further than empty rhetoric and empty bravado, and that violent resistance had to be organized elsewhere. Several members of the AWB's Chief Council, including its deputy leader, the editor of the AWB's newsletter, *Sweepslag*, had resigned, joined by about 400 rank-and-file members each month (*Sunday Times*, 10 October 1989; interview, Wim Booyse, 11 April 1991). The defection of large numbers of its members was followed by the organization having to move out of its offices in Pretoria to the western Transvaal town of Ventersdorp.

In 1986 the AWB began to establish paramilitary units, *Brandwag* (Sentries), in every large town outside the Cape, whose main purpose was to crush a possible black uprising if the government was unable or unwilling to do so. It also infiltrated neighbourhood watches throughout the country (Welsh 1988: 6;

Kemp 1990: 159). Later an élite paramilitary youth wing, the *Stormvalke* (Storm Falcons), was formed, and links were established with a private security firm, Aquila (Kemp 1990: 161). By 1993 the AWB had transformed these into military-style commandos, of which the largest was on the east Rand under the leadership of 'general' Hagar Thompson.

Terre Blanche frequently emphasized the aspect of violence in fiery speeches: 'When law and order are non-existent in this country, the AWB will not run away like other white colonialists did, we will stay and fight' (*Pretoria News*, 25 June 1988); 'Our main task is to be there when this government sells out the country, to restore law and order when it vanishes, to ensure our women and children are not maimed and raped by ANC murderers' (cited in Leach 1989: 104).

In April 1993 the AWB's violent posture claimed its first high-profile victim when a paid-up member of the AWB, Janusz Walus, almost single-handedly succeeded in unleashing a race war by assassinating the leader of the SACP, Chris Hani. Terre Blanche's callous comment was that if Walus had not committed the murder, he would have wanted to do so himself (*The Sunday Times*, 25 April 1993). In May Terre Blanche gave the government the most explicit ultimatum to date: 'We give the government six months to restore law and order and to negotiate self-determination with us. If they do not meet this we will negotiate over the barrel of a gun' (*The Times*, 31 May 1993). In June a group of right wingers, consisting mostly of AWB members, occupied the World Trade Centre where the multiparty negotiations were under way, disrupted the proceedings and assaulted black negotiators.

However, although the AWB regained some stature through its membership of the Afrikaner Volksfront, Terre Blanche's reputation as a buffoon and his ludicrous antics, e.g. twice falling off his horse while being televised, have relegated him to a minor figure within the right wing. It is doubtful whether his poor public image was improved by the introduction in 1993 of a new 'haute khaki' two-colour AWB uniform (with a gold braid on Terre Blanche's cap), or by the AWB's launch of its own 'air force' in July 1993, consisting of six or seven single-engined aeroplanes borrowed from private owners. Terre Blanche's image problem was exacerbated by the emergence of the Angola

War hero and former head of the SADF, Constand Viljoen, as leader of the AVF. It is not surprising therefore that Terre Blanche humbly offered to 'serve as a corporal' in Viljoen's 'Boer' army (*The Times*, 31 May 1993).

The Boere Weerstandsbeweging (BWB) (Boer Resistance Movement)
The BWB is closely linked to the Boerestaat Party. Its leader is Andrew Ford and the organization had an estimated membership of 18,000 in 1990 (*The Argus*, 15 October 1990). Although Ford boasted in April 1993 that he has the support of 'thousands' of Boer warriors, it is unlikely that the BWB could muster more than 100 men in a crisis (*The Sunday Times*, 25 April 1993). The BWB has organized itself into self-defence units and provides military training for its members. The organization also had its own counter-intelligence unit to prevent government agents from infiltrating it. Like Terre Blanche, Ford has issued an ultimatum to the government and the multiparty conference: 'The day a one-man, one-vote election is called it's war' (*The Sunday Times*, 25 April 1993).

The Blanke Bevrydingsbeweging (BBB) (White Liberation Movement)
This organization was founded in 1987 by Johan Schabort and had the same paramilitary characteristics as the AWB. It believed that the whole of South Africa and Namibia belonged to whites and embraced other extreme racist ideas. It was banned by the government in 1988, changed its name to the *Blanke Nasionale Beweging* (BNB) and was banned again. Schabort also formed a political party by name of the *Blanke Party* (Bekker et al 1989: 40-41). In 1990 the BBB disbanded and Schabort joined the CP.

The World Apartheid Movement (also known as the World Preservatist Movement)
This organization is under the leadership of Koos Vermeulen and is suspected of having links with international right-wing movements including the Basque Separatists and the British movement DARE, the Companions of Justice, the French neo-Nazi movement L'Assault and the Ku Klux Klan (*Vrye Weekblad*, 30 November 1990). It has Belgian and British citizens as members and its total membership was estimated in 1990 at 800 (*South African Foundation Review*, September 1990). The

organization was suspected of planning to use biological and chemical weapons to kill large numbers of blacks, and to assassinate cabinet members (*Rapport*, 18 November 1990).

Orde van die Dood (The Order of Death)
This organization was also suspected of planning to kill members of the cabinet, and two members of its Vaal Triangle (Pretoria–Johannesburg–Vereeniging) cell, Lottering and Goosen, were convicted in 1990 for the murder of a black taxi driver. They claimed that the murder was committed to aid the survival of the *volk* and could be justified on biblical grounds.

Orde Boerevolk (Order of the Boer People)
This organization, founded the late 1980s by Piet Rudolph, achieved notoriety on account of several acts of violence, e.g. the bomb attacks on Melrose House the Anglo–Boer War Museum, the offices of the NP, the *Beeld* newspaper, the black trade union FAWU, and the theft of arms from the Air Force headquarters in Pretoria. One of the weapons stolen during the latter theft was used three years later to assassinate Chris Hani. A member of the organization, Eugene Marais, was found guilty of killing seven blacks in 1990 in retaliation for the murder of whites in Durban by black youths.

Wit Wolwe (White Wolves)
This organization was long thought to be a figment of the imagination of the racist mass murderer Barend Strydom, who had murdered eight blacks in Pretoria in its name. However, other acts of terror committed in the name of the White Wolves during recent years, and the creation of an organizational structure, have changed this perception. The secretary-general of the organization is one 'Boerestaat' Bosman, who admitted in March 1993 that his organization had committed retaliatory attacks on blacks in response to the killing of whites.

Pretoria Boere Kommando Group (PBKG)
The leader of this group is former AWB second-in-command, Jan Groenewald, and it was founded in 1992 in Pretoria. It quickly enlisted a membership of 1,000 divided into 14 different commandos in the Pretoria area, with a command

structure based on a chief commandant, commandants and field cornets (*The Weekly Mail & Guardian*, 10–16 December 1993). The PBKG regards Pretoria as the shrine of Afrikanerdom and as the capital of its proposed *volkstaat*. A few of the members of the organization occupied Fort Schanskop in Pretoria, an old military structure dating from the Anglo–Boer War, in December 1993, but the occupation ended peacefully.

Right-wing elements within the NP and government institutions

Within the National Party

As indicated previously, there have been divisions within the NP since its founding. In the post-1966 era the terms *verlig* and *verkramp* were used to describe the ideological divisions within the party. The terms (coined by Willem de Klerk) were meant to distinguish between those more open to change and those less open to change. There was a considerable group within the NP caucus by 1974 which supported the apartheid status quo, consisting of one-third to one-half of the caucus (Hanf et al 1981: 127–44). The breakaway of right-wing groups from the NP in 1969 and 1982 served to subdue tensions within the NP to a large extent during the remainder of the 1980s, although the party did not succeed in ridding itself of its continuing ideological rift.

By 1989, according to Willem de Klerk, the NP under P.W. Botha could be divided into a conservative reformist group (about 75 per cent of the NP caucus), and a liberal reformist group (the remaining 25 per cent). The latter were also known as the 'New Nats' and were in favour of greatly speeding up the reform process by scrapping all apartheid laws while the former adhered to the principle of group rights and had a vision of a race federation (Leach 1989: 54–7). Other analysts such as Lipton (1986: 328) and Eschel Rhoodie (1989: 213) differ in their estimates of the size of the NP's *verkrampte* wing, but it is evident that a considerable number of the NP caucus remained within this category when F.W. de Klerk came to power in 1989. Between 1989 and 1993 the rift between the 'new' and the 'old' NP appeared to grow as the *verkramptes* attempted to obstruct or slow down the pace of reform. After most of the hard-line ministers and securocrats dating from the P.W. Botha era eventually had resigned, retired or been removed to less sensitive positions (e.g. Magnus Malan from Defence to Forestry and Adriaan Vlok from Police to Prisons), the right wing of the NP was led by members of the cabinet who were unhappy about aspects of the constitutional proposals. Those who wanted the NP to form an alliance with the IFP rather than with the ANC included Tertius Delport, Kobie Coetzee, George Bartlett, Hernus Kriel, Rina Venter, Andre Fourie and Danie Schutte (*Rapport*, 1 August 1993; 12 September 1993).

The NP also experienced discontent among MPs and members of its provincial congresses who were alarmed by the speed of the negotiation process and by the perception that the NP had lost control over the process of reform. In 1992 the chief secretary of the NP, Stoffel van der Merwe, euphemistically admitted that 'a degree of confusion and restlessness' existed among members of the NP caucus. During a caucus meeting before the opening of parliament in February 1992, back-benchers refrained from greeting the state president with the customary standing ovation (*Sunday Times*, 26 January 1992). Even the Cape MPs, who were traditionally regarded as the 'liberals' within the NP, expressed their concern in September 1990, concern which almost turned into a full-scale rebellion two years later when they declared that they no longer had confidence in the state president (*Sunday Times*, 19 October 1992). In Natal and Transvaal many MPs were unhappy with the tension that existed between the NP and the IFP (which they regarded as a natural ally for whites against the ANC). As a result two MPs, Jurie Mentz and Hennie Becker, defected from the NP early in 1993 to join the IFP.

The Civil Service.
The appeal that the CP would have for white bureaucrats is not difficult to understand, for as long as such bureaucrats felt that their jobs, pensions and promotions were being threatened by reforms and the prospects of a black-ruled government, they would oppose the process that led to such a government. As Adam and Moodley observed: 'The former politicization of the Afrikaner civil service with wide discretionary power, based on the underlying consensus of the incumbents, also seems to

backfire now. No longer do all officials automatically implement orders from above; rather, they interpret them according to their own views' (1986: 64).

Although Charney (1984: 277–8) claimed that constant pay-offs and the discipline of government patronage had kept most of the civil service loyal to the NP after the split in 1982, certain categories of the bureaucracy have constantly displayed a wavering loyalty during the Botha era and especially under de Klerk. This was particularly the case with the middle and lower echelons of the civil service (Bekker and Grobbelaar 1987; Adam 1987).

Although it is difficult to prove specific examples of bureaucratic obstruction within government departments, an incident concerning the Group Areas Act provides a clear example of the negative bureaucratic sentiment towards reform well into the de Klerk era: in December 1990 the Department of Local Government, Housing and Works refused to grant a coloured headmaster of a school in Bellville a permit to buy a house in a white suburb of the city. What makes this so remarkable (apart from the racism behind the Group Areas Act which caused the incident in the first place) is that the headmaster's new neighbours apparently approved of his buying the house, and his application enjoyed the support of the NP MP for Bellville. Even more telling is the fact that the incident occurred in December 1990, after the government had already said that the repeal of the Group Areas Act would officially be announced two months later (the announcement was in fact made in February 1991).

Within the security forces
The security forces maintained a very powerful position throughout the 1980s. Botha created a system of Joint Management Committees which included police and army representatives, which effectively took control of many areas of public administration and policy-making. They bypassed parliament and were accountable only to the State Security Council. This resulted in the security forces being drawn into everyday politics, accountable only to themselves and a small body of securocrats, as members of Botha's creation became known. Although the securocrats became a law unto themselves,

they remained firmly loyal to the government's ideology at the time.

The increasingly powerful position of the security forces and the government's waning ability to curb their abuse of power during the late 1980s and early 1990s are illustrated by the ongoing incidence of deaths in detention, even though this practice resulted in worldwide condemnation and extreme embarrassment to the government. A further example was the continued support which Renamo (National Resistance Movement of Mozambique) received from military sources inside South Africa, even after the government had officially claimed to have stopped its support to its former protégé. In 1989 the SADF became involved in a further controversy in Namibia when rogue elements rigged radio messages in an attempt to disrupt the Namibian peace process.[10] After F.W. de Klerk became president in 1989, allegations were rife concerning the disloyalty towards the government and an anti-NP sentiment among the police force. Reforms such as the release of political prisoners, allowing mass rallies, the desegregation of beaches and the unbanning of black resistance movements caused open dissent among parts of the police force. Many members of the force resigned (although this was exacerbated by poor pay and long hours) and there were fears that many in the junior ranks might deliberately try to sabotage the reform process. At this stage much of the resentment in the ranks of the security forces originated in the request by the government that the police should ignore the strict provisions of the law, e.g. to refrain from interfering in the mass rallies under ANC banners. A typical response of the police to this inconsistency was: 'If the government don't want us to enforce the law then they must change the law' (Daily Dispatch, 2 November 1989). An indication of the dissent in the police force came from a BBC documentary in 1991 in which members of the Cape riot police claimed that 99 per cent of their force did not trust the government (Cape Times, 16 April 1991). A 1991 M&M survey concluded that the CP enjoyed the support of approximately one-third of the Defence Force and possibly more than half of the police force.

Towards the end of 1989 the activities of the secretive Civil Cooperation Bureau (CCB) became the object of public scrutiny after a member of a CCB death-squad, Almond Nofomela, confessed to his involvement in the murder of a black anti-apartheid lawyer. The CCB was a secret SADF organization which was involved in the calculated elimination of leading opponents of the NP government and had a chain of command allegedly leading to the Minister of Defence. The *Vrye Weekblad* (17 November 1989), a liberal Afrikaans newspaper, published the revelations of a former captain in the security police, Dirk Coetzee, who claimed to have led a death squad sanctioned by senior police officers. His allegations supported those of Nofomela and implicated several high-ranking officers, such as the chief of the police's forensic branch, General Lothar Neethling (today a prominent right-wing supporter), the Commissioner of the South African Police, General Johan Coetzee, and an NP-member of the President's Council, Craig Williamson. After intense pressure the State President appointed the Harms Commission to investigate the activities of the CCB, but as most of the evidence regarding the organization was carefully destroyed beforehand, the Commission did not fully succeed in opening the Pandora's Box of state-sponsored terrorism. However, long-held suspicions about the CCB were confirmed in January 1991 by the findings of the Supreme Court Judge, Mr Justice Kriegler, who found that Coetzee spoke the truth when he implicated Lothar Neethling as an important figure in the death squad saga. These findings confirmed what most South Africans suspected, and although the Kriegler findings were overturned on appeal in December 1993, there is little doubt today that the CCB existed and that its clandestine activities were sanctioned by the apartheid state and led to the death or disappearance of almost 200 anti-apartheid activists.

However, the CCB cannot be described as right wing *per se*, as it was merely an extension of the Botha government – if one classifies the CCB's activities as right wing, then the whole state structure of the Botha era should also be classified as such. It can, however, safely be assumed that the majority of the CCB's members defected to the right wing during the de Klerk era, especially since they were so reluctant to allow themselves to be disbanded after the government had given a promise to this effect. Although officially disowned by the de Klerk administration, this did not imply that the goals and private agendas of some of its members had been extinguished. In fact, the remnants and certain of the goals of the CCB were transferred to Military Intelligence (MI) and its Directorate for Covert Operations, who operated from plush offices in Pretoria under a front company called the Africa Risk Analysis Company, until it was uncovered in November 1992 by the Goldstone Commission set up to investigate the causes of political violence in South Africa. The extent of the military's involvement in covert operations against anti-apartheid forces in destabilizing the transitional process and hampering negotiations became clear when President de Klerk dismissed 16 senior officers and suspended seven others (only some of whom were later reinstated) in December 1992 after an internal military investigation.

On the basis of these facts, it can be concluded that the activities of certain groups within the military, such as MI, in trying (presumably) to wreck the negotiation process without the knowledge of the State President, clearly categorizes them as to the right of the government, and therefore as aligned with the goals of the formal right wing. Furthermore, it is very likely that elements within and former members of these organizations were active throughout the largest part of the de Klerk era as a 'third force', their only goal being to prevent power slipping away from the white minority. Their *modus operandi* was straightforward: firstly, to undermine and weaken the ANC and to destabilize the country by helping to fan violence between the ANC and the IFP by arming the latter, and, secondly, by providing arms and logistical support to militant right-wing organizations which were intending to launch a civil war.

English-speaking support for the right wing
Contrary to their liberal image, political conservatism and racial prejudice have never been alien to the mentality of a considerable proportion of English-speaking white South Africans. Since early times large sections of the two million English-speakers shared the Afrikaner's fear of being outnumbered and hence overwhelmed by blacks. Racism among English-speakers was further strengthened by the influx of immigrants from Britain in the decades after 1945. South Africa was especially popular among those British immigrants who

already carried with them the baggage of racial prejudice and were attracted by South Africa's image of being a country 'where the white man knew how to keep the black man in his place' (Leach 1989: 256).

During the 1960s, 1970s and 1980s South Africa experienced a further influx of immigrants from the former European colonies of Angola, Mozambique, Southern Rhodesia (now Zimbabwe), South West Africa (now Namibia) and, to a lesser extent, the Belgian Congo, Kenya and Northern Rhodesia (now Zambia). Immigrants from these territories were fleeing the protracted civil wars which brought about the end of white minority and colonial rule. The 100,000 or so whites who left Zimbabwe included many who refused to accept black rule and were unreconstructed racists; because of strict exchange controls they had lost most of their wealth, and many came to South Africa determined not to let the process be repeated (Welsh, cited in Leach 1989: 257).

Most English-speakers chose the former United Party as a political home for many decades, not because its ideology was that much more liberal than that of the NP, but because it kept close ties with Britain, and provided an alternative to the rampant Afrikaner nationalism of the NP and latent anti-English sentiments prevalent among many Afrikaner nationalists. This was especially the case during the period between 1948 and 1960, until Verwoerd realized that he would need the support of English-speakers to win the referendum on a republic in 1961. Verwoerd's rapprochement with the white English-speaking community was continued by Vorster, and during the 1970s support among English-speakers for the NP was further strengthened as the NP expanded its ethnic base to a more inclusive white nationalism. The policy of rapprochement met with fierce resistance in some Afrikaner circles, including many prominent nationalists such as Albert Hertzog and Piet Meyer. Meyer insisted that a policy of deliberate 'Afrikanerization of English-speakers' was the only solution to the threat posed by the Anglicization of Afrikaners, according to which the English-speakers would gradually accept Christian National ideals and the Afrikaner's language and history as their own.

In the heyday of NP rule, a commonly used election strategy was to scare English-speakers with the *swart gevaar* (the black peril) to coerce them to vote against the liberal opposition.[11] The anti-black propaganda which was meant to ensure English-speaking support for the NP worked so efficiently that it led to unexpected consequences when the NP started to move in the direction of a broader, non-racial South African nationalism in the late 1980s. As in the case of Afrikaners, for many English-speakers the ideological shift came altogether too suddenly, resulting in the perception that the NP was surrendering to the black majority. In this way the English-speaking community became prey to the right wing during the 1980s. During the early 1990s many English-speakers, especially in Natal, shifted their support to the IFP with the intention of preventing the ANC from dominating the province.

Although the electoral success of the CP was rooted in the resurgence of Afrikaner nationalism, the party was eager to compete for English-speaking support, on condition that Afrikaner nationalist ideals and leadership were accepted. The primacy of the Afrikaner culture was never doubted by English-speaking supporters of the CP, as the English supplement to *Patriot* (under the guidance of Clive and Gayle Derby-Lewis) had illustrated: 'While nobody denies that Afrikaner nationalism is the driving force of active conservative politics in South Africa today, thousands of English-speakers have declared their support for a party and a policy that they know will secure their future in a very dark continent' (*Patriot*, 15 March 1990). It appeared that most of the English-speaking supporters of the right wing were probably prepared to accept Afrikaner domination, as long as they could return to the levels of white prosperity and security of the 1960s (Bekker et al 1989: 51).

In exchange for the acknowledgment of the primacy of Afrikaner nationalism, the CP, unlike the HNP, accepted that English would be an official language when it came to power. The party distanced itself from phrases like *Boerevolk* and *Boerestaat* and preferred to use the terms 'white' or 'Afrikaner', the latter having fewer emotional connotations in the English psyche than 'Boer'.

From 1990 until the split in the CP in 1992, opposing viewpoints over the role of English-speakers were causing a rift in the party. According to Clive Derby-Lewis, CP member of the

President's Council and unofficial spokesman for the English-speaking section of the CP, the CP was co-founded by English-speakers and ample English-speakers were elected to top posts in the party (interview, 10 September 1990). Derby-Lewis further argued that the English-speakers were never a threat to Afrikaner nationalism, and that patriotism should be the only criterion for membership of the CP. He received support from Treurnicht, who said that the CP's strong performance in a by-election in the mainly English-speaking constituency of Umlazi had proven that the English-speakers had crossed their Rubicon: 'When it came to cultural interests, these were no longer obstacles in the way of cooperation for the sake of white survival as a white nation' (*Patriot*, 10 August 1990) [translation]. Andries Beyers, the CP's former chief secretary, argued that English-speakers could be assimilated into the Afrikaner nation in a similar way that the Afrikaner evolved from his Dutch, French and German ancestors (interview, 11 April 1991).[12] Ironically, this was one of the issues which caused Beyers to leave the CP 16 months later; by then, however, he had adopted a radically different position, namely a definition of Afrikanerdom which included Afrikaans-speakers of all races, but not English-speaking conservatives.

Following its split in 1992 the CP emphasized the difference between its own position of speaking on behalf of 'Afrikanerdom and those of Anglo and European stock who are one of the Afrikaner', and the ethnic, racially inclusive definition of the AVU (*Patriot*, 19 March 1993). The position of the AVF with regard to the definition of Afrikanerdom appeared to hover between the AWB and AVU; its leader, Constand Viljoen, refers to his constituency as the 'Afrikaner-Boer' (*Rapport*, 5 September 1993).

The overall English-speaking support for the right wing has been showing an upward trend. According to M&M surveys the average English-speaking support for the CP between January 1988 and March 1991 was 9 per cent. The sentiments of English-speakers on the pace of reform show considerable support for the right: according to an M&M survey of January 1990, 47 per cent of English-speaking whites regarded de Klerk's pace of reform as satisfactory, 40 per cent regarded it as too slow, while 13 per cent thought it was too fast (the logical assumption being that the latter group consisted of CP supporters). Of particular relevance is the CP's good performance over the past two years in the predominantly English-speaking constituencies of Umlazi and Maitland. In Umlazi the CP increased its share of the vote from 9 per cent in 1987 to 20 per cent in 1989 and to 44 per cent in 1990, while the swing to the right in Maitland was 27 per cent between 1989 and 1991.

Organizations
The Stallard Foundation was the only significant right-wing organization to cater specifically for English-speakers. It was founded in 1985 and named after a conservative English-speaking segregationist who was also a staunch monarchist and member of the Natal-based Dominion Party. The organization was headed by Clive Derby-Lewis and claimed a membership in 1988 of approximately 1000 (Zille 1988: 59). The Stallard Foundation's goal was the promotion of a conservative brand of politics, and it sponsored right-wing conferences and hosted foreign visitors sympathetic to the right-wing cause.

In 1991 Derby-Lewis founded the Republican Unity Movement of South Africa (Rumosa), which claimed the Cape Province and Natal on behalf of the descendants of the British settlers (*Die Burger*, 17 April 1993). Derby-Lewis also had extensive contacts with the extremist 'Western Goals Institute', based in London and founded to promote values of Western civilization. He was elected its president in February 1992 in the place of the notorious Salvadoran right-wing death-squad leader, Roberto d'Abuisson. Derby-Lewis and his wife, Gaye, were arrested in April 1993 in connection with the assassination of Chris Hani by a Polish immigrant and member of the AWB, Janusz Walus. Derby-Lewis was later convicted of conspiracy to murder and sentenced to death; his wife was acquitted.

Financial support for the right wing
There has never been much affinity between the business sector and the CP since its founding in 1982. Dominant Afrikaner businesses such as the insurance corporation Sanlam and Nasionale Pers have always been strong supporters of the Cape NP, while other groups such as *Federale Volksbeleggings* formed the core of the party's Transvaal financial support. However, in

the Transvaal, Volkskas Bank and the Perskor newspaper group were closely intertwined with civil servants, farmers and white workers, who, in turn, had a strong association with CP (Charney 1984: 276).

The right wing's standing in the business community received a severe setback in the aftermath of the Boksburg episode in 1988 when the CP-controlled town council reintroduced petty-apartheid measures. These were meant to prevent blacks from using public facilities, which, technically, was still legal. However, it resulted in a black consumer boycott of white-owned business in Boksburg and gave the business community a taste of a future South Africa dominated by a party intent on reimplementing a policy of undiluted racial discrimination. White business vehemently condemned the CP policy as turnover in stores and shops in the town dropped by between 10 and 90 per cent. The Boksburg town council's decision was followed by that of Carletonville and others, with the same disastrous consequences.

The very negative attitude of the business community towards the CP manifested itself during fundraising efforts by the party during the 1989 general election. While the NP received almost half of its campaign funds from big business, the CP received almost nothing. Clive Derby-Lewis explained that, as a result, the party did not even waste its time approaching businesses (*Business Day*, 6 September 1989). The CP's standing among businesses improved marginally after it became the official opposition in parliament. Relations with Volkskas, in particular, had improved and it became easier for the party to obtain loans from that bank. Volkskas was also the only well-known corporate name that regularly supported the CP's mouthpiece, *Patriot*, by placing advertisements in it.[13]

The CP's attempt in 1990 to launch its own publishing concern, Volkspers, was not greatly successful, as only R1.2 million of the R20 million needed in the form of public contributions had been received by 1991. By 1992, after its decisive defeat in the referendum, the CP began experiencing financial difficulties as donations from its members began to dry up (*Rapport*, 16 August 1992).

Right-wing alliances

Lack of cooperation and disunity between the CP and HNP at electoral level had cost the combined right wing a number of seats on several occasions, but did not really affect the total number of right-wing votes. Attempts during the 1980s to form a unified right wing were unsuccessful because of the HNP's unrealistic demands, policy differences, and personality differences between the leaders of the HNP and CP. Other right-wing organizations did not have much success either – the AWB, HNP and Boerestaat Party formalized a right-wing unity front during the 1989 general election, but this was only temporary.

The first significant attempt to create a right-wing alliance, albeit of a temporary nature, was during the referendum campaign in March 1992, when the CP, HNP and AWB joined hands to campaign for a No vote. Although the referendum alliance had helped to streamline the No campaign and to present a united right-wing front, this was partly offset by the differences within the CP between the moderates and the traditionalists over party policy. In addition, the AWB's radicalism and Terre Blanche's public image repelled some CP supporters and persuaded some disaffected NP voters who had intended to abstain to vote Yes. Not surprisingly, following its defeat, the members of the alliance went their own separate ways, and in August 1992 the right wing was split further with the founding of the AVU.

However, towards the end of 1992 the white right succeeded in forming the Cosag alliance with the black right, and in May 1993 the white right wing came as close as it ever has been to unity with the creation of the AVF.

The Concerned South African Group (Cosag)/Freedom Alliance
Cosag was founded in September 1992 by the CP, AVU, Vekom and three conservative black homeland leaders, Mangosuthu Buthelezi of KwaZulu, Lucas Mangope of Bophuthatswana and Oupa Gqozo of the Ciskei. The intention was to act as a counter to bilateral negotiations and agreements between the ANC and NP, and to oppose any moves in the direction of creating a unitary South Africa. Generally speaking, the white members of the alliance, with the exception of the AVU, propagated the idea

of a South African confederacy consisting of sovereign states, while the black members are hovering between a federal and confederal system. Buthelezi, for example, is supposedly in favour of a federal South Africa, but the draft constitution released by the IFP in December 1992 implied the virtual secession of Natal/KwaZulu from the remainder of South Africa, while both Gqozo and Mangope have indicated on occasion that they would not consider surrendering the 'independence' of their homelands.

Relations between the CP and the black members of Cosag were shaky from the start. Apart from the racism which still formed an inherent part of the CP's general philosophy, differences also existed over the CP's earlier reluctance to participate at the Convention for a Democratic South Africa (Codesa) and over constitutional policies. Tension was heightened by the end of 1992 by Hartzenberg's reference to the city of Durban, the industrial and financial heart of Natal/KwaZulu, as an 'ideal basis' for a white homeland (*Insig*, November 1992). In turn the IFP has rejected the CP's *volkstaat* proposals as 'racist' (*Vrye Weekblad*, 8 June 1993), while Mangope said his support for a confederation did not imply support for a 'white secessionist confederation' (*Rapport*, 11 October 1992). Relations between the CP and the IFP took a turn for the worse following the invasion of the venue of the multiparty negotiation forum by the AVF in June 1993 – apart from the blatant racism displayed by the protesters, IFP delegates who were assaulted by right-wingers received no help from the CP delegates. In response Buthelezi said that he would have to reconsider his relationship with the other members of Cosag (*Rapport*, 27 June 1993). In addition, the rapid growth in the white support of the IFP implied that the CP and IFP were competing in the same electoral segment, namely conservative whites. A Markinor poll of June 1993 suggested that 27 per cent of whites in the Witwatersrand supported the IFP, but this figure is probably even higher in Natal, where Buthelezi hopes to build an anti-ANC alliance crossing racial and ethnic barriers.

The CP joined the IFP in leaving the negotiation forum in July 1993 protesting the consitutional proposals of the multiparty forum, and they were joined in October by Ciskei and Bophuthatswana and a part of the AVU. In the same month the members of Cosag, joined by the AVF, founded the Freedom Alliance to coordinate their efforts to resist the interim constitutional proposals which they believed were aimed at creating a strong central government and weak federalism. The members of the new alliance now consisted of the AVF (representing more than 20 right-wing organizations), the CP, the IFP/KwaZulu-government and the governments of Bophuthatswana and Ciskei.

During its early stages the multiracial right-wing alliance was representative of little more than a flirtation between entities on the right of the political spectrum who had no true common ideology, and were linked only through their collective over-emphasis on ethnonationalism and the use of bluster as methods of maintaining political relevance and ensuring a regional power-base. However, as the transitional process edged closer to the creation of the Transitional Executive Council (TEC) and an interim constitution towards the end of 1993, the alliance members drew closer together and presented a more cohesive strategy of opposition to the multiparty forum and the government.

Towards the end of October 1993 the Freedom Alliance received a considerable boost to its morale when an opinion poll conducted by Lawrence Schlemmer of the Human Sciences Research Council indicated that the Alliance enjoyed about the same level of electoral support as the NP (*Financial Times*, 27 October 1993). This opened up the possibility (in theory at least) that the NP might only come third in the April 1994 elections, a result which would enable a member of the right-wing Alliance to become vice-president of South Africa. A development of even greater significance for the fortunes and coherence of the Freedom Alliance occurred in November 1993 with the finalization of the interim constitutional agreement by the multiparty negotiating forum, which was ratified in the tricameral parliament on 22 December 1993. The interim constitution, although ostensibly federal, turned out to grant significantly fewer powers and rights to the regions and to ethnic and cultural minorities than originally demanded by the NP. The Freedom Alliance accused the NP of having caved in and capitulated to the ANC, and saw the opportunity to position itself as the sole defenders of 'true' federalism and the only guarantors of regional autonomy and self-determination of peoples.

Informal negotiations between the ANC/NP and the Freedom Alliance during November 1993 were not particularly success-ful, but by now the Alliance had at least clearly defined their minimum requirements for entering the constitutional process, even if there were considerable differences between the various members' views on the definition of self-determination. The demands of the Freedom Alliance at that stage, in summary, were as follows: an expansion of the proposed legislative and taxation powers of the regions, the right of regional governments to draw up their own constitutions, a minimum 60 per cent threshold for constitutional decisions by a future parliament, and a dual ballot system for local and central elections (as opposed to one ballot counted twice). In return for placing these demands on the agenda for negotiations, the government and the ANC demanded an unconditional commitment from the Alliance not to boycott the elections, but for the time being neither side was able to overcome the deadlock.

However, early in December the Freedom Alliance decided to restart the constitutional talks without fully accepting the government's preconditions, a step which over the next three weeks led to further progress towards an agreement following three-way talks between the NP, ANC and the Alliance. On 21 December 1993, after a near-collapse of the talks, a compromise was reached which would bind the Freedom Alliance to the transitional process and participation in the TEC and the 1994 elections, on the condition that its constitutional demands were met. The negotiators of the Freedom Alliance agreed to submit the proposals to their leaders and report back before 24 January 1994, the deadline for any further amendments to the interim constitution. The January deadline passed without an agreement being reached. It became apparent that extra-ordinary measures would be required to break the impasse but that neither side were yet prepared to make the fundamental shift in their policies that would have facilitated such a breakthrough.

The Afrikaner Volksfront (AVF)
The AVF was founded as a direct result of the violence and racial tension that erupted after the assassination of Chris Hani in

April 1993 and in response to the leadership vacuum that emerged after the death of the leader of the CP, Andries Treurnicht. The process of unity began when four former generals of the South African Security Forces came together to form the sinister-sounding 'Committee of Generals' (CoG) in April 1993. CoG consisted of Constand Viljoen, the former chief of the Defence Force, Koos Bischoff, Cobus Visser, and Tienie Groenewald. Its goals were to unite and to mobilize the right wing, in order to pursue the goal of Afrikaner self-determination more effectively.

On 7 May 1993 the committee succeeded in launching the long-awaited united right-wing front, called the Afrikaner Volksfront, under the leadership of Constand Viljoen. The AVF incorporates 21 right-wing groups, but Viljoen insisted that these all maintain their own identity and political culture. He emphasized that the AVF was not a political party but would act as the 'cement' to bring the right wing closer together in an effective alliance. As some of the right-wing parties , e.g. the CP and AVU, differed considerably over fundamental issues, keeping the alliance together has proved to be Viljoen's first major task. The first problem arose in May when the AVU refused to sign the AVF's founding act because it contained a 'racist' clause concerning the citizenship provisions of the *volkstaat*. Although the other members of the AVF wanted to suspend the AVU, Avstig, SABRA and the AV (including Viljoen as member of the AVU), only Hartzenberg's intervention prevented the early demise of the alliance. The AVU eventually signed the founding act conditionally by not endorsing the offending clause.

In June 1993 right-wing protesters, in particular the AWB, ignored Viljoen's pleas for a peaceful protest and physically took over the venue of the multiparty forum at the World Trade Centre in Kempton Park in Johannesburg. Although Viljoen criticized the violence, he compared the event to the storming of the Bastille and warned that it was only a taste of what was to come should the Afrikaner's 'right' to self-determination be ignored. The AVF also suggested that the events at the World Trade Centre were part of a 'people's mobilization' to force the government and ANC to recognize its demands. Altogether 98 forms of passive resistance, referred to as the 'Ten Plagues',

were considered by the AVF; these include mass civil
disobedience, deliberately engineered power failures, industrial
sabotage, the non-payment of taxes, a unilateral referendum
among Afrikaners, the forming of an alternative government,
and, ultimately, securing a *volkstaat* through violent secession.
In September 1993 the AVF launched its own FM radio station
called Radio Pretoria, labelled as the 'radio *with* borders'.

In July 1993 the AVF submitted its proposals for the creation
of a *volkstaat* to the technical committee of the negotiation
forum. The proposed area of the *volkstaat* comprises approximately 16.5 per cent of the country's surface and is inhabited by
2.3 million whites and 2.1 million blacks. It includes Pretoria,
parts of the northern, eastern and western Transvaal (excluding
the Witwatersrand), the northern part of the Free State,
Kimberley and northern Natal. However, the constitutional
proposals released by the multiparty conference in August 1993
made no reference to the AVF's proposals. In September the AVF
announced four basic demands underpinning its demand for a
negotiated *volkstaat*. These included a separate constitution
without (presumably racial) discrimination, separate defence
and police forces, the right to levy taxes, and the right to secede
from South Africa in case of irreconcilable differences.
Although Viljoen denied that these implied an agreement to a
federal state within South Africa, he agreed that many
constitutional variations existed. While his demands are in many
respects similar to the powers normally granted to a federal unit
within the parameters of democratic federalism, it also implies a
greater degree of autonomy than is the case in strong regional
governments such as Quebec in Canada and Catalonia in Spain .

With the collapse of the AVU in late 1993, there were
indications of renewed tension within the AVF. With his
'sponsoring' party and the voice of realism gone, Viljoen found
himself, and his willingness to negotiate and compromise, under
attack from hard-liners in the CP and the AWB. Although he was
forced by the Hartzenberg faction in October 1993 to suspend
his talks with the NP and the ANC, it was obvious that he did so
reluctantly. At this point Viljoen had to decide whether to
submit to the dictates of the hard-line faction in the AVF or to
force their hand once and for all. If he opted to stand up to his
opponents, there was a considerable risk of splitting the AVF. On

the other hand, as the most popular right-wing leader by far, he would most likely have succeeded in taking with him a considerable number of moderate CP supporters, and he would probably also have been assured of the support of large numbers of disaffected NP supporters who admired Viljoen but could not see themselves in the same camp as the racists within the CP.

By early November 1993 it became obvious that the CP had realized how powerful Viljoen had become, and that the party's options became more limited with each passing week. Later that month the AVF came forward with a new plan for a *volkstaat* based on a territory consisting only 14 per cent of South Africa's land mass, with only limited autonomy (rather than full independence) for Afrikaners within that territory. At the same time blacks would have only limited voting rights, insofar as they would be allowed to vote for the central but not the regional government, which would ensure that the regional government of such an Afrikaner province-state would be controlled by Afrikaners. This was seen as a more agreeable way of ensuring Afrikaner control in a region in which Afrikaners would possibly be in a minority, rather than the alternative, which was population transfers of blacks out of the region. Although the ANC rejected qualified voting rights for blacks within the *volkstaat*-province, negotiations between the two organizations were now in full swing and both parties declared that they were moving closer to one another. Mandela declared that 'the more we talk to the right wing, the more we understand one another', while a joint ANC/AVF delegation left for Europe to study the local and regional government systems of Belgium and Switzerland (*Rapport*, 5 December 1993). It also appeared that by the end of November 1993 Viljoen had agreed with the ANC that Afrikaner independence was out of the question and had committed the AVF to this much, with the ANC in turn offering the AVF the eastern Transvaal Pretoria as its capital and as a base for its federal region within a united South Africa. However, the mutual enthusiasm of the ANC and AVF was not shared by the whole of the CP – its leader, Ferdi Hartzenberg, announced in parliament that his party remained 'utterly committed' to confederalism, i.e. an independent Afrikaner homeland (*Cape Times*, 27 November 1993). In spite of the recalcitrance of the main component of the AVF (the CP), Viljoen pushed ahead with negotiations with the NP and the ANC, but his surprising 'UDI'-announcement on 29 November 1993, that the AVF was unilaterally going to establish a *volkstaat*, was clearly an attempt to pacify the more militant members within the AVF, in particular Hartzenberg.

Viljoen's efforts came to fruition on 20 December 1993 when the AVF announced that it had reached an agreement with the government and the ANC and that it was entering the transitional process. Over the next 24 hours the agreement hovered on the brink of collapse as Viljoen, under pressure from his partners in the Freedom Alliance, had to announce that he could not sign the deal because 'of the attitude of the people in the Cape', presumably referring to the government rejection of the AVF's proposed recommendations to the interim constitution (*Business Day*, 22 December 1993). However, he emphasized that the provisional agreement which had been reached on regional autonomy and participation by the right wing in the 1994 elections was not nullified by his failure to sign it, and that it could be signed at a later date. The agreement reached between the ANC and the AVF stated that both organizations were determined that the aspirations of many Afrikaners to govern themselves in their own territory should be addressed. In addition, a joint working group has been set up to examine the financial and economic viability of a *volkstaat*, the civil rights of Afrikaners outside the *volkstaat*, and its relationship with local, regional and central government structures. The working group was to report back before 24 January 1994, but this date passed without agreement being reached. After this latest failure, Viljoen again came under severe criticism from the hardliners within the AVF, and was publicly humiliated when he was shouted down and his request for a peaceful solution ridiculed by 10,000 supporters of the AVF during a rally in Pretoria. During the same event the AVF elected an Afrikaner 'interim' government with Hartzenberg as 'president'.

3· The Electoral Struggle for Control of the Afrikaner Destiny: 1981–92

The struggle between the CP and the NP during the 1980s and early 1990s was an extension of the pattern of *broedertwis* which has racked Afrikanerdom for most of the twentieth century. It was essentially a struggle for the ideological soul of the Afrikaner, i.e. between those 'more open' and those 'less open' to the influence of modernization. At the core of this struggle were different interpretations of how best to use the state to protect the status and identity of the Afrikaner. Those holding right-wing and *verkrampte* positions defined Afrikaner national-ism exclusively by emphasizing its primordial characteristics, while the *verligtes* defined it inclusively by emphasizing racial and later territorial aspects.

The overt antagonism between these two ideological strains and the numerous spheres in which the intra-Afrikaner conflict was being fought were an illustration of the permeative and pervasive nature of conflicts even *within* a single ethnic group, i.e. an intra-ethnic conflict. In this respect this chapter is largely dependent on the work of Donald Horowitz, who contended that an attempt by an ethnically based party in a divided society to move to the centre by becoming a multiethnic party or alliance would result in the formation of ethnic flanking parties. Such flanking parties, he argued, would take a firm position on ethnic issues and would differ fundamentally from the centrist party on inter-ethnic relations: 'The sense of betrayal and the disagreement with the substance of the compromise give rise to electoral opportunities on the ethnic flanks' (1985: 411).

As the NP attempted to become multiethnic and multiracial by shifting from a purely Afrikaner and white nationalism towards a territorially based South African nationalism between the 1960s and the early 1990s, ethnonationalist flanking parties emerged on the right, first in the form of the HNP in 1969 and then the CP in 1982. Throughout this period the right wing and the NP attempted to outbid each other for the electoral support and allegiance of the Afrikaners by following opposing ideologies and strategies. While the CP clung to Afrikaner ethnonationalism with its emphasis on primordial characteristics such as the Afrikaner language, culture, mythology, a common fatherland and pigmentation, the NP, on the other hand, broadened its definition of Afrikanerdom to a non-racial South African nationalism based on common values and interests, what Linz (1985) described as territorial nationalism. The conflicting views on how the identity and status of the Afrikaner could best be protected resulted in the bitter electoral rivalry between the NP and the CP. As the NP moved further to the centre, the CP positioned itself firmly to its right to garner the votes of those who did not share the NP's new vision.

This chapter deals mainly with the rivalry between the CP and the NP, but because of the HNP's exceptionally strong performance during the 1981 general election, the latter date is regarded as the beginning of the right as a significant electoral force.

The 1981 general election

The election of P.W. Botha as prime minister in 1978 had a direct impact on the electoral fortunes of the HNP. In contrast to his reputation as a 'hawk' and a hard-liner while serving as minister of defence, Botha adopted a reformist stance early in his career as party leader. His references to apartheid as a 'recipe for permanent conflict' and his warning to the white electorate to 'adapt or die' had set the tone for his reform programme: in 1979 he announced a 12-point plan which made provision for power-sharing between whites, coloureds and

Indians, and committed the NP to the elimination of racial discrimination.

In 1979, Botha also attempted to draw the business community closer to the government with the Carlton Conference, a meeting he held with top business leaders in order to mobilize their support for his reforms. The reports of three commissions – two of them that same year – were also significant. The Wiehahn Commission recommended the abolition of statutory job reservation, the opening of apprenticeships to blacks and the registering of black trade unions; the

Table 2
Results of the 1981 general election (abridged)

Party	Votes	Percentage votes	Seats	Percentage seats
Cape				
NP	229,033	59.1	43	78
HNP	35,386	9.1	–	–
NCP	1,573	0.4	–	–
Transvaal				
NP	396,425	59.9	67	88
HNP	119,379	18.0	–	–
NCP	17,156	2.6	–	–
Natal				
NP	67,282	37.4	7	35
HNP	8,206	4.5	–	–
NCP	520	0.2	–	–
OFS				
NP	84,818	72.4	14	100
HNP	29,333	25.2	–	–
Total				
NP	777,558	57.8	131	79
PFP	265,297	19.7	26	16
NRP	106,764	7.9	8	5
HNP	192,304	14.3	–	–
NCP	19,249	1.4	–	–

Riekert report chiefly recommended that urban blacks be granted greater mobility, and the de Lange report that all races should receive education of equal quality. With Botha's acceptance of the Riekert and Wiehahn recommendations and partial acceptance of the de Lange report, he sent a clear message to the white working class to the effect that its days of preferential treatment were over. The labour reforms resulted in large-scale disaffection among white workers and lower-echelon civil servants, who rightly perceived it as a direct threat to their economic security. Their resentment was transformed into support for the HNP, which enabled the party to win an average of 40 per cent of the vote in three by-elections in 1979 in the blue-collar constituencies of Koedoespoort, Rustenburg and Germiston. In contrast to its dismal electoral performance during the 1970s the right wing started the 1980s with new enthusiasm and received a further boost from the general election of 1981.

As can be seen from Table 2, above, the NP won 131 seats although its electoral support declined from 67 per cent in the 1977 general election to less than 58 per cent. The right-wing parties collectively received almost one-third of the Afrikaner and 16 per cent of the total vote (compared to the 3 per cent which the HNP received in 1977). Due to the distorting effect of the 'first-past-the-post' electoral system, the right-wing parties failed to win any seats, but under proportional representation they would have had about 25 seats. The NP interpreted the election results as a vindication of its reformist direction and as a mandate for devising a power-sharing structure with the coloured and Indian communities. However, the NP had lost one-third of its traditional constituency to the right wing; during the few months after the election, the growing discontent among members of the NP's *verkrampte* wing, under the leadership of Treurnicht, posed a considerable challenge to P.W. Botha's reforms and leadership.

Political developments and elections in 1982–83
During the remainder of 1981 Treurnicht's course of resistance and his obstructionist actions caused a rift within the cabinet and the NP caucus, and finally led to the split in the NP in 1982 over the issue of power-sharing and the founding of the CP in March 1982.

During the course of 1982 the government implemented the Black Local Authorities Act which gave urban blacks greater authority to govern themselves. At the same time, Botha's iron fist took a still tighter grip: the government-appointed Steyn Commission proposed that firmer control should be placed on the media; the Rabie Commission proposed stronger security legislation, while the Defence Force launched 'preventative' counter-insurgency attacks on ANC and SWAPO bases in Angola and Lesotho. Such incursions into neighbouring countries became a common method during subsequent years of demonstrating to the white electorate that the NP, in spite of its reforms, had not lost its capacity for strong-arm tactics.

In by-elections held in Walvis Bay, Stellenbosch and Parys in November 1982 the right-wing parties were convincingly beaten, an indication that the convergence between the CP and the NP on basic ideology, and the fact that the CP was still struggling to establish its own identity so soon after the split, had acted to its detriment. The possibility of an early settlement being reached in Namibia became a major issue in these elections, but on this there was no difference between the NP and the right. Both rejected any settlement which would have led to a SWAPO victory on the grounds that a 'communist government would be unacceptable' (*Cape Times*, 2 November 1982). In addition, there was little difference between the NP and the right wing in 1982 on the ultimate goal of Afrikaner hegemony, apart from disagreements over power-sharing and social apartheid. Even on the possibility of blacks in the central government, there were no substantial differences between the two parties. The NP's policy at the time was to strengthen the ties between urbanized blacks and the homelands with the intention of giving each urban black the vote, as long as those votes were cast in the 'independent' homelands. P.W. Botha was very clear on this topic: 'No National Party can accept the principle of majority rule in one state. That we reject. But we are prepared to consult with the black leaders ... to carry out a system in South Africa which will make it possible for them to achieve their own independence' (Pottinger 1988: 124).

There were several important political developments in 1983, the most important of which were: the referendum to test white support for the new tricameral constitution, the founding of the internal black resistance movements, the United Democratic Front (UDF) and National Forum; further 'pre-emptive' strikes by the SADF on ANC and SWAPO bases in neighbouring countries; and the strike by the ANC on the Air Force HQ in Pretoria. The latter event, in which several white soldiers and black civilians died, caused a strong reaction among white voters, and during the following round of by-elections in the Transvaal in 1983, also known as the 'battle of the bergs', the two right-wing parties experienced a swing of respectively 11 and 27 per cent in their favour. Although the NP won three of the four seats contested, its majorities declined considerably. In the Soutpansberg constituency, the NP saw its majority reduced from 3647 in 1981 to 621 (a swing of 10.7 per cent). In the Waterberg constituency the CP overturned the NP's majority of 1461 over the HNP in the 1981 election to a CP majority of 1894. In Carletonville the NP held on to the seat with a majority of 1359, but the combined right-wing vote surpassed that of the NP by 314 votes. In Waterkloof the NP received a majority of 1951 over the PFP, but the CP managed to attract 2887 votes in spite of the fact that no right-wing party had contested this seat during the previous election. The NP had received slightly fewer votes in the four constituencies combined than its rivals on the right: 21,578 votes to 21,774.

The by-election results indicated that the NP would have to compete in future with a much stronger right wing, the CP having overtaken the HNP, but the prime minister insisted that this would not deter the government from its path of reform (*Die Burger*, 12 May 1983). The NP's poor performance was attributed to the fact that the CP took over about 80 per cent of the NP's party organization in certain constituencies when the split occurred in 1982, and that the proximity of certain constituencies to the northern border with Zimbabwe and Mozambique had made whites uneasy over reform.

The 1983 referendum
During 1983 the NP government enacted into law a new constitution which provided for power-sharing with coloureds and Indians at central government level. The CP and HNP strongly opposed the new constitution on grounds that the white grip on power would be weakened and that it would inevitably lead to the inclusion of blacks in parliament.

The referendum on the new constitution was not held on a constituency basis, as would be the case in a general election, but instead the white electorate was divided into 15 referendum regions, each consisting of several parliamentary constituencies. Voters could cast their ballots in whichever referendum region they happened to be present on the day. The results are shown in Table 3.

Table 3
Results of the 1983 referendum

Region	Yes	No
Beaufort West	22,509	7,733
Bloemfontein	52,019	26,960
Cape Town	221,511	71,456
Durban	123,783	44,442
East London	53,202	15,087
George	31,256	11,426
Germiston	113,600	60,241
Johannesburg	194,396	85,554
Kimberley	34,815	17,898
Kroonstad	55,486	32,321
Pietermaritzburg	50,519	20,060
Pietersburg	31,403	34,827
Port Elizabeth	60,661	25,901
Pretoria	209,763	157,433
Roodepoort	105,307	80,238
Total	1,360,223	691,577

The tricameral constitution was approved by two-thirds of white voters, but because the No votes were not differentiated between left and right in the ballot, it was virtually impossible to determine how many voters opposed the new constitution from each of the two opposing sides on the political spectrum. According to Laurie (1987: 254–62), who projected the 1981 and 1987 general election results onto the 1983 referendum results, the right-wing share of the total vote was approximately 555,000 (27 per cent).

Reform, unrest and the by-elections in 1984–87

The signing of the Lusaka and Nkomati accords in 1984 gave evidence of more regional cooperation between Southern African states, but it soon became obvious that the South African government had no intention of refraining from its destabilizing activities. At the parliamentary level the coloureds and Indians turned out in only small numbers to vote for representatives to the Houses of Delegates and of Representatives in August 1984. Of registered voters, only about 30 per cent of coloureds and 20 per cent of Indians voted, but it nevertheless signalled the end of exclusive white rule and of the Westminster system. At the same time the exclusion of the black majority stirred up waves of resentment which took the form of unrest, violence, school boycotts, strikes, consumer boycotts, sabotage and attacks on co-opted black officials. On the labour front the National Union of Mineworkers was founded in November, and a mass stay-away on the Reef gave an indication of the growing power of black workers.

The first by-elections following the referendum were contested in the constituencies of Soutpansberg in February 1984, Primrose, George and Parow in November 1984. The result at Soutpansberg, where the NP lost the seat to the CP, indicated a further erosion of the NP's support-base in the northern Transvaal. In the other two by-elections the CP focused its election campaigns on the poor state of the economy and on the claim of the finance ministry that the country was 'technically bankrupt'. The CP also claimed that voters were not made aware before the referendum of the fact that coloureds and Indians were going to be joining the cabinet, nor did they know that 93 per cent of the portfolios were going to be general affairs and only 7 per cent own affairs. In response the NP candidate in Parow at the time, Hernus Kriel, hastened to reassure concerned NP supporters that 'our policy is still separate development' (*The Argus*, 10 November 1984). Although the CP did not win any of these three by-elections, the results indicated that there was a swing towards the right of up to 22 per cent. The outcome in the Transvaal constituency of Primrose, where the NP majority declined from 4399 to 748, was a clear indication that many formerly safe NP seats in the Transvaal had now become marginal.

In spite of the electoral setbacks during 1984 the NP introduced several important reform measures in 1985. These included the repeal of the Mixed Marriages and Immorality Acts and the repeal of the Prohibition of Political Interference Act. In May 1985 the government announced the creation of institutions to accommodate black political rights and the granting of self-determination to groups without one population group dominating another. These proposals, which were totally unacceptable to most blacks, resulted in an increase in political unrest during the course of the year and caused the government to introduce a state of emergency in 36 magisterial districts in June. The year also saw the founding of the non-racial trade union body, COSATU (Congress of South African Trade Unions), and further labour unrest and school boycotts.

In September 1985 P.W. Botha's infamous 'Rubicon' speech caused reverberations throughout the world. The disastrous tone and contents of this speech were a result of a combination of Botha's own obstinacy (allegedly urged on by – at the time – a *verkrampte* F.W. de Klerk) and the accusation by sections of the white population that the government was caving in to foreign pressure. The Rubicon speech, which was promoted beforehand by Pik Botha as the watershed in South African politics, was a disaster in terms of reform and the country's international standing. More than anything else, its total rejection of international demands opened the way for large-scale disinvestment, economic sanctions, and hastened the drastic decline in the value of the local currency. Apart from the Rubicon speech, the year of 1985 contained a mixture of political reform and repression, but with the killing of 19 black protesters in Uitenhage in the eastern Cape, the pattern for the hard-line approach of the second half of the decade had been established.

The CP had another chance to test its strength against the NP during the October 1985 'mini' general election when by-elections were held in Bethlehem, Port Natal, Sasolburg, Springs and Vryburg, covering a large part of the northern provinces. The results once again came as a shock to the NP, as its majorities declined in three of the five constituencies by between 50 and 70 per cent, while it lost Sasolburg to the HNP. In all, the average swing to the right wing was 16.3 per cent. The

NP blamed the swing on the recession, drought and unrest which plagued the country, while P.W. Botha expressed his concern over the disunity among whites in the face of the threats facing the country (*Cape Times*, 1 November 1985). Botha also criticized 'outside' attempts to prescribe to South Africa and to weaken its economy. What emerged from these by-elections was that if an urban NP seat like Sasolburg could fall to the right and a previously safe NP Reef seat such as Springs became marginal, the right wing would stand a good chance of gaining a considerable number of seats in the next general election.

The official end of South Africa's 'Prague Spring' and by-elections in 1986
Significant political developments during 1986 included the repeal of the Influx Control measures which controlled the migration of blacks to urban areas, the KwaZulu/Natal Indaba, the visit of the Commonwealth Eminent Persons Group (EPG), and the proclamation of a national state of emergency. The EPG's mission to South Africa was intended to broker a settlement between the government and the ANC, but was wrecked by cross-border raids by the SADF on ANC bases in three neighbouring black states. Apart from wrecking a possible breakthrough in negotiations with the ANC, the raids also achieved the expected and desired result of proving to the white electorate that the government had not gone soft on the external threat and was not caving in to foreign pressure. The introduction of a national state of emergency in June 1986 led to large-scale state suppression of most forms of anti-government protest, including pre-publication censorship, the transfer of great powers of discretion to even junior members of the security forces, and resulted in the detention of 25,000 people in the 11 months after its proclamation. These events led to what was described as the 'end of South Africa's Prague Spring', i.e. the end of the reformist and enlightened period of the P.W. Botha era (*Sunday Times*, 16 August 1987).

Under these circumstances the Kliprivier by-election was contested in September 1986. As usual the NP tried to straddle two chairs, fighting left and right at the same time. The minister of national education at the time, F.W. de Klerk, explained that his party's middle-of-the-road policy was the only viable one, which ensured an own community life, own schools, and a built-in guarantee for white survival and security. He added that the voters of Kliprivier should reject not only the 'flagrant racism and the pie-in-the-sky' solutions of the right, but also the 'suicidal' policy of one-person-one-vote as proposed by the PFP (*Die Burger*, 15 September 1986). In spite of de Klerk's assurances, the NP's majority in Kliprivier declined by 22 per cent.

The general election of May 1987
The general election of 1987 took place under a countrywide state of emergency, which resulted in the prominent position which security and law and order issues took during the election campaign. The NP's election strategy was based on the twin pillars of reform and security, as its election slogan exclaimed: 'Reform yes, surrender, no'. The NP relied on the tried-and-tested *swart gevaar* and 'total onslaught' tactics to scare voters away from the parties on the left, and in this it succeeded so well that it chased some of its own supporters into the right-wing fold.

The right-wing parties focused on the 'failure' of power-sharing. The CP argued that the worsening unrest in the country, the economic decline and increased foreign pressure were proof that power-sharing did not work. To avoid the damaging results of a split right-wing vote, unsuccessful attempts were made by the AWB to broker an election agreement between the HNP and CP. To force the issue, Eugene Terre Blanche threatened to activate the AWB's Blanke Volkstaat Party, but because of the HNP's insistence on a 50–50 division of seats, nothing came of his efforts.

The most important patterns which emerged from the election (Table 4) were the increase in its electoral support for the combined right wing from about 14 per cent of the total vote in 1981 to almost 30 per cent in this election. The number of right-wing seats had increased from zero in 1981 to 22 in 1987.[1] The CP had become the official opposition, an event of great symbolic value for the party. The outcome also indicated the demise of the HNP, as it had lost its deposit in all but four of the seats it had contested, leaving the CP as the true representative of the right. However, the lack of an election agreement between the two right-wing parties had cost the CP eight seats.

Table 4
Results of the 1987 general election

Party	Votes	Percentage votes	Seats	Percentage seats
Cape Province				
NP	335,739	60.6	47	84
CP	82,366	14.8	0	0
HNP	14,006	2.5	0	0
Transvaal				
NP	526,919	48.7	45	59
CP	383,176	35.4	22	29
HNP	32,499	3.0	0	0
Orange Free State				
NP	93,497	55.0	14	100
CP	60,958	37.3	0	0
HNP	10,505	5.6	0	0
Natal				
NP	119,299	49.9	14	70
CP	21,059	8.8	0	0
HNP	4,446	1.3	0	0
Total				
NP	1,075,454	53.0	120	72
CP	547,559	27.0	22	13
HNP	61,456	3.0	0	0
PFP	288,547	14.0	19	11
NRP	38,494	2.0	1	1
Ind.	27,149	1.0	1	1
Vacant			3	

The results showed that support from the right wing was largely concentrated in the Transvaal, but that it also enjoyed considerable support in the Free State. Its support in the Transvaal was mostly concentrated in the rural districts, especially in the northern Transvaal where it received 57 per cent of the vote compared to the NP's 43 per cent. In the eastern and western Transvaal, a mixture of mining and agricultural towns, the right wing received 52.6 per cent and 54.3 per cent of the vote respectively, in the Vaal Triangle 46 per cent, in the west Rand 42 per cent and in Pretoria 39 per cent of the vote. The NP's support declined from 58.3 per cent of the vote in 1981 to 53 per cent in 1987. The PFP–NRP alliance fared poorly and the PFP was replaced by the CP as official opposition in the House of Assembly. It was obvious that many liberal voters were influenced by the scare tactics of the government and believed that security took priority over reform. However, the NP's emphasis on the 'total onslaught' and its *laager* mentality backfired badly: it lost more Afrikaners to the CP than it gained from the English-speaking community.

Newspaper headlines were almost unanimous in their verdict that the election results were a decisive move back to the *laager*: 'No one can ignore the swing to the right' (*Rapport*, 10 May 1987); 'Voters crossed all cultural, religious and language barriers to enter the white laager and to shut out the rest' (*Business Day*, 8 May 1987); 'Swing to the right reduces pressure for reform' (*Southern Africa Report*, 8 May 1987); 'Those who did not scurry back into the *laager* took another frightened step back to the ox-wagon days by voting for the CP' (*The Sowetan*, 8 May 1987).

Only a minority of political analysts shared the CP's view that the election results implied a swing to the right. In this vein it was argued that the CP could win the next election if a 12 per cent of NP voters switched to the right – such a swing would give the CP 850,000 votes and 84 seats in parliament (Donald Simpson, cited in *The Argus*, 23 May 1987). The author Alan Paton agreed that white voters had moved 'decidedly and spectacularly to the right', a turn of events which he blamed on the international sanctions campaign and on the need for security – whites feared the future, the UDF, Cosatu, the ANC, and thought that the NP could best provide it. Paton (with some foresight) predicted that the government, with half-a-million right-wing voters looking over its shoulder, would use the tools of repression, the army and police, over the next two years to maintain the status quo and would only reform at its own slow pace (*Sunday Times*, 17 May 1987).

In contrast, many analysts held the view that the swing in white politics was actually to the left. It was argued that the result implied a funnelling of support to the white centre, and since this centre had shifted to the left (which left the right wing in the position of the NP under Vorster), the support for rigid separate development and partition had declined between 1977 and 1987 from 64 to 30 per cent (Schlemmer 1987: 321). Elsewhere it was suggested that the policies of the CP in 1987 were identical to those of the NP in 1981, in that blacks were excluded from the central political institutions, influx control and independence for homelands including urban blacks, i.e. support for 'conservative' policies declined from 57 per cent in 1981 to 30 per cent in 1987 (*Weekly Mail*, 15 May 1987). Both these sources correctly argued that the media were under the mistaken impression that there had been a swing to the right because of failure to recognize that the centre of politics had moved to the left over the past few years.

The NP faced international condemnation for its policies, and sanctions and disinvestment began to have a strongly detrimental effect on the economy. Foreign pressure intensified because the election was also interpreted internationally as a move towards self-imposed isolation, e.g. the statement by the Australian acting minister of foreign affairs, Gareth Evans, that 'the whites-only election appeared to have entrenched white supremacy' (*Cape Times*, 12 May 1987). In addition the NP was facing increasing pressure from the more *verligte* members within its own ranks such as Albert Nothnagel, who was soon removed from local politics by being posted to The Netherlands as ambassador. The NP also had to contend with a determined onslaught from the new right-wing official opposition, which, together with the HNP, commanded the support of almost 600,000 voters, as opposed to the one million or so who voted for the NP.

Having carefully considered all the above issues, the NP opted to slow down its reform programme and to focus upon security. During the next two years P.W. Botha repeatedly made overtures to Treurnicht to help restore unity among Afrikaners for the sake of Afrikanerdom, reminiscent of the relationship between Smuts and Hertzog after 1913. However, his efforts to appease the right wing and to win back former NP voters met with little success, and resulted in the NP losing support to left and right in the run-up to the next general election in 1989.

The by-elections and municipal elections of 1988
The by-elections in Standerton, Schweizer-Reneke and Randfontein in March 1988 gave the CP the first opportunity to test its

strength against the NP in its capacity as the new official opposition. Standerton, in particular, was of great symbolic significance as it was here that the former UP prime minister Jan Smuts was defeated by the NP in 1948. It had been NP territory since then, but the CP won the seat in 1987.

The CP focused its election strategy on the 'negative' consequences of the reforms implemented by the NP, in particular on the effects of sanctions and disinvestment, the unrest in Natal, the failure of the tricameral parliament, the 'chaos' on selected desegregated beaches in Durban, the 'greying' of suburbs like Hillbrow, the freezing of salaries of public servants. It also accused the government of selling out the whites, and fought a successful campaign on the personal unpopularity of P.W. Botha in the Transvaal.

The NP responded to the CP's electoral campaign with its usual strong-arm tactics just before the election by ordering the SADF to attack ANC bases in Angola and by banning 17 anti-apartheid organizations. To balance its over-emphasis on security issues, certain NP leaders emphasized reform, most notably F.W. de Klerk, who argued that it was possible to change the constitution in order to accommodate blacks, although not without asking for white permission first by way of a referendum. He also said that separate residential areas were not always 'practical' (*The Star*, 25 March 1988).

The results of these three by-elections, all of which were won by the CP, were not unexpected, but still came as a shock to the NP because of the extent of the swing towards the right and because of the analogy with Smuts in Standerton. In the Schweizer-Reneke constituency the swing to the right was 5 per cent, in Standerton 8 per cent and in Randfontein 9 per cent. The results confirmed that the CP's support was not confined to rural or blue-collar areas, and came as a tremendous boost to its prospects in the countrywide municipal elections due in October 1988.

The media expressed its concern at the strong performance of the right. The English-speaking sections of the media with their anti-NP tradition, which normally expressed their delight in any setback in the fortunes of the NP, began to show signs of dismay at the seemingly unstoppable growth of the right. Their headlines read: 'Routed! Nats lose election by a landslide – Conservatives rampant' (*The Argus*, 30 March 1988); 'Secret cabinet talks on CP threat' (*Sunday Times*, 7 March 1988); 'CP could topple Nats if election rules not changed' (*The Argus*, 5 March 1988); 'By-elections thrashing! – PW slams foreign elements' (*Weekly Mail*, 4 March 1988); 'CP says it can win the next election' (*Cape Times*, 4 March 1988). Even those newspapers sympathetic to the government became more critical and suggested that the NP would have to address white fears and insecurity. *Die Burger* (4 March 1988) mentioned that the racial problems experienced at Durban beaches and the relaxing of the Group Areas Act were symptoms of the wider phenomenon of white fears of being 'swamped'.

From his response to the by-election results, it was clear that the leader of the NP, P.W. Botha, had decided that he had to address these insecurities of white voters if the growth of the CP was to be contained; Botha said that the government would from now on 'give priority to the security of South Africans' and only there-after would continue with reform (*Die Burger*, 4 March 1988). Other senior NP members also admitted privately 'that a brake would now be placed on racial reform' (*Die Burger*, 4 March 1988). It was clear that after these by-election setbacks, the NP leadership had lost its nerve and would freeze reform until the swing to the right had been reversed or brought into perspective.

The municipal elections of October 1988

The municipal elections (Table 5) had a symbolic value as they were the first ever in which people of all races could go to the polls in a countrywide election (albeit in separate polls). The further significance lay in the fact that many of the reforms introduced so far, such as the gradual opening of certain beaches, the creation of 'grey' areas and the opening of central business districts to all races, brought many whites into social contact with other races for the first time. The CP, which fiercely opposed desegregation at any level, realized that, although it could not prevent the government from repealing apartheid legislation, it was within its power at least to obstruct the implementation of reform. Its plan was to gain control of as many town and city councils as possible, and to use these to guarantee the existing racial order at local government level.

The NP, realizing that it faced a determined onslaught from the CP in the sphere in which the right was at its most powerful,

Table 5
Results of the 1988 municipal elections

Province	Party	Percentage control of local authority
Transvaal	NP	38
	CP	53
	NP/CP (doubtful)	6
OFS	NP	78
	CP	18
	NP/CP (doubtful)	4
Cape	NP	90
	CP	3
	NP/CP (doubtful)	4
Natal	NP	87
	CP	0
	NP/CP (doubtful)	2
Total	NP	71
	CP	22

was initially reluctant to contest the elections on a party-political basis. However, because the CP was using the NP's reluctance for propaganda purposes and because it was virtually impossible to fight any kind of election on a non-political basis in the highly politicized atmosphere which pervaded South Africa at the time, the NP eventually entered the fray under its own banner, although many of its candidates stood as independents.

The CP concentrated its electoral efforts on the Transvaal and Orange Free State and it managed to win the majority of contested local authorities in the Transvaal. The party received 37 per cent of votes under its own banner, as opposed to the 27 per cent of the NP. These percentages were adjusted to 42.4 per cent of the vote (343,344 votes) for the CP, and 42.1 per cent of the vote (341,347 votes) for the NP, after the ideological persuasions of the 'independent' and 'doubtful' councillors became known. The CP gained control over 101 (67 per cent) out of a possible 150 local councils in the Transvaal (*CP Information pamphlet*, February 1989). More neutral commentators estimated the CP's election gains in the Transvaal to be slightly lower, at 53 per cent. More specifically, the CP won 43 of the 65 councils in cities and large towns, and 19 of the 28 smaller town councils.

The CP regarded its performance in the municipal elections as a mandate to halt and reverse political reforms implemented by the NP. Many cities and towns under CP control began to re-implement petty apartheid measures soon after these elections. The local government of Boksburg and Carletonville were the first to do so by closing recreational halls, public parks and swimming areas to blacks. The response of blacks took the form of consumer boycotts which had such severe economic consequences on white businesses, that it soon became a serious impediment to the continued growth of right-wing support. In Boksburg, a CP candidate who contested a local by-election previously held by the CP, lost by a landslide a few weeks later, and during the general election of 1989, the CP was soundly beaten by the NP in towns on the East Rand that had re-implemented petty-apartheid measures (see also Chapter 4 for greater detail).

The general election of September 1989
An important issue which accompanied the 1989 general election was whether the forces inherent in the 'first-past-the-post' electoral system would allow the CP finally to obtain a number of seats proportional to its electoral support. After all, the same forces which gave the NP 72 per cent (120) of the seats in parliament but only 53 per cent of the total vote during the 1987 general election were due to start working in favour of the CP as well; the CP had the same basic matrix of support as that of the NP when it came to power in 1948 with only 44 per cent of the vote. As indicated earlier, on a proportional basis the CP would have had close to 50 seats in parliament instead of 22.

The CP entered the election campaign with great expectations. Not only had the party experienced a 7 per cent average swing in its favour during the two years since 1987, but a damaging leadership struggle erupted within the NP during the months leading up to the election. This struggle rocked the party and culminated in P.W. Botha's (forced) resignation as state president. The leadership struggle between de Klerk and Botha began when Botha suffered a stroke early in 1989, whereupon he resigned as leader of the NP and requested that the posts of party leader and president be separated. The NP caucus elected F.W. de

Klerk as new party leader in February, but then decided to reject Botha's proclamation of the separation of the posts. This led to the start of a five-month power struggle between Botha and the NP caucus. The situation became acrimonious, with Botha refusing even to attend functions in his honour given by the NP and by his attempts openly to discredit de Klerk's style of governing. Botha finally resigned as state president in August 1989, and took a final public swipe at de Klerk by implying that de Klerk was guilty of treacherous behaviour because of his talks with Kenneth Kaunda of Zambia. As R.W. Johnson observed, 'it is not often that one sees a retiring president accusing his duly chosen successor – on prime time TV – of being a liar and virtual traitor' (*The Times*, 17 August 1989). To limit the pre-election damage Pik Botha in turn accused his former leader of having lost his 'memory' (probably implying senility).

The NP feared that the controversy surrounding P.W. Botha would be exploited as an election issue by the CP and damage even further the NP's unity. An M&M survey of July 1989 concluded that the Botha affair had little effect on the electorate, with 12 per cent indicating that Botha's departure would lead them to vote for the NP, 9 per cent saying that Botha's departure might cause them not to vote for the NP, and 73 per cent remaining unaffected by it all. Botha's demise as a political force gave rise to the 'Give F.W. a chance' slogan, which was a plea from the NP to voters to give the new state president an opportunity to prove that his style of government would be different – it was intended to draw the *gatvol en keelvol* (exasperated and fed-up) voters back to the NP, and de Klerk's own brother and founder-member of the DP, Willem de Klerk, was among the people who proclaimed this view. De Klerk's political initiatives during 1989, even before he became state president, gave many *verligte* NP members hope that a new approach might be in the offing. Even de Klerk's visits to Zaire and Zambia were conducted in such a way as to project a new and fresh presidential image which was expected to reflect favourably on the tired image of the NP (*Rapport*, 23 August 1989). The NP's election campaign was based on the following fundamental principles: group control over own affairs would be retained; each racial group would have its own voter's roll, its own community life, and separate residential areas and schools; racial groups to participate as such in government; public amenities would be opened to all races where necessary and where it could be achieved without causing racial conflict (Five Year Plan of Action, 1989).

The CP's election campaign concentrated on three major issues: firstly, it accused the NP of 'selling out' the whites with its reforms; secondly, it said the NP had mismanaged the economy and impoverished whites through its redistributive policies;[2] thirdly, it said the settlement in Namibia was not in the interests of that country's whites and might have similar implications for South African whites (Bekker et al 1989: 11–12). As a solution the CP offered its own policy of partition, which, it claimed, would result in the creation of separate states for each population group; total segregation in all spheres of society; no power-sharing with any non-white group; the reinstatement of influx control.

A comparison of the policies presented to the white electorate by the NP and the CP suggested that as late as 1989 both subscribed to a rejection of majority rule, refused to negotiate with the ANC, and insisted on the right of whites to an own community life. As it turned out, the 'F.W.' factor made little difference to the NP's prospects, as NP supporters deserted the Party in large numbers. The election was the NP's worst electoral performance since 1948 (Table 6, below). The party suffered losses to both left and right and it received its lowest number of seats since 1953. The NP lost 29 seats, of which 17 went to the CP and 12 to the DP. Even though the NP maintained an overall majority in parliament (without the nominated MPs, the NP had 94 seats against the 72 of its opponents), it had lost its overall majority in votes (1,031,566 for the NP against 1,108,779 for the opposition parties). The CP increased its share of the vote by only 3 per cent compared to 1987, but increased its number of seats by 77 per cent, from 22 to 39, i.e. although the right wing did not greatly increase its number of votes, it almost doubled its number of seats. The CP also made a breakthrough outside the Transvaal by winning six seats in the Orange Free State and two in the Cape. A large number of former safe NP seats became marginal – these included the seat lost to the NP because of HNP intervention, seven seats where the NP majority was less than 500 votes, nine seats with an NP majority of less than 1000 and 14 seats with an NP majority of less than 1500, a total of 31 marginal seats. However, the party failed to win any seats on the Reef

Table 6
Results of the September 1989 general election

Party	Votes	Percentage of vote	Seats	Percentage of seats
Cape				
NP	315,956	54	42	75
CP	106,376	18	2	4
DP	162,887	28	12	21
Transvaal				
NP	520,034	46	34	45
CP	453,826	40	31	41
DP	159,383	14	11	14
HNP	3,308	0.28	0	0
OFS				
NP	88,490	51	7	57
CP	80,068	46	6	43
DP	4,382	3	0	0
Natal				
NP	107,077	44	10	50
CP	32,809	13	0	0
DP	103,547	42	10	50
Total				
NP	1,031,557	48	93	56
CP	673,079	31	39	23
DP	430,199	20	33	20
HNP	5,501	0.25	0	0
Vacant			1	

industrial belt or in Natal, and did not capitalize on its strong showing in urban areas during the 1988 municipal elections.

Another prominent characteristic of the results was a large-scale defection of English-speaking support from the NP. English-speakers displayed a remarkably consistent pattern of rallying to the NP when the latter was in need of electoral support; this was the case during the 1987 general election, when the NP received over 40 per cent of the English-speaking vote, and led to a perception that English-speakers had 'become a permanent and integral part of the National Party structure' (Schlemmer 1988: 24). As reform came to a virtual halt between 1987 and 1989, however, the result was a considerable loss in support for the NP among English-speakers, from over 40 per cent in 1987 to about 28 per cent in 1989 (*Sunday Times*, 10 September 1989).

With the CP enjoying the support of almost half of Afrikaners, the NP had little choice but to accelerate the pace of reform in order to win over the English-speakers from the DP, rather than to attempt to win back the core of its traditional support-base from the right. This partly explains the NP's new direction after September 1989, but with the CP lurking in the background and increasing its strength with every new reform measure, the NP began to realize that even its greater English-speaking support could not guarantee its continued dominance in white politics. Over the following 24 months a fast-changing political environment, together with the growing risk that the government might not survive another right-wing electoral onslaught, brought about a realization within the NP that there could not be another whites-only election. This was to be the clear message from the by-elections between the general election of September 1989 and the referendum of March 1992.

The de Klerk presidency and the by-elections after September 1989
After September 1989 the process of political change gained momentum. In October 1989 the government released the seven remaining Rivonia trialists,[3] excluding Nelson Mandela, and the welcome rally organized for them in Johannesburg implied the *de facto* unbanning of the ANC. In November the government ordered the opening of beaches to all races, and in response to a mass defiance campaign by the UDF and other organizations, announced its intention to repeal the Separate Amenities Act. It also gave permission for a protest march in Cape Town, led by Archbishop Desmond Tutu, the mayor of the city and other dignitaries. The first 'Free Settlement Areas' were proclaimed, and in December of 1989 the president received a visit from Mandela at Tuynhuis, his official residence.[4] In Namibia SWAPO won the election with a convincing majority in spite of the South African government's financial backing of opposition parties.

Having to deal with the cautious steps which characterized de Klerk's first few months as state president, and with the prospects of further political changes in the back of their minds, the voters of the traditionally safe Cape NP seats of Ceres and Vasco went to the polls for by-elections in late November 1989. Since 1934, when D.F. Malan founded the Purified NP with the help of the Cape Nationalists, the western Cape has been an NP stronghold. The CP had never succeeded in gaining a foothold there, but hoped that recent political developments would bolster its support in the traditional heartland of the NP. Although the NP retained both seats, there was a swing to the CP of 5 per cent in Ceres and of 13 per cent in Vasco; the NP's majority declined in Ceres from 2519 to 1570 and in Vasco from 3899 to 1243.

The results were a clear indication that the minor political changes announced by de Klerk up to November 1989 had claimed their first victims, in the form of the defection of about 4000 NP supporters to the CP in two constituencies. For many voters even the limited reforms of the first few weeks of the de Klerk era, such as the opening of beaches and the proclamation of the first free settlement areas, were too much to bear. Despite these setbacks the government accelerated its reform programme and with de Klerk's speech on 2 February 1990 for the first time ever gave the impression that it was serious about dismantling white domination. The early part of 1990 saw the following dramatic changes: the release of Nelson Mandela; the formal unbanning of the ANC, SACP, PAC and other resistance organizations, the first meeting between the government and the ANC/SACP; the government's declared commitment to repealing the Group Areas and Population Registration Acts, its intention to open white schools to all races (with certain provisions) and to shorten military service, and a moratorium on executions.

The NP's new direction met with strong opposition from the right wing. Following de Klerk's epoch-making speech Treurnicht accused the government of implementing 'revolutionary' measures and threatened that the CP would intensify its struggle for survival on all fronts. Terre Blanche said that the NP had surrendered its honour and given in to the wishes of leftist radicals, while Jaap Marais argued that de Klerk had now become the 'prisoner and Mandela the warder' (*Vrye Weekblad*, 9 February 1990).

While the reaction of the right generally was predictable and amounted to little more than empty racist and nationalist rhetoric, one issue stood out above all, an issue which became the focus of the CP's whole election strategy over the following two years. It concerned the NP's alleged lack of a mandate for its reforms. The CP argued with great conviction that the NP had deceived the white electorate by not spelling out the full implications of its reforms: 'If you had spelled out your current policy to the voters before the 1989 general election, you would have lost that election' (Treurnicht, cited in *Patriot*, 9 November 1990) [translation]. The CP based its argument on the discrepancies which it believed existed between the reforms proposed by the NP before the election, and the actual reforms implemented afterwards. One example cited by the CP concerned the NP's commitment to maintain population groups and separate voters' rolls as the building blocks for its constitutional reforms. However, the NP had dissociated itself from the group concept during 1990–91 and repealed the basis of racial group classification, the Population Registration Act. Furthermore, the CP argued, the NP broke its promise that 'own residential areas are and will remain NP policy', by repealing the Group Areas Act in 1991, and, contrary to its election promises, the NP unbanned the ANC and began negotiating with the organization before it suspended violence. These 'discrepancies' formed the basis of the CP's claim that the NP had no mandate for its radical reforms, and that the government had to resign because it no longer represented the wishes of the electorate.

However, as the subsequent by-elections results indicate, not all the opposition to the reforms came from the right wing. Through the rapid pace of reform the NP appeared to have left behind large numbers of its own supporters. An M&M survey of February 1990 indicated that 32 per cent of all whites, 43 per cent of Afrikaners and 6 per cent of NP-supporters disapproved of Mandela's release; 43 per cent of all whites, 58 per cent of Afrikaners and 25 per cent of NP-supporters disapproved of the unbanning of the ANC, SACP and PAC. The repeal of the Separate Amenities Act evoked a similar ominous response: 35 per cent of all whites, 51 per cent of Afrikaners, and 15 per cent of NP-supporters disapproved. These figures indicated that the NP faced an uphill battle in trying to convince its traditional supporters of the benefits of reform. The party realized that it had to educate white voters and accustom them to the idea of fundamental reform, but it was a task which it had no hope of completing in the short-term, and definitely not before the Umlazi and Randburg by-elections scheduled for 1990.

The Umlazi by-election

The Umlazi by-election was held in a predominantly working-class constituency of Natal where 80 per cent of the voters were English-speaking. It had been a safe NP seat, but the government's intention to repeal the Group Areas Act, together with the violence in Natal, murders of white farmers on the Natal south coast and the overcrowding of Natal beaches introduced an element of doubt to the expected result.

The CP more than doubled its support in Umlazi since the 1989 general election, representing a swing of more than 20 per cent to the right. It increased its share of the vote from 9 per cent in 1987 to 20 per cent in 1989 and 43.6 per cent in 1990, showing that it now enjoyed considerable support in Natal, even among English-speakers. Treurnicht claimed that the results showed growing white rejection of proposals which would lead to majority rule; in his view this was proof that the NP did not represent the majority of white voters any more (*Cape Times*, 7 June 1990).

The NP's reaction was that it would not be deterred from its path of reform; de Klerk stated that whites could not turn back the clock and take refuge in the past (*The Argus*, 8 June 1990). On the day the results became known (8 June 1990), he lifted the state of emergency and for the first time used the word 'irreversible' to describe his reforms. The NP-supporting press saw the results in a more serious light: *Die Burger* argued that no NP seats in Natal were safe after Umlazi and cited several political analysts (e.g. Schlemmer and Simpson) who claimed that these results showed that the CP could defeat the NP if a general election were held. *Citizen* (8 June 1990) once again warned the NP that it was leaving its supporters behind by reforming too fast, and even the liberal *Business Day* (8 June 1990) warned that white South Africans needed to be reassured over issues that caused panic, such as their future in a black-dominated South Africa, their personal safety, the loss of democracy, the security of their savings, the destruction of their schools, and in general, anarchy.

In contrast, the *Cape Times* (8 June 1990) argued there would not be another whites-only election, mainly because the NP knew it could not win such an election, while the *Sunday Times* (11 June 1990) claimed that in the absence of another whites-only election, any anxiety about the CP's electoral strength was unnecessary. This was confirmed by the former minister of constitutional planning and development, Gerrit Viljoen, as well as by the state president.[5]

The Randburg by-election

The NP experienced a further setback in the Randburg by-election in November 1990. The seat had been won by Wynand Malan in 1987 as an Independent candidate and again by him in 1989 for the DP. The DP did not put up a candidate this time, hoping for an election pact with the NP, but although the NP backed out of such an election deal at the last minute, its reformist stance resulted in certain DP leaders calling on its supporters to vote for the NP.

The results of the Randburg by-election represented a swing of 10.9 per cent to the CP since the 1989 election, as the party increased its share of the vote from 4.7 per cent in 1989 to 15.6 per cent. Although the NP obtained an overwhelming majority of 8913 over the CP, it received 5500 votes less than the combined NP/DP support of 14,400 in 1989, while the CP's support increased from 755 to 1969 votes. Even though the CP lost its deposit, it still managed to triple its support in a constituency with a 50 per cent English-speaking component consisting mostly of upper-middle-class and urban voters, a socio-economic category that had never favoured the CP in the past. A 10 per cent swing towards the CP in such a constituency implied a swing of much greater proportions elsewhere in the country.

Randburg was the last by-election in 1990, and towards the end of the year the government began to prepare the white electorate for the repeal of the last major apartheid legislation, to be announced at the opening of parliament in February 1991. There was no indication that the by-election setbacks caused too much concern among members of the government or resulted in it having second thoughts about its direction. In fact, if anything, the reform programme was accelerated: in February 1991 the state president announced the repeal of the final major apartheid legislation and issued a manifesto spelling out his vision for the future: this included a commitment to a free and democratic political system, universal franchise, equality before the law, a bill of rights, government based on the consent of the governed and freedom of expression, religion, movement and association, and a free and equitable economic system. The former obsession with group and minority rights was replaced in this manifesto by references to 'the right to an own community life for each community that so desires' (*Hansard*, 1 February 1991).

The Maitland by-election
Shortly after de Klerk's 'second Rubicon' speech in February 1991, in March, a by-election was held in Maitland, an NP-held seat close to Cape Town. Maitland was an urban lower-middle-class constituency and had been regarded as a safe NP seat for many years, with the main opposition coming from the PFP in 1987 and the DP in 1989. The combined right wing had managed to attract only 14 per cent of the total vote in 1987 and 3.5 per cent in 1989. The CP's electoral strategy emphasized the NP's 'capitulation to the black majority' and the 'selling-out' of white interests, but in particular, it repeated its accusation that the NP was acting contrary to the mandate it received from the electorate during the 1989 general election.

Although the NP managed to double its previous majority, the results in Maitland represented a 27 per cent swing to the CP, described by Treurnicht as the largest ever swing in the history of South African politics (*Patriot*, 8 March 1991). The swing itself was not unexpected, but its extent and the fact that it occurred in a former UP seat with a large English-speaking component came as a shock to the NP.

The Ladybrand by-election
The results of the Ladybrand by-election two months later, in May, confirmed the previous pattern. It was the only one of the series of by-elections after September 1989 to be contested in a rural constituency, and was also the only one in a seat previously held by the CP. The by-election was symbolic in the sense that it

was the last to be contested before the final apartheid laws were scrapped in June 1991. The run-up to this by-election was heavily influenced by political developments which largely benefited the CP. Apart from the countrywide violence which had been raging unabated during the months before the election, the ANC suspended its dialogue with the government, and Winnie Mandela[6] was convicted of kidnapping by the Rand Supreme Court. In addition, the scheduled repeal of the Land Acts caused great consternation among the white farmers in this rural constituency, which was exacerbated by the events near Ventersdorp in the western Transvaal where several hundred white farmers who attempted to destroy a squatter camp were shot at by the police. The proverbial last straw was the racially inspired riot which erupted on the day of the election in Maseru, the capital of Lesotho, which is just a few kilometres from Ladybrand. The residents of the town saw hundreds of whites fleeing Lesotho in fear of their lives and arriving in Ladybrand with rumours of 'fearsome atrocities' which had been committed against whites in Maseru. The effect that images of whites fleeing for their lives from 'black hordes' can have on the white psyche was analysed earlier (see Chapter 1); in Ladybrand this was no different, and the NP's already slim chances of defeating the CP disappeared completely.

The CP won the Ladybrand by-election with a majority of 1258, up from its majority of 70 in 1989, a swing of 7.8 per cent to the CP. The percentage poll of 81 per cent indicated an unusually high level of interest for a by-election. The CP saw the election results as a vindication of the power of 'true nationalism' and as a major defeat for the 'Tuynhuis–ANC Alliance' (*Patriot*, 4 May 1991). According to Andries Beyers the CP would easily win a general election, and that the government now had a moral obligation to call such a general election (interview, 11 April 1991).

De Klerk claimed that the result was not a setback for the government as the majority of whites countrywide supported the reforms. *Die Burger* (24 May 1991) cautioned that the NP should be careful not to neglect its traditional support-base (the Afrikaners). However, by now it was very doubtful whether the NP still had access to the supposed 'traditional' support-base, as the Ladybrand by-election confirmed suspicions that the CP now possibly enjoyed the support of the majority of Afrikaners. In return, the NP, having taken over most of the DP's policies, enjoyed the support of a majority of English-speakers. Following de Klerk's reforms the DP's support levels declined from 28 per cent in September 1989 to 18 per cent in February 1990 and to about 10 per cent in 1991, according to M&M polls. The NP also increasingly received support across racial lines, as was illustrated by the defection to the NP by almost half the members of the (coloured) Labour Party during the weeks after the Ladybrand by-election.

The Virginia by-election

The final by-election of 1991 was held at Virginia in the Free State, but at this stage political developments outside parliament had largely overtaken white electoral politics. The by-election was overshadowed by the preparations for Codesa One (Convention for a Democratic South Africa) in December 1991. The imminent commencement of multiparty negotiations instilled into the CP a new sense of urgency, insofar as only a very strong showing of the party at future by-elections would keep up the pressure on the government to consult the white electorate again. As the NP had already excluded the possibility of a general election under the existing constitution, it was clear to the CP that it had to focus on the whites-only referendum. Once a referendum was won, the CP had no doubt that it could enforce a general election in which a right-wing victory would be a foregone conclusion.

Virginia was situated in the politically conservative Orange Free State where the CP already held six of the 14 parliamentary seats. Crime and violence had reached epidemic proportions and the economy was in the midst of a severe recession, with almost one million whites living below the bread-line (*Sunday Times*, 29 November 1992). The CP successfully incorporated these issues into its by-election campaign, which also emphasized the 'forced integration' in the suburbs of mining towns and the violence and bloodshed at a Free State gold mine shortly before the election. It also benefited from the anger which many whites felt over the ANC's insistence that the Springbok emblem, and the national flag and anthem, be removed as symbols for South African sport as a precondition to the country's re-admittance to international sport.

In the mind of the white voters of Virginia these issues overshadowed the increasingly vocal disagreements within the CP between its traditional and *volkstaat* wings, and such internal party conflicts appeared to have had little effect on the electoral performance of the CP at Virginia. The party overturned an NP majority of 47 in the 1989 election into a CP majority of 3,166. The results represented a 15.8 per cent swing to the CP, which exceeded the 14 per cent average swing to the right in other by-elections during the previous two years. While the NP blamed poor economic conditions and the violence in Welkom for its defeat, the CP viewed its victory as a powerful demonstration of Afrikaner nationalism and its quest for self-determination. Although the poor state of the economy did play a role in the resounding CP victory, especially in a strongly working-class constituency such as Virginia, the main contributing factor was the perception that the government's reforms were weakening the political position of whites in relation to the ANC. The fact that the ANC was taking control of South African sport by tying international participation to racially integrated sporting bodies and the rejection of state emblems illustrates this point.

The outcome of the Virginia by-election increased the pressure on the government to test the opinions of whites regarding the general political direction, but another conclusive by-election defeat three months later at Potchefstroom was required to bring about the long-awaited referendum.

The Potchefstroom by-election
This by-election was the most important one since the 1989 general election, for several reasons. The first was the perception, not only within the CP, that a convincing victory would prove once and for all that the party enjoyed the support of the majority of whites, a perception which would seriously compromise the legitimacy of the government and its ability to negotiate on behalf of whites. This view was shared by various analysts, e.g. the leader of the DP, Zach de Beer, who suggested shortly before the by-election that the CP's support was possibly as high as 50 per cent (*Sunday Telegraph*, 31 January 1992). Secondly, the NP realized that its political future and the success of the negotiation process depended to a large extent on a

convincing victory over the CP. Potchefstroom had a long history of being a Nationalist stronghold and was therefore crucial to the NP's prestige and self-confidence. It was one of only three constituencies in the country in which the NP increased its majority over the CP during the 1989 general election. It was a typical middle-class Afrikaner constituency with a mixture of academics, students, civil servants, business people and army personnel. In addition, the headquarters of the Reformed Church is located here, its most famous member being the state president himself, who also received his university education in Potchefstroom. The NP was convinced that this western Transvaal, middle-class, Afrikaner constituency, devoid of the working-class and agricultural segments which had tended to favour the CP on previous occasions, would be a true reflection of the mood of Afrikaners at the time. During the by-election campaign the state president suggested on more than one occasion that the Potchefstroom results would be the most conclusive indication yet of the white electorate's views on reforms under the de Klerk administration. By committing himself in this fashion, it was obvious that an NP defeat would leave the party with no face-saving device other than de Klerk's resignation, a referendum or even a general election.

The by-election at Potchefstroom in February 1992 was preceded not only by the historic events at Codesa in December 1991, but also by increasing dissension within the CP and the NP. The CP, which refused to participate in Codesa, now began to experience openly rebellious behaviour from members of its pragmatic wing, but the pending Pothchefstroom by-election prevented the issue from coming to the boil.

The CP's candidate at Potchefstroom was Andries Beyers, the party's chief secretary. Beyers achieved hero status in right-wing circles after he spent two weeks in prison in 1991 for refusing to reveal his source of allegations that the state was involved in the kidnapping of witnesses in a murder trial involving Winnie Mandela. Beyers oscillated between the pragmatic and hard-line factions of the CP and (like Treurnicht) preferred not to commit himself to either side. During the campaign he avoided references to traditional aspects of apartheid and instead emphasized self-determination as the only logical alternative to the 'unitary state envisaged by the NP–ANC alliance' (*Rapport*, 12

February 1992). The key element of the CP's campaign was the demand for self-determination of the Afrikaner and other white people, to be achieved through partition. By now the CP had adopted the example of Boris Yeltsin's Commonwealth of Independent States as a model for its own proposal of an ethnic-based 'commonwealth of independent South African nations', economically linked but politically separate (*Rapport*, 9 February 1992). To 'boost' its by-election campaign, the CP enlisted the services of Brigadier Oupa Gqozo, military ruler of the Ciskei. Following a meeting between the latter and Treurnicht early in February 1992, Gqozo claimed that both parties envisaged the 'same kind of self-determination' and were opposed to a unitary South Africa (*Rapport*, 9 February 1992).

Apart from the state president having metaphorically painted himself into a corner on the outcome of the by-election, his candidate and the NP-supporting press did not help the NP's cause much either. The NP candidate decided early on in the campaign that the best way to contain a rampant CP was to concentrate upon the similarities between the two parties rather than emphasize the differences: he chose to ignore his own party's stated policy of 'nation building' and instead focused his campaign on those pre-1986 elements of the NP's policy which emphasized the 'diversity of South Africa's peoples' (*Rapport*, 12 January 1992). To make matters worse, the *verkrampte* editor of *Rapport*, Izak de Villiers, argued in an editorial (which must have sent cold shivers through the spine of the NP) that he would vote for 'partition' if the CP would indicate the exact borders of the *volkstaat* (*Rapport*, 2 February 1992).

The CP won the Potchefstroom by-election with a majority of 2140, a reversal of the NP's majority of 1583 in 1989. The results represented an 11.2 per cent swing to the CP, and, all things being equal, the CP now theoretically enjoyed the support of about 45 per cent of the white electorate (the average by-election swing of 14 per cent to the right plus the 31 per cent support the CP had received in the 1989 general election). Purely on the basis of the NP's election victory in 1948 (with 41 per cent of the vote), 45 per cent of white voter support would have allowed the CP to win a general election but not quite enough to win a referendum (where a total of 50 per cent plus 1 is required). The CP realized this, and renewed with great vigour its demand for a whites-only general election, on grounds that the NP had lost the support of the majority of whites.

However, this was not to be, for the better the CP's prospects were of winning a general election, the less became the chance that the NP would risk such an election. On the other hand, the NP had no choice but to consult the white electorate. As the state president committed himself unambiguously before the by-election to accepting the result as a barometer of white support for reform, his options were now severely limited: it was simply a choice between resigning and consulting the white electorate. In addition the growing resistance among disaffected white voters provided greater authenticity to the CP's claims that the NP lacked a mandate, and undermined the credibility of the NP to such an extent that even its opponents at Codesa questioned whether the party could still speak on behalf of whites. It was primarily this growing lack of political credibility that eventually forced the NP to opt for an earlier-than-planned referendum, not to ask for the approval of white voters for a new constitution, but rather for the renewal of its mandate to negotiate such a constitution.

The March 1992 referendum
The referendum was announced in parliament on the day after the Potchefstroom by-election, an indication of the sense of urgency which the NP's dismal showing had instilled in the government. F.W. de Klerk explained his reasons for calling the referendum as follows:

> [The CP] had achieved some success in cultivating a suspicion that I no longer represent a majority of the very voters who in the first place elected the National Party in 1989.... People want to negotiate with people who can deliver. I have no doubt that I have majority support for what I am doing, but this perception has been cultivated and the way in which to settle it without any doubt is the democratic way (*Sunday Times*, 23 February 1992).

However, the NP's desire to restore its status among the white electorate and to strengthen its hand at Codesa constituted only two of the reasons for the urge to consult white voters. The NP had to contend with growing discontent among MPs who were alarmed by the speed of the negotiation process and by the perception that the NP had lost control over the process of reform. Linked to this was the deterioration in the morale of the NP caucus and indications of dissent within the security forces. The London-based weekly *Africa Confidential* speculated that the referendum was a pre-emptive move to stave off the possibility of a military coup from increasingly discontent security forces (cited in *The Argus*, 24 February 1992).

Contributing to the NP's troubles was dissent from erstwhile allies. The former leader of the NP and previous state president, P.W. Botha, took the unprecedented step of aligning himself with the No campaign of the right wing. He claimed that Codesa was a 'tower of Babel' and that the government's negotiations would lead to a process of abdication and suicide by whites, and would eventually result in the domination of South Africa by an ANC–SACP alliance (*Rapport*, 8 March 1992). Furthermore, another former ally, Buthelezi, decided that the referendum provided an ideal opportunity to score political points against the government. Although he stopped short of endorsing the No vote, he accused the government of 'being in bed' with the ANC, an allegation also central to the CP's referendum campaign. To exacerbate matters, a leader of the Transvaal branch of the IFP concluded a 'non-aggression' pact with the AWB one week before the referendum. Buthelezi eventually distanced the IFP from this step, but it marked the turning point in the previously cosy relationship between the IFP and NP.

The NP's Yes campaign received the full backing of the DP, the media, the international community, and the vast majority of commercial institutions, artists, sports personalities, parties and organizations across the political spectrum. The South African cricketers participating in the World Cricket Cup in Australasia were among the host of public figures who openly supported the Yes campaign. Nelson Mandela personally appealed to white voters and white supporters of the ANC to vote Yes for the sake of the negotiation process: 'A [Yes] vote means we will sit around a table as South Africans and work out the best method of installing a democratic system in which all the country's inhabitants feel secure. A [No] vote will be a declaration of war against the majority in this country' (*Sunday Times*, 8 March 1992).

The right wing's No campaign received no such endorsements or financial backing from any large companies, and it was scant compensation that the DRC opted to remain neutral, or that the PAC and AZAPO rejected the referendum as racist. To complicate matters further for the CP, it had less than 12 hours within which to celebrate its victory at Potchefstroom before the referendum was announced in parliament by the state president. Although one of its MPs, Casper Uys, immediately accepted the challenge to participate in the referendum, the CP caucus had second thoughts when the full implications of it became clear. The party realized that the referendum could be crucial to its own future as well, and that the NP–DP alliance had a massive advantage in the form of financial resources, access to the media, the support of the outside world, and the final say over the formulation of the referendum question. Realizing that the odds were heavily stacked against his party, Treurnicht insisted that participation depended on certain preconditions being met, in particular a right of veto over the formulation of the referendum question and equal time on the national television and radio network.

Following the government's refusal to consider the CP's demands, the party's executive committee decided by seven votes to two not to participate in the referendum (*Rapport*, 1 March 1992). The decision immediately evoked a rebellion in the caucus. The pragmatists under the leadership of Koos van der Merwe insisted on participation and threatened to split the party should their demand be refused. After a fierce debate the caucus decided to overturn the party executive's decision.

A total of 1,924,186 white voters (68.6 per cent) voted Yes, against the 875,619 who voted No (31.2 per cent). This was the highest ever turn-out in South Africa's electoral history, namely 2.8 million voters in an 85 per cent poll (Table 7, below). An estimated 62 per cent of Afrikaners and 79 per cent of English-speakers voted yes (*Die Burger*, 20 March 1992).

The referendum result was a victory for the government's reform policies rather than for the NP itself, for a substantial number of Yes votes came from DP supporters. If all No votes are regarded as support for the CP, it is obvious that all the CP's electoral gains since September 1989 had been lost, leaving the party with the same level of support as it had then, namely 31

Table 7
Results of the March 1992 referendum

Referendum region	Yes votes	No votes	Yes majority	Poll
Beaufort West	18,941	11,798	7,143	84
Cape Town	355,527	63,325	292,202	88
Bloemfontein	58,066	41,017	17,049	89
Durban	204,371	35,975	168,396	87
East London	66,675	18,498	48,177	82
George	40,075	21,211	18,864	96
Germiston	164,025	86,844	77,181	81
Johannesburg	324,686	89,957	234,729	84
Kimberley	33,504	27,993	5,511	86
Kroonstad	54,531	51,279	3,252	79
P'maritzburg	66,500	21,023	45,477	80
Port Elizabeth	87,216	29,909	57,307	85
Pretoria	287,720	213,825	73,895	89
Roodepoort	124,737	113,145	11,592	78
Pietersburg	37,612	49,820	(−12,208)	88
Total	1,924,186	875,619	1,048,567	85

per cent. Even in the referendum regions where the CP controlled a majority of parliamentary constituencies, e.g. Roodepoort (10 out of 14), Pretoria (13 out of 23) and Kroonstad (four out of seven), it failed to obtain a No majority. Its sole victory was in the northern Transvaal referendum region of Pietersburg.

The right wing's chances of a victory were doomed from the moment it accepted the NP's challenge to participate in the referendum. Several factors contributed to the decisive defeat of the No campaign.

The wording of the referendum question was formulated to indicate a simple choice between approval or disapproval of the government's reform programme as initiated on 2 February 1990, i.e. a choice between white domination on the one hand and a non-racial democracy on the other. Although the NP's referendum campaign focused on the goals of minority protection and power-sharing, it provided no guarantees on the final nature of a new constitution. The referendum question furthermore neglected to inform the white electorate that it was probably the last time that it would have an exclusive veto over its political destiny. Considering these points, it can be assumed that it was highly unlikely that all those who voted Yes fully understood the ultimate implications of their vote.

The right wing had to contend with a media blitz such as had never been experienced in South Africa before. Virtually all of the country's major publishing houses and independent newspapers campaigned for the same cause. Opposing this overwhelming media onslaught, the right-wing parties fielded their insignificant mouthpieces, *Patriot* and *Die Afrikaner*, with little success.

Scare tactics and doomsday scenarios were employed by the Yes campaign with great effect: the referendum was presented as a simple choice between peace and an outright racial war. Apart from the ANC's blunt warning that a No vote would be regarded as a declaration of war against blacks, the outside world warned white South Africans of dire consequences in the form of sanctions, boycotts and blockades should a No vote prevail. From within the white community, employers warned their employees that a No vote would mean harsh sanctions and the loss of their jobs, and estate agents warned that house prices would plunge; the list was seemingly endless.

The CP's financial and human resources were spread thinly across the country, and in contrast to the by-elections, the party could not concentrate all its organizational efforts in one area. Furthermore, without the financial support of any large companies, its funds were severely stretched. According to estimates the No campaigners had approximately twenty times less money to spend than their opponents (*Cape Times*, 19 March 1992).

Although the alliance between the CP, HNP and the AWB helped to streamline the No campaign and to present a united right-wing front, this was partly offset by the differences within the CP between the *volkstaters* and the traditionalists over party policy. In addition, the AWB's radicalism scared off some CP supporters and persuaded some disaffected NP voters who had intended to abstain to vote Yes. Terre Blanche's own contribution to the failure of the No campaign was considerable. Due to a lack of communication between the CP and Terre Blanche, the latter's announcement to the media that the right-wing alliance would not participate in the referendum directly contradicted the decision to participate made only hours before by the CP. Terre Blanche caused further embarrassment by falling off his horse twice while parading through the streets of Pretoria. Repeated screenings of this episode on SABC TV and media references to him as the 'horseman of the Apocalypse', detracted strongly from the image the CP was trying to project. The Yes campaign strongly emphasized the role of the AWB in the right-wing alliance and portrayed the organization as consisting of hooded terrorists and neo-Nazis. As an example of this, in full-page advertisements, the AWB was represented by a hooded thug with menacing pose and large calibre revolver and the headline: 'Free with every CP vote, the AWB and all they stand for' (*Cape Times*, 12 March 1992).

If the image of Terre Blanche caused many undecided voters to vote Yes, so did the personal efforts of de Klerk. The state president, accompanied by the press, undertook a successful American-style, countrywide 'hearts and minds' tour to convince undecided voters through personal contact to vote Yes.

Ultimately, however, the right wing's decision to participate in the referendum was probably its biggest tactical error to date. Giliomee estimated that, due to voter apathy, the poll could have been as low as 30 per cent without the CP's participation (*Cape Times*, 10 March 1992). Has this been the case, 30 per cent of the white electorate would have voted Yes while the remaining 70 per cent would have been in the No/undecided/apathetic category. Such a result would have vindicated the CP's claim that only a minority of whites actively supported the NP reform initiatives.

The CP's defeat in the referendum left the party in a much weaker position than it had been shortly after the Potchefstroom by-election. Some party officials blamed 'traitors' for the defeat, no doubt referring to the *volkstaat* faction. Ever since the Anglo–Boer War the word 'traitor' has had a highly emotional meaning in Afrikaner nationalist terminology, and it was obvious that tensions within the CP had finally reached breaking point. In August 1992 five MPs under the leadership of Andries Beyers resigned from the CP to found the AVU (see also Chapter 4).

From a historical perspective its defeat in the referendum was the turning-point in the CP's seemingly irreversible electoral advance, which accelerated after the NP began its transition to a representative democracy under the de Klerk administration. The referendum established the core of right-wing support at slightly less than one-third of the white electorate. Although the uncertainty and violence which accompanied the NP's last two years in power following the referendum resulted in a further rush towards the right, by early 1994 the transitional process had become irreversible, and speculation on the level of support for the right wing became purely academic.

In the final instance, however, since all further general elections and by-elections under the tricameral constitution have been suspended, the 1992 referendum should be seen as the end of the CP's role within the narrow confines of white politics. Its role as a potential spoiler and as an electoral bogey had finally been laid to rest, and it was up to its supporters to decide whether to draw back to their *laagers* and await Armageddon, or to participate in the shaping of a new role for the Afrikaners in a non-racial society. Should the white right decide to participate in the non-racial election in 1994, it would realistically be possible for it to receive between 4 and 5 per cent of the seats in a non-racial parliament under a system of proportional representation, based on the number of votes it received in the referendum.

4· The Right Wing in the de Klerk Era: from Schism to Unity

From its founding in 1982 the CP espoused parliamentary politics, believing that it stood a good chance of winning a general election at some point in the future. Such an election victory would have allowed the party to reverse the reforms of the Botha era and to implement the CP's policy of partition. However, the CP's hopes of achieving power through constitutional means received a serious blow in 1990 when the government suggested that it did not foresee the country having another general election under the tricameral constitution. The implication was that the CP would never again have an opportunity to contest a general election under the present electoral circumstances, since the next general election would have universal franchise and a single, non-racial voters' roll. Apart from a reliance on a total collapse of the negotiation process between the NP and the ANC, the remainder of the CP's political strategy up to March 1992 rested on a promise made by the NP that it would test white support for a new constitution by way of a referendum, which the CP believed would be rejected by the majority of whites. This did not mean that the CP at any stage relinquished its attempts to force the government to call a general election. In fact, the party intensified its campaign of putting pressure on the government by using the results of by-elections to indicate that the NP had lost the support of the majority of whites and therefore lacked legitimacy, and, furthermore, that it had acted contrary to the mandate it had received from the electorate in the 1989 election.

The scope of the political reforms initiated by the de Klerk administration which led to the repeal of the final pillars of apartheid in June 1991, and the consequent political developments relating to a negotiated settlement and the demise of white domination and free elections by April 1994 were not foreseen by the right before 2 February 1990. The political landscape was virtually transformed overnight to such an extent that the right wing, and in particular the CP, was caught unprepared, and struggled to adjust its Verwoerdian-based policies to reflect the new realities. As a result the CP spent a considerable time during the de Klerk era trying to re-define its basic philosophy and its approach to issues such as: does the party represent Afrikaners or whites as a whole?; was it still realistic to expect a return to Verwoerdian apartheid?; should it enter into multiparty negotiations?; where were the boundaries of the mythical Afrikaner/white homeland?; would passive and non-violent resistance against the government be sufficient to attain the objective of self-determination or would right-wing terrorism, an armed insurrection or a coup d'état be more effective?

These issues formed the basis of the fierce debate which had raged between the CP's pragmatic and hard-line wings in the early 1990s. The position of the CP's pragmatic wing, the *volkstaters*, could be described as the rejection of partition in favour of a policy incorporating the demand for a smaller territory as the basis for an Afrikaner fatherland. In contrast, the hard-line faction argued that the size of the white homeland had already been determined by the grand apartheid policy of Verwoerd. As the party struggled to reconcile the growing tension between its two wings over matters such as the size, location and ethnic composition of the proposed fatherland, Treurnicht, who was caught in the middle, compromised in both directions. To appease the hard-line faction the CP adopted a more militant stance, while subtle changes to its policies were made to appease the moderates.

However, the CP's rigid apartheid-based partition policy did not lend itself to speedy reform or rapid modernization, with the result that the party experienced a defection by some of its members to the moderate centre with the founding of the AVU in 1992. The right wing now appeared more divided than ever, but the leadership vacuum left by the death of Treurnicht led to the first successful efforts of unity in the history of the right, with the founding of the AVF in May 1993. However, incompatible policies and the Afrikaner tradition of *broedertwis* put even this new-found unity under strain.

Broedertwis revisited: apartheid or self-determination?

Transforming outdated constitutional policies
The main objective of Afrikaner nationalists after 1948 was to turn South Africa into a homogeneous Afrikaner and thus white state. These attempts at constitutional engineering were coined 'grand' apartheid which had as goal the unilateral removal of blacks from 'white' South Africa through the creation of homelands. The CP duplicated virtually the entire NP policy in 1982 and renamed it partition. Apart from the CP's proposal of creating coloured and Indian homelands (the NP attempted to co-opt these two racial groups within the white parliamentary structure), the two parties had the same ultimate goal – the creation of a homogeneous white state through the removal of other races, either physically by forced removals and expulsion, or by re-drawing political boundaries. Although the NP had eventually realized by the late 1970s that demographic developments had made a successful implementation of grand apartheid impossible, the CP argued that the NP's failure to implement 'meaningful' partition was the cause of the failure of the homeland system. However, by 1990 it had also become obvious to moderate elements within the CP that it was impractical and absurd to propagate a policy aimed at turning back the clock 20 years. Under this moderate influence the CP, with great reluctance, attempted to adapt its policies relating to Afrikaner and white self-determination to reflect the new realities, but the strong resistance offered by the party's hard-line wing made this very difficult.

The first indication that the CP had deviated from traditional apartheid/partition came in May 1990 when Treurnicht announced in parliament that the CP was 'no longer prepared to … prescribe to black peoples what they should do' [to organize themselves constitutionally] (*Hansard*, 11 May 1990). This theme was repeated at a CP congress in October 1990, and the idea that whites should be able to lay claim to their own territory without being prescriptive to other groups suggested a considerable shift away from the '13-nation-states' philosophy of original partition. The implication was that, in order to ensure the formation of a white state, partition did not necessarily have to be applied to the remaining part of 'black' South Africa. This deviation was also perceptible in the party's revised set of policy guidelines of 1990, in which the term 'Republic of South Africa' (the CP's name for a white South African state) was replaced with the term 'our fatherland'; furthermore, references to the creation of Indian, coloured and new or consolidated black homelands were also dropped, although the amended policy document stated that the party still believed that black interests would best be served by separate geographic areas (*The Argus*, 18 October 1990; interview, CP MP Connie Mulder, 11 February 1991).

The rejection of prescriptive policies appeared also to have been a victory for the pragmatic faction within the CP and for their proposals of a smaller white homeland, albeit with unspecified borders. Although it was not always evident from his comments, a leading member of this group was CP MP Koos van der Merwe, who strongly advocated that the party focus solely on the 'white nation': 'While the CP's policy in the past had placed much emphasis on a separate state for each black nation, the scope of reference today has narrowed solely to the white nation, leaving the black nations to decide for themselves on the issue of a unitary state' (*Vrye Weekblad*, 14 September 1990) [translation].

Although van der Merwe merely echoed what Treurnicht had said in parliament a few months earlier, clearly not all members of the party shared this view, as illustrated by the comments of hard-line CP MP Jan Hoon, who contended that the borders of the homelands had already been determined by legislation, while the area where coloureds and Indians were allowed to live was prescribed by the Group Areas Act (interview, 7 February 1991).

Having coerced the CP 'not to be prescriptive' over how the rest of South Africa organized itself constitutionally, the moderate faction of the party now began to propagate the idea that the CP would have to be satisfied with a much smaller white homeland than the 87 per cent of the land formerly envisaged. This led to further conflicting declarations by members of the opposing camps within the party. The CP's official position was reiterated by Treurnicht during the party's national congress in October 1990, when he said that the white state consisted of everything outside the present black homelands, in accordance with the Land Act of 1936, although the final borders could be negotiated with their respective governments (*The Argus*, 16–18 October 1990). In contrast, other CP members, most notably van der Merwe, argued that while the CP was not interested in a smallholding like the town of Morgenzon (page 83), partition should recognize the historical, logical, legal and economic realities. He subsequently added that certain parts of 'white' South Africa had already become racially integrated to such an extent that these areas would have to be left out of the proposed white fatherland: 'We will have to sacrifice important land, but I can't tell you which land. People will have to think for themselves' (*Vrye Weekblad*, 14 September 1990; *The Argus*, 26 October 1990). Van der Merwe's viewpoint on the CP's possible renunciation of claims to 'important parts' of South Africa was repudiated by Treurnicht and Andries Beyers (*Die Burger*, 1 November 1990). Six months later Beyers acknowledged that the CP might be prepared to make 'much greater sacrifices' with regard to territory than previously stated in public, but without specifying what he had in mind (interview, 11 April 1991).

By mid-1990 the CP's unofficial think-tank, *Toekomsgesprek*, joined the moderate wing of the party in arguing that, in the light of 'irreversible' political and demographic realities, the CP should envisage a much smaller homeland. By now the numbers of the moderates/pragmatists (later known as the *volkstaters*) had grown to approximately one-third of the caucus, and in October 1990, encouraged by *Toekomsgesprek*, they formulated their philosophy in a policy document entitled *Strategie vir 'n Veranderende Situasie* ('Strategy for a Changing Situation', also known as the 'Koos document'). Written by Koos van der Merwe and other senior CP MPs, the document referred to the impracticality of repatriating seven million people to the homelands and argued that because blacks have become a permanent fixture of 'white' South Africa, the CP will have to settle for a smaller state to be created by way of 'sacrificial partition' (van der Merwe et al 1990: 37). It represented a shift towards the secessionist philosophy upon which the *volkstaat* proposals of Carel Boshoff were based, i.e. creating a much smaller white state which would separate itself from the rest of South Africa, as opposed to the traditional partition policy which envisaged the forced separation of black homelands from the rump of the greater white state. The leak of this confidential document caused considerable embarrassment to the CP, resulting in its being rejected by the party leadership and also leading to Van der Merwe's dismissal from his position as head of the CP's Information Committee in 1991.[1]

In September 1991 the CP once again reaffirmed that the official party line remained a white state with borders based on the existing 'white' territory, but admitted that this would merely be a starting-point for negotiations with homeland leaders (*Patriot*, 13 September 1991). Treurnicht also indicated that the CP supported the creation of an ethnic confederation or commonwealth of independent South African states, economically linked but politically independent. This view was strongly supported by the foremost proponent within the party of the 'greater white state' philosophy, deputy leader Ferdi Hartzenberg.

One month later, however, Treurnicht appeared to have changed his previous stance by mentioning the possibility of accepting a smaller white homeland, and this was held forth by van der Merwe as evidence that the party's leader now endorsed the *volkstaat* proposals of the pragmatists. Hereafter, the position of the *volkstaters* was boosted by several positive events, such as acceptance by the Free State congress of the CP of a 'twelve-point plan', which argued for an Afrikaner homeland rather than for the reinstatement of grand apartheid (*Insig*, November 1991). Following the CP's refusal to participate in Codesa in December 1991, the *volkstaters*, who feared that the party was being left behind by events, became more brazen in their demands and some MPs became openly rebellious: the leader of the CP in the Free State, Cehill Pienaar, stuck his neck out further than any CP MP had ever done by suggesting that the CP should consider the option of a federal unit for whites within a greater South Africa (*Die Burger*, 25 November 1991), while Koos van der Merwe and Koos Botha came out strongly in favour of negotiations with all parties.

The CP's decision to participate in the March 1992 referendum strengthened the hand of the pragmatic wing of the CP because its position on participation overruled those of both the executive and the hard-line faction under the leadership of Ferdi Hartzenberg. Although by now the party had accepted in principle that it would have to be satisfied with a smaller fatherland, it remained reluctant to indicate how much smaller, and where the borders of this state would be. A further indication of van der Merwe's 'going for broke' approach during the referendum campaign was his interview with an American television channel in which he stated unequivocally that the CP did not want to reinstate apartheid or dictate to other peoples, but only wanted self-determination for the Afrikaners in a smaller territory. He further rejected a pillar of the CP's policy, namely the creation of a coloured homeland, in favour of the reincorporation of 'brown Afrikaners' into a future white homeland. Van der Merwe received support from Cehill Pienaar, who commited further 'sacrilege' by boldly stating that the father of apartheid and ideological icon of the CP, H.F. Verwoerd, would be 'out of place in today's times' (*Die Burger*, 28 February 1992).

Not surprisingly, both van der Merwe and Koos Botha were expelled from the CP shortly after the party's heavy defeat in the referendum. Their other colleagues in the *volkstaat* wing decided to remain with the party in order to change its policies from within. In June 1992 five members of this group submitted a document, *Die Pad Vorentoe* ('The Road Ahead') at a special CP congress, in which they demanded that fundamental changes be made to the CP's constitutional policies, in particular with regard to a smaller Afrikaner *volkstaat*. The document argued that the country should be divided into ten ethnic regions, each capable of constituting a separate autonomous state within a confede-ration; the Afrikaner state would consist of a continuous territory, which would partly be in the north of the country, but there could also be one or two Afrikaans-speaking states in the south which could include the coloured community; each of the ten states would have the right to secede from the confederation or to amalgamate into a single state.

The rejection of this proposal by the CP's executive in August

1992 led to the resignation of five MPs under the leadership of Andries Beyers and the formation of the AVU. The major policy differences between the AVU and the CP concerned the new AVU's emphasis on a smaller homeland, the right to self-determination (not apartheid) and an emphasis on the Afrikaner 'ethnic' group rather than the white 'racial' group. Treurnicht's initial response was that the differences between the two parties were insignificant as they pertained largely to the size and location of the white homeland: 'You try to get the most land instead of the least. Our friends in the AVU want far too small a homeland' (*Sunday Times*, 23 August 1992). However, realizing that there were still many disaffected *volkstaat* supporters in the CP, he announced a policy deviation in August 1992: the proposed white homeland would consist of the 41 constituencies in the 'possession of the CP'. Treurnicht omitted to mention that the CP now had seven fewer constituencies after the split and expulsions. It comprised an area covering almost the whole northern part of the country, excluding the homelands and urban strongholds of the NP and DP.

This remained the CP's official view throughout most of 1993. During the multiparty planning conference in March the CP's constitutional platform was outlined by the CP's chief negotiator, Tom Langley. He stated that the only alternative to the unitary and federal proposals of the NP and ANC was Afrikaner (and white) self-determination in a sovereign state, economically linked to a commonwealth/confederation of independent South African states (*Patriot*, 19 March 1993). The fact that the term 'partition' had by now been replaced by 'self-determination' showed a narrowing of the gap between the CP and the AVU, while a CP negotiator even conceded at the multiparty forum in June 1993 that his party did not want a confederation immediately: 'We could begin with cooperation treaties. Confederation could develop in due course. There is opportunity for interpretation' (*The Times*, 30 June 1993). However, unlike the AVU, the CP steadfastly refused to present any detailed map of the location of its envisaged white homeland.

With the founding of the AVF in May 1993 both the CP and the AVU found themselves in a dilemma as certain of the AVF's founding principles contradicted elements of their party's policies. While it was not the AVF's intention to dictate to its individual member organizations, the AVF submitted its own proposals in July 1993 to the multiparty forum for an Afrikaner homeland with precisely defined borders in an area comprising 16 per cent of South Africa's territory. This was a direct contradiction of the CP's strategy of not specifying the size and location of the envisaged white homeland, but as the CP constituted the largest part of the leadership core of the AVF, it decided to endorse the proposal. The AVU again refused to support the article in the AVF's founding acts which stipulated that only whites would enjoy citizenship rights in a *volkstaat*. In September 1993 the AVF announced that, in line with the policy of the AVU, there would be no racial discrimination in the *volkstaat*, although this was later refuted by its denial of black voting rights.

Towards the end of 1993 the CP's policy on size and location remained ambivalent. Although the Party entered into negotiations through the AFV with the ANC, it stuck to its hard-line position that the borders of the Afrikaner *volkstaat* should comprise parts of northern and eastern Transvaal, a part of the Free State and northern Cape (*Rapport*, 5 December 1993). The CP also announced that on the basis of a poll conducted among the whites in the Free State – which comprise 16 per cent of that province's population – that the whole of the province should be declared an Afrikaner state.

This remained the position of the right at the end of 1993, and if the territorial demands of the CP, and to a lesser extent the AVF, appeared both excessive and absurd, the obvious answer was that these represented the maximum gains. However, as the country entered the new year, there was little doubt that the right wing could ask at most for a small part of the Transvaal as the core of a semi-autonomous Afrikaner federal region and perhaps one or two other subregions within other federal units where Afrikaners would form a majority – in addition, perhaps as a bonus, with Pretoria as its capital city.

The issue of negotiations
Ever since the freeing of the political process in February 1990 the right wing had rejected the possibility of participating in constitutional negotiations on the grounds that it refused to

negotiate with 'communists and terrorists', and later, because it did not recognize the legitimacy of Codesa. However, negotiations with 'recognized and democratically elected black leaders', i.e. the array of co-opted and autocratic homeland administrations and selected church leaders, had long been part of the CP's strategy to overcome its isolation outside white politics. The common denominator had been the rejection of violence and a common view on the self-determination of nations. To this end a meeting was organized in October 1990 between the CP and the IFP. Buthelezi argued that the CP represented a large constituency, and although the two parties differed on the political models to accommodate the various groups in South Africa, both subscribed to 'Christian principles, and rejected communism, terrorism and domination' (*Cape Times*, 3 November 1990). The CP described the significance of this meeting as follows: 'It has been a while since the standard-bearer of Afrikaner nationalism and the representative of the majority of Afrikaners (if not whites) had an opportunity to deliberate with the leader of the party to which most Zulus belong' (*Patriot*, 9 November 1990) [translation]. The relative success of the meeting was not a surprise, considering that both parties were strong adherents of the philosophy of ethnonationalism. Jan Hoon claimed afterwards that Buthelezi had mentioned the possibility of the Afrikaners and Zulus having to fight the ANC 'shoulder by shoulder' at some point in the future (interview, 7 February 1991). In March 1991 Treurnicht met with the military leader of the Transkei, General Bantu Holomisa, at the latter's request. Treurnicht described the meeting as 'an honour' but insisted that he met with Holomisa in his capacity as the leader of an independent state, and not in his capacity as a member of the ANC (*The Argus*, 2 March 1991). The fact that Holomisa requested the meeting caught many observers by surprise, especially as the Transkei at the time was strongly supportive of the ANC, but this could partly be explained by the acrimonious nature of the relationship between the South African and Transkei governments at the time.

The official stance of the CP until late 1992 was not to participate in any multiparty negotiating forum, whether it be Codesa or another. Corné Mulder pointed out that negotiations had always been a part of the Afrikaner history, as those between

Piet Retief and the Zulu leader, Dingane, and between Paul Kruger and Britain had illustrated, although in neither of these cases did it result in any benefits for the Afrikaner (interview, 11 February 1991). However, he argued, 'The CP will never negotiate over certain fundamental values, rights and freedoms which it embraces, and the CP is therefore not prepared to negotiate over the right to self-determination of the Afrikaner or the surrender and capitulation of whites' (*Patriot*, 16 November 1990) [translation]. Mulder also stated that the CP was not prepared to negotiate with the ANC or any other 'terrorist/communist organization which committed violence', a viewed shared by Jan Hoon, who claimed that he would not remain a member of the CP if the party did eventually decide to enter all-party negotiations (interview, 7 February 1991).[2]

By early 1991 the CP's official stance to eschew multiparty negotiations came under increasing pressure, not only as a result of agitation by its own moderate wing, but also from the ANC and the NP. Thabo Mbeki of the ANC suggested that the right wing would be welcome to bring its proposals to the negotiating table and that all proposals which might help to dispel right-wing fears would be taken into consideration by the ANC (*The Argus*, 6 October 1990). Invitations to the CP to put forward its case also came from the NP via President de Klerk (SABC TV, 17 February 1991) and cabinet minister Gerrit Viljoen (*Hansard*, 4 February 1991), while government-supporting newspapers actively encouraged members of the CP who supported negotiations to 'make themselves heard' (*Rapport*, 10 February 1991).

The most severe pressure to negotiate came from the CP's pragmatic wing who feared that the party was being left behind by the fast-moving political developments and would miss out on the opportunity to put its case for Afrikaner self-determination at the negotiation table. However, for the moderates, negotiation was conditional on the CP's rejection of the concepts of partition and racism, as only then could the party, free from the baggage of apartheid, legitimately pursue the goal of ethnic self-determination. Koos van der Merwe and other members of the Party's pragmatic wing expressed their doubts over the tenability of the CP's policy on negotiations. In the Koos document he demanded the freedom to make contact with any organization, including the ANC/SACP, and proposed participation at the future multiparty conference, the only precondition being that the government accept white self-determination as one of the 'options to be negotiated' at such a conference (*Rapport*, 3 February 1991; *Vrye Weekblad*, 8 February 1991).

This precondition differed considerably from the party's official stance (as amended late in 1990), that white self-determination should be the *guaranteed* result of any process of negotiation, a view also espoused by the traditionalist wing of the CP. In February 1991 van der Merwe's statement that the CP would join negotiations if the government acknowledged the right of self-determination of groups was contradicted by Hartzenberg's reply, that the CP would not participate under any conditions in negotiations over a new constitutional dispensation for South Africa (*Vrye Weekblad*, 8 February 1991).

During this period Treurnicht's main concern was to prevent a split in the CP, as his ambiguous stand on the issue of negotiations illustrated: 'We have not excluded negotiations in principle, but the government has positioned itself politically so distant from the demand for self-determination for whites, that it would be almost practically nonsensical to enter into negotiations with it, let alone with the ANC' (*Die Burger*, 15 February 1991) [translation]. It is important to note that he used the word 'almost', thereby leaving a door open if new developments necessitated a change in policy.

However, van der Merwe gave no indication that he would back down on this issue. In parliament he said that 'the era during which whites could prescribe to blacks had long passed and that the CP would listen to suggestions from blacks on how to solve problems affecting them, as long as it would not involve the right to self-determination of whites' (*Die Burger*, 7 March 1991) [translation]. At about the same time both van der Merwe and Thabo Mbeki were invited to speak at a conference in Switzerland, where they were photographed together in a friendly pose (*Die Burger*, 13–14 March 1991).

In the Koos document van der Merwe suggested that the CP was in danger of becoming irrelevant if it stuck to its present policy, and it would be forced to watch from the sidelines how other organizations determined the future of its followers. It accused the traditionalists within the party who opposed

negotiations with the ANC, SACP and PAC of being unrealistic and
said their objections could not be morally justified as they were
prepared to talk to other 'former terrorists and communists' in
Angola and Mozambique. The document argued that the CP join
the negotiation process immediately on the single condition that
the important parties recognize the principle of self-
determination.

The rejection of the Koos document by the party leadership
and contradictory statements from van der Merwe and
Treurnicht accentuated the differences which by now had
clearly emerged between the moderate and traditional wings of
the CP. In October 1991 the two appeared at a public meeting
and supported the idea of participation in the negotiating
process with certain preconditions, chiefly, the recognition of
the right of whites to self-determination. An elated van der
Merwe claimed afterwards that Treurnicht's position now
corresponded with his own (*Rapport*, 13 October 1991). His
optimism turned out to be premature, for shortly afterwards
Treurnicht reiterated that the CP 'cannot and will not be a
fellow-negotiator to sell out our own people' (*The Argus*, 26
October 1991). However, the pro-negotiation faction received
further support from the CP's Free State congress, which
approved a 12-point plan (sponsored by *Toekomsgesprek*, the
right-wing think-tank), which incorporated an approval of
negotiations (although the more powerful Transvaal congress
rejected it).

With the commencement of Codesa in December 1991 the
impatience of the pro-negotiation faction within the CP became
palpable. Koos van der Merwe appeared briefly at the Codesa
venue in Johannesburg during its first session, ostensibly to
introduce two obscure Angolan businessmen to the minister of
finance, Barend du Plessis.[3] The CP issued a statement
condemning van der Merwe's appearance, but did not act
against him. At Codesa the NP agreed to one of the CP's chief
demands for participating in the negotiations, viz. placement of
the demand for self-determination on the agenda (the ANC had
made a similar offer two weeks previously). Although
Treurnicht rejected both invitations on the grounds that he had
no mandate to negotiate with 'communists' and that Codesa first
had to be reconstituted on the basis of 'nations', the *volkstaters*

strongly rejected this position. By now the ranks of those openly advocating CP participation in negotiations included van der Merwe, Cehill Pienaar and Koos Botha.

After the expulsion of van der Merwe the pro-negotiation faction struggled unsuccessfully to change the CP's position on negotiations. With the founding of the AVU, Beyers indicated his willingness to negotiate with all parties: 'We want to discuss our idea with everybody across the political spectrum. We want to bring it across that the Afrikaner is not selfish and that we are interested in peace and harmony' (*Sunday Times*, 16 August 1992). The AVU's pro-negotiation stance placed enormous pressure on the CP to follow suit, as the latter feared that the perception could develop that the AVU was the sole representative of Afrikaner nationalism. However, while the CP had decided in principle to join the negotiating process, it was unsure of how to go about it without losing face in the light of its earlier determination not to negotiate unless 'the right of self-determination of the whites' was recognized. Such an opportunity presented itself with the founding of Cosag in September 1992. As the CP's black allies in the alliance, the IFP, the Ciskei and Bophuthatswana, were committed to negotiations, it became possible for the CP to join the negotiations through its association with Cosag.

Accordingly, in October 1992 the party grudgingly announced that it would join multiparty negotiations, but only in conjunction with a renewed commitment to the 'struggle'. According to CP MP Pieter Mulder, the concepts of 'negotiation and struggle' were interrelated insofar as a lack of progress at the negotiation table would allow the CP to opt for a violent struggle to achieve its objective of self-determination. Mulder drew an analogy with the ANC/SACP's 'policy of negotiation and struggle', and said that the 'struggle', as in the case of the latter organizations, would also strengthen the hand of the CP negotiators. He also rejected the AVU's position on negotiations as useless: '[without the struggle] you are not going to achieve anything by sitting at the negotiation table with a friendly face and a good plan, as the AVU is doing' (*Rapport*, 18 October 1992). The CP also argued that it had no problem with sitting around the same table as the ANC, as the latter 'did not dictate the process anymore', but insisted that it would not engage in bilateral talks with the ANC (*Die Burger*, 8 March 1993).

In March 1993 the CP participated in the planning conference for the multiparty forum, but the party's lack of cooperation within the forum and its negative attitude during the actual proceedings were a clear indication that its heart was not fully in negotiations. This was possibly because the CP had realized early on that there was no realistic chance that it would attain its objective of a sovereign white state. In June 1993 the CP, joined by the IFP, withdrew from the forum because it had been agreed that the final constitution would be written by a democratically elected body after the election. This issue also led to a split and the eventual demise of the AVU in late 1993.

The pro-negotiation stance of the leader of the AVF, Constand Viljoen, received an initial setback when members of the organization physically disrupted the proceedings at the multiparty negotiation forum in June 1993. However, after this event the organization entered into bilateral negotiations with the government and the ANC and even submitted its constitutional proposals to the multiparty forum in July 1993.

On the issue of negotiations, the AVF continued with unofficial negotiations with the ANC and the government throughout the remainder of 1993 and later entered into bilateral negotiations with the ANC. Viljoen's style of negotiations were so accommodating and reasonable that Mandela himself admitted the ANC had developed a new understanding of the right wing's position: Mandela said 'the more we talk to the AVF, the closer we get to one another'.

Non-violent resistance to reform
Up to the decisive referendum of March 1991 the CP firmly believed that it could win a whites-only general election if given the opportunity. Its two-pronged political strategies were therefore aimed at ensuring that such as an election or at least a referendum would be called before a transition to majority rule began.

The first component of these strategies had moral undertones and dealt with the NP's legitimacy: the CP argued that the NP was acting contrary to the mandate it had asked for in the 1989 general election. As Treurnicht pointed out: 'It is blatantly misleading and immoral to promise voters a certain policy

before an election but to follow a different one afterwards....
Today you do not represent the majority of whites, and for this
reason, you owe the whites an election' (*Patriot*, 9 November
1990) [translation]. Furthermore, the CP claimed that the
by-election results and the average 14 per cent swing to the right
since September 1989 were a clear indication that the NP had lost
the support of the majority of whites.

The second component of the CP's strategy was linked to the
first insofar as the party viewed extraparliamentary –
supposedly non-violent – strategies as a logical response to an
'illegitimate' government. At this stage the CP still believed that it
could re-implement apartheid if given the opportunity, and it
countered the NP's slogan that 'the process of reform was
irreversible', with its own version of the same slogan: 'nothing is
irreversible, except for NP rule'.[4] During the first two years of
the de Klerk era the goal of attaining power and reversing
reforms became the guideline for the CP's strategies of passive
resistance.

Following the announcement of the repeal of the remaining
apartheid legislation in February 1991, the early phase of
passive resistance was characterized by the formation of an
all-inclusive *volksaksie* (people's front) (*Rapport*, 8 April 1990).
The goal of this front was to coordinate the various elements of
passive resistance; it became known as *Operasie Spierwys* (literally
an action of flexing the Party's muscles) (*Rapport*, 3 February
1991). The early proposals for non-violent opposition were
based on organizing resistance against reform at various levels
such as the media, the business sector, trade unions, education,
religion and local government; it also included right-wing
protests in the form of marches and gatherings and the
interruption of NP political meetings; also considered were the
options of strikes, the refusal to pay taxes, the refusal to
acknowledge call-ups for military service, and to issue a separate
identity document for right-wing whites.

It was only after the resounding defeat of the right-wing
forces during the referendum that the inevitability of the end of
white domination in South Africa became obvious even to the
die-hards within the CP. From this point onwards, the emphasis
of right-wing resistance shifted from attempting to reverse

reforms and taking control of the government to an emphasis on pressuring the NP and ANC into recognizing Afrikaner claims to self-determination. This entailed mass mobilization and a programme of active opposition to the process of transition and the democratization of South Africa. It included the creation of a 'mobilization secretariat' with an extensive structure, and threats to create a people's army and an alternative government, and, as has been mentioned, to launch a comprehensive campaign of civil disobedience and ultimately violence. The right wing referred to its programme of resistance as the 'Ten Plagues', an analogy with the biblical account of Moses and Pharaoh. The implicit understanding here was that should the 'plagues' – meaning non-violent resistance – not bring about the desired goal, the right would implement the final strategy, i.e. violence, again with reference to the biblical account of the tenth plague, the death of firstborn children.

White labour
The reasoning behind labour-related white opposition to reform was explained in a typically exaggerated fashion by the CP mouthpiece:

> The most important element in White resistance is the ordinary working man; the man who keeps the wheels of South African industry going. Without him, South Africa would collapse. There would be nobody to keep the water supplies going, no one to repair the typewriters and computers, no one to make the bread, keep the water pure, fix the cars, aeroplanes and trains; no one to maintain roads, control the traffic lights, manufacture the furniture, keep the milk pure (*Patriot*, 3 November 1989) [translation].

To enhance the political strength of white workers, the CP advocated the creation of an overarching trade union body. The all-white MWU indicated its desire for a trade union which would be more capable of fending off 'the onslaught on white workers from the combined forces of massive black trade unions, left-wing employees and an unsympathetic government' (*Patriot*, 1 February 1991) [translation]. After negotiations between six white unions in October 1991, plans were announced to form an overarching union in 1992, with an expected membership of 100,000 white workers (*Patriot*, 25 October 1991). However, nothing concrete came of these plans and the closest white labour unions came to unity was through their common affiliation with and membership in the AVF.

Towards the end of 1993 white unions again threatened to paralyse the economy through one-day strikes, and to engage in industrial sabotage at strategic institutions such as ESCOM, nuclear power plants, water boards, airports, etc. According to one report the right-wing supporters at ESCOM came very close in September 1993 to cutting off the largest part of South Africa's electrical supply, but refrained from doing so for 'humanitarian' reasons (*Rapport*, 12 September 1993).

Mass public protests
These became an increasingly important feature of right-wing opposition to reform early in the de Klerk era. The concept was regarded by the right as a legitimate component of the peaceful intensification of the 'people's freedom struggle', but frequently ended up in violence. One of the largest displays of mass protest was organized on 15 February 1990 in Pretoria, attended by about 30,000 people. Another mass meeting held on 31 May 1990 at the Voortrekker Monument, also in Pretoria, was attended by between 60,000 and 150,000 right-wing supporters (estimates varied). These were followed in 1991 by two mass rallies involving between 12,000 and 20,000 disaffected right-wing farmers, protesting at labour legislation. In May 1993 the AVF organized a mass meeting which was attended by approximately 5000 right-wing supporters at the government's administrative headquarters at the Union Buildings in Pretoria, to issue an ultimatum to the government to open talks on Afrikaner self-determination within six months or face armed rebellion (*The Times*, 31 May 1993). The most visible public protest to date occurred one month later, when 3000 right-wingers, under the auspices of the AVF but led by the AWB, stormed and occupied the World Trade Centre building in Johannesburg in which the multiparty negotiations were in progress. The attackers assaulted delegates, caused damage to property, and showed that the police did not have the will to

stand up to the right – in fact many members of the police force were on friendly terms with the protesters, while others allowed themselves to be intimidated into participating in the singing of the anthem and joining in prayers by right-wing officials.

Petitions

To intensify its pressure on the government to call an election, a petition was circulated in 1991 with the aim of gathering one million signatures. This campaign became known as *Aksie Een Miljoen* (Action One Million), but was singularly unsuccessful. Treurnicht later admitted the failure of the campaign and argued that it was more difficult to collect one million signatures than it would be to get one million votes during an election (*Die Burger*, 15 February 1991). The party blamed the failure of the campaign on a 'misunderstanding', but nevertheless claimed that a few hundred thousand signatures had been collected up to February 1991 (interview, Andries Beyers, 11 April 1991).

The media

The lack of a sympathetic press had been one of the CP's main weaknesses since its founding in 1982. The party mouthpiece, *Patriot*, had limited circulation and functioned mainly as an information/propaganda pamphlet, rather than as a proper newspaper. Shortly after the split of the NP in 1982, Marius Jooste of Perskor had threatened to switch his allegiance to the CP, but apart from some early sympathetic coverage of CP activities, Perskor remained committed to the NP. Since then the CP could at most rely on some marginally sympathetic editorials in the *Citizen* and later *Rapport*. As a result the CP decided that there was a definite need for an independent right-wing newspaper. Treurnicht claimed that there was a 'hunger' in the country for a medium which could convey to the right-wing whites the message of nationalism and 'survival of our nation' (*Patriot*, 1 June 1990).

By mid-1990 efforts to launch such a paper were in full swing. A prospectus was issued with the goal of creating a capital fund of R20 million. The prospectus recommended the creation of the publishing firm Volkspers, on the grounds that there was a great need for the publication of a newspaper representing the right wing. It appeared, however, that the average right-wing supporter did not feel obliged to make money available for this project, irrespective of how worthwhile he thought a CP-supporting newspaper would be. Consequently, by February 1991 only R1 million of the projected R20 million worth of shares in the venture had been sold, and by August 1991 this figure stood at a paltry R1.2 million (*Patriot*, 1 February 1991; 9 August 1991). This was in spite of the fact that only R30 each was required from the 670,000 people who voted for the CP in 1989. By 1993 the proposed newspaper had not yet appeared on the streets and it is doubtful whether it ever will, especially against the background that even the low-key *Patriot* had suffered losses amounting to hundreds of thousands of Rand during the last few months of 1991 and the first half of 1992 (*Die Burger*, 16 August 1992).

Disrupting NP meetings

Another strategy implemented with great success concerned the disruption of NP meetings in various constituencies. As a result several meetings had to be cancelled and others were held in a tense atmosphere with the help of massive police protection. During the state president's meeting in Ventersdorp in August 1991 a violent confrontation resulted in the deaths of three right-wing supporters.

Treurnicht defended this form of protest as follows: 'Mr de Klerk is being too hasty in pointing a finger at the CP. He knows very well that political meetings can become a little robust ... he stirred up the *volk*. Now he wants me to calm them down' (*Sunday Times*, 19 August 1990).

Local government

One of the most effective strategies employed against reform occurred at the level of local government in CP-controlled local authorities. The intention was to obstruct the repeal of apartheid legislation without breaking any laws, and in some cases, blatantly to overrule the directives of the government. Ironically, up to 1990 the CP's policy at this level was not much different from the official NP policy, as the CP merely adhered to a strict interpretation of the racial laws promulgated by the NP government. Finally, towards the end of 1989, a firm commitment was made by the de Klerk government to abolish

the Separate Amenities Act in 1990, but with some provisions
being scrapped with immediate effect, e.g. beach segregation
and the opening of the central business districts of cities and
towns to all races. These measures came as a serious blow to the
CP's ability to implement its policies at the level of local
administration, as its freedom to act in terms of central
government legislation had disappeared.

The reaction of the right wing was characterized by
frustration and anger. At Boksburg's newly opened recreational
facilities blacks were physically assaulted by right-wingers. In
more than one instance the Boksburg police and traffic officers
refused to intervene and sided instead with the attackers (*Sunday
Times*, 10 December 1989). In response to the government's
request that all beaches be opened with immediate effect in
November 1989, several councils, including Richards Bay,
Mossel Bay, Hartenbos and Durban, indicated their determination to enforce beach apartheid until the law was repealed by
the government. Mossel Bay's mayor insisted that his town's
beaches would remain segregated, 'as it is the only way by which
white rights can be protected', and he rejected government
interference in local affairs (*The Argus*, 21 December 1989). In
1991 the final repeal of discriminatory legislation made it more
difficult for the CP to obstruct its reforms at local government
level. Consequently the CP resorted to other methods: in
response to black consumer boycotts, several CP-controlled town
councils cut off water and electricity supplies to neighbouring
black townships. The town council of Carolina refused to
reconnect the services to the neighbouring black township of
Silobela, even after the Transvaal Provincial Administration
(TPA) had directly ordered it to do so (*The Star*, 9 April 1991).

The CP, being in control of the Transvaal Municipal
Association, exerted a powerful influence on such decisions.
During a meeting of all CP local councillors in Pretoria in
January 1991, the party challenged the government to disband
'democratically elected' city councils which refused to become
racially integrated in line with the recommendations of the
Thornhill Report. The CP claimed that integrating local
government would lead to the 'deterioration of the standard of
services to that typical of the Third World' and that white
municipal taxpayers would have to pay more tax to subsidize

black residents (interview, H.J. Coetzee, Chairman of the CP's General Municipal Committee: 15 July 1991). The leader of the CP in the Pretoria city council, Paul Fouche, predicted a fourfold increase in the municipal rates if that council became racially integrated (*Patriot*, 15 March 1991). The proposed integration of the local government structures of Durban was described by *Patriot* as 'legalized plunder', because of the suspected 'subsidization' of black residents by Durban's white taxpayers.

Several individual CP-controlled towns took it upon themselves to hold local whites-only referendums on these matters, and up to March 1991, the towns of Nigel, Phalaborwa, Mossel Bay, Calvinia, Warrenton, Bloemhof, Villiers, Kraaifontein and Ottosdal were among those to reject the racial integration of their town councils. Further obstructionist action by certain CP-controlled councils followed the repeal of the Separate Amenities Act in October 1990. These councils used existing vagrancy and rights-of-admission by-laws legally to obstruct the process of desegregating amenities. The retention of their municipal facilities for whites only was guaranteed by the following measures: Springs closed its municipal pool rather than open it to all races; Sasolburg allowed only season-ticket holders, available only to residents from within the 'white' boundaries of the town, to use its pool; Vanderbijlpark residents had to show their water and electricity accounts to avoid an entrance fee to the municipal pool; in Witbank, 'non-residents' had to pay a R20 deposit for each book borrowed from the library; Bethal charged R500 and Pietersburg R100 membership fees per year to 'non-residents' of the 'white' town to use their libraries; Newcastle refused to accept any new members to its library; Potchefstroom increased the entrance fees to the local dam. The strategy was simply to prevent blacks from using public facilities by making such facilities private and allowing existing 'members' (whites) only, to use them, or alternatively to charge exorbitant fees to 'non-members' (blacks). Although the government tried to stop these practices by the force of law, it was very difficult to prove whether a higher entrance fee implied the practice of racial discrimination *per se*, especially since this is the convention in many 'exclusive' resorts all over the world.

Some of these local authorities received support from

privately owned resorts within their municipal boundaries. Some resorts turned into private and exclusive clubs for the use of their (white) members only – the Silversands resort in Gordons Bay sold holiday units on the basis of 'joint ownership', i.e. a certain number of pre-selected white owners jointly bought a unit which remained theirs for the rest of their lives. The promoters of Silversands stated openly that every buyer who showed his CP membership card would receive a R2000 discount.

The action of right-wing local councils in preventing blacks from using public facilities and discriminating in other ways against them evoked a severe response from blacks in the form of consumer boycotts of white business in these towns. The significance of consumer boycotts was that white racists had to put a price on their desire for racial exclusivity. For many of the shop-owners who helped to vote the CP into power in towns and cities of the Transvaal and Free State in 1988, the idea of directly paying a price for apartheid was a novel one. Until then, these whites had only read about the effects of sanctions, disinvestment and boycotts – admittedly, they had to get used to such minor inconveniences as a limited selection of consumer products, the lack of British programmes on television, no international sport tours or direct flights to the USA, Australia or Japan; but racist whites had never had to consider the direct costs to themselves when erecting a 'whites-only' sign in a park, on a beach or at a public swimming-pool. Events in Boksburg and Carletonville changed all this: the re-implementation of 'petty' apartheid by CP-controlled local authorities led to a black consumer backlash with significant implications for the CP. What the CP either did not realize or refused to acknowledge was that the socio-economic position of blacks in relation to that of whites had improved markedly over the past few years. By 1988 black consumers represented more than half the country's buying power, and in one conservative town in the Transvaal, Boksburg, blacks accounted for two-thirds of retail spending (*Newsweek*, 12 December 1988).

The announcement of the Boksburg CP-controlled city council to close its parks, halls and swimming areas to blacks in 1988 led to a boycott by black consumers of all white-owned shops in the city. The effect of this on the turnover and profit margins of white-owned businesses was devastating: the retail food chain, Checkers, reported that its branch in Boksburg had lost about 50 per cent of its business in the five months following the start of the boycott. A local retailer, Champions Clothing, reported a 40 per cent decline in sales, while the overall turnover of businesses in Boksburg dropped by between 10 and 90 per cent between December 1988 and February 1989 (*Sunday Tribune*, 7 May 1989). The medium-term consequences were even worse: in Boksburg nine businesses and 18 shops had to close down towards the end of 1989; the turnover of furniture shops declined by 30 to 40 per cent and that of hardware stores by 20 to 25 per cent; the development of a hypermarket worth R110 million and a shopping centre worth R30 million was shelved, while approved house plans declined by 40 per cent (*Finance Week*, 15 December 1989).

The town of Carletonville was equally hard hit: 44 per cent of businesses suffered losses in turnover of between 70 and 100 per cent, and 61 per cent of businesses indicated that they could last for only another month under similar trading conditions. The OK Bazaars in the town saw its turnover reduced by 50 per cent after nine weeks of boycotts (*Sunday Tribune*, 7 May 1989). In contrast, in neighbouring Fochville where the CP-controlled town council decided to maintain the status quo, the OK Bazaars branch saw an increase of 90 per cent in its turnover.

Although these figures were a clear indication of the financial implications of the CP's policies, the party's response to what happened in Boksburg and elsewhere was one of recalcitrance. It argued that the NP and the media were presenting a false picture of the events. According to CP Town Councillor, T.J. Ferreira, the town had received a mandate from the voters and would therefore keep Boksburg white, even if sacrifices had to be made: 'I'm also a businessman but I'm prepared to make sacrifices to survive as a white community. There are a lot of *hensoppers* who will sell out the white man for a few rands' (*The Argus*, 1 April 1989). Concurring, Treurnicht admitted that the Boksburg boycott might have had a 'temporarily negative effect', but insisted that when 'a people's real freedom is at stake a choice has to be made' (*Leadership*, Vol. 7, 1988: 8–11).

The reaction of the white voters indicated the opposite: in a municipal by-election in Boksburg in December 1988, a liberal candidate defeated the CP candidate by a large majority. A survey conducted in Boksburg confirmed the shift away from the CP after the effects of its policies were fully realized by the town's white citizens. The survey, conducted early in 1989 by the Policy Research Unit of the American Chamber of Commerce, indicated that, following the boycotts, 54 per cent of Boksburg's white residents were prepared to share power at local government level with the coloured people from neighbouring Reiger Park in a racially integrated municipality (it mentioned nothing about the blacks of neighbouring Vosloorus). The CP also performed poorly in the 1989 general election in the East Rand constituencies where social apartheid had been re-implemented; while the median swing towards the CP in the Transvaal had been 3 per cent, in some of these towns the CP experienced a decline in support, e.g. Vanderbijlpark (−3.4 per cent), Potchefstroom (−5.6 per cent) and Krugersdorp (−5.7 per cent). The conclusion drawn from the events in Boksburg and elsewhere was that racial segregation was becoming too expensive to enforce at local government level because of the growing power of black consumers, trade unions and better organized black resistance.

By mid-1993, 87 right-wing town councils in three provinces were trying to maintain racially segregated local government structures and facilities within the 'white' town boundaries on the one hand, and the increasingly agitated black civic associations fighting back with consumer boycotts on the other. The worsening race relations in many such towns resulted in high volatility and numerous incidents of violence. In the town of Koppies in the Free State right-wingers terrorized the inhabitants of a squatter camp and declared the town centre a 'no-go' area for blacks in response to a black consumer boycott; in Bothaville a violent confrontation was narrowly avoided when the AWB conferred the freedom of the town on Eugene Terre Blanche on the same day as the adjacent black township did the same for Joe Modise, leader of the ANC's military wing; and in the town of Bothaville the right wing prevented Harry Gwala, a senior ANC official, from opening the local ANC branch.

Against this background, the government announced in 1993 that it intended to implement legislation which would have integrated all local councils across racial lines by October 1993, on the recommendation of the Local Government Negotiation Forum. The implication would have been to implement power-sharing by creating non-racial local councils in which non-statutory bodies such as the Civic Associations would contribute half of the members of the combined town councils. As was to be expected, the CP-controlled town councils, supported by the Transvaal and Free State Municipal Associations, vowed to resist any attempts to integrate local councils by not paying taxes, light and water bills and by confiscating the financial resources of the towns. The CP threatened that it would resist this infringement on its last remaining power-base to the hilt, including violent resistance and the destruction of the infrastructure of towns: 'We will not allow blacks to run this council, and if anyone tries to force us, there'll be a revolution ... police will have to arrest councillors and mayors.... We will make the towns ungovernable' (*Sunday Times*, 4 July 1993).

The severity of the reaction emanating from the CP-controlled local councils appeared to have shaken the government, and by August 1993 it announced that these plans would be put on ice for the time being. However, in December 1993, the government regained its courage in the face of vehement opposition from the right, and introduced the Local Government Transitional Bill, which gave considerable powers to provincial administrators to regulate the reform of local government. According to the Bill, the administrators, in conjunction with local government provincial committees (to be established by the TEC), will have the power to encourage or enforce the establishment of non-racial local and metropolitan councils by April 1994 – should existing whites-only councils not devise their own transitional models according to non-racial guidelines, they would run the risk of being dissolved by the administrator and be replaced by a non-racial transitional council and the winding-up of all assets and rights of the recalcitrant council. The CP's response in rejecting the Bill was that 'forced integration' of local councils would be met with the boycotts of taxes and rates by whites, but the Party suggested no new strategy to counter what at this stage has become inevitable, even in CP-held towns. It did, however, announce in December 1993 that 21 towns in the Transvaal and two in the Free State had indicated through referenda that they would like to be included in the proposed *volkstaat*.

The government's decision to give right-wing and other conservative councils the choice to either integrate voluntarily or be forced to do so, made a strong impression on the Pretoria city council, for in December 1993 this citadel of Afrikaner nationalism with a strong right-wing presence, agreed, in conjunction with the ANC, to the formation of the multiracial Greater Pretoria Transitional Metropolitan Forum.

Agriculture

The CP enjoyed considerable success in mobilizing farmers to oppose reforms. The CP used its control of both the powerful Transvaal and Free State Agricultural Unions as a basis from which to oppose land, labour and other reforms. Reaction in the farming community was particularly fierce over the repeal in 1991 of the Land Acts of 1913 and 1936 and over the Urban Foundation's recommendation that black farmers who were able to obtain financing should be allowed to buy out white farmers who were saddled with heavy debts.

Towards the end of 1990 disgruntled Transvaal farmers met in Pretoria and threatened to take measures that could 'surpass the boundaries of decency' if the government did not respond in a satisfactory way. The government relented with regard to further financial assistance to farmers, but insisted that the Land Acts were definitely to be repealed. In January 1991, between 1500 and 5000 farmers (the estimates varied considerably) staged a disruptive rally in the streets of Pretoria to voice their opposition to the intended scrapping of the Land Acts and the alleged lack of state assistance to the agricultural community. When the farmers resorted to violence and refused to leave the central business districts, their arrest provided the CP caucus with the opportunity to fly from Cape Town to Pretoria to lend moral support to the farmers. The fiasco in Pretoria provided the CP with a political victory, as the CP's promise to stand by the farming community contrasted sharply with the state president's condemnation of the protest and the clashes between a number of farmers and the police. A referendum held by the TAU two weeks later, in February 1991, showed that 95 per cent of Transvaal farmers were against the repeal of the Land Acts, i.e. firmly in line with the policy of the CP (*The Argus*, 15 February 1991).

Right-wing resistance reached a peak when the White Paper on Land Reform was published in March 1991. The White Paper proposed that there would be no more racial restrictions on land ownership in South Africa. The CP warned that these proposals were an attempt to deprive the *volk* of its collective property ownership, and promised that it would meet with fierce resistance from the right wing. The TAU regarded the White Paper as a 'declaration of war' against white farmers, but besides the symbolic burning of the White Paper in public, and vague proposals to form closed corporations to buy all white land, no other concrete action emerged from the TAU threats. The reaction of farmers and organized agriculture outside the Transvaal to the CP's call for mass protest was lukewarm. By mid-April 1991, i.e. two months after the government announced its intention to repeal the Land Acts, only the TAU and a few district agricultural unions had testified before the parliament's Joint Committee on Land Reform.

In May 1991 a combination of about 1000 militant farmers and AWB members became involved in another clash with police and SADF troops, after they had taken the law into their own hands to drive squatters off the farm Goedgevonden near Ventersdorp in the Transvaal. The farmers claimed that the government was too 'cowardly' to act against the squatters, leaving the farmers with no choice but to remove the squatters by force. Several farmers were wounded when the police were forced to use buckshot to protect the squatters. The CP accused the government of 'shooting its own people to protect anarchists' and compared the government's actions with that of the British government during the Slagtersnek rebellion in 1815 (in which Afrikaner rebels were executed) (*Cape Times*, 15 May 1991). Ferdi Hartzenberg warned that the security forces might have come off second best if the farmers had shot back, and suggested that a monument should be erected to honour them for refraining from doing so (*Hansard*, 14 May 1991). The right wing strongly emphasized the 'civil war' aspect of the Goedgevonden incident: it was the first time that government forces had fired on whites since the mineworkers' strike of 1922. Later Hartzenberg accused the government (without supplying proof) of intending to shoot up to 1000 right-wing supporters at Ventersdorp (*Die Burger*, 28 November 1991).

The actual repeal of the Land Acts in June 1991 resulted in little physical protest and nothing came of the threats by the TAU that the government would have to 'kill' Afrikaners before it would be able to take their land away. Shortly after the repeal of these acts, the right wing's clamour about the sanctity of Afrikaner land met its match in market forces: a white farmer and member of the AWB, Bill Ruthvin, sold his Delmas farm in July to a black millionaire, Charlie Moloi, after having received an offer he could not refuse (*Die Burger*, 22 July 1991).

An important gathering of right-wing farmers took place in May 1993, when between 12,000 and 20,000 farmers met in Potchefstroom to issue an ultimatum to the government and the ANC, and to welcome Constand Viljoen as their political saviour. The farmers expressed in no uncertain terms their rejection of the transitional process, of multiracial security structures, and of new labour legislation. They also insisted that negotiations with 'communists' be suspended, that a night-time curfew be introduced in rural areas, and that farmers be incorporated into commando structures (*Die Burger*, 7 May 1993; *Patriot*, 14 May 1993). The protest gathering was held against the background of a heightened terror campaign against white farmers; six white farmers had been killed the week before. The perpetrators of the murders were mostly members of the PAC's military wing, Apla, but the farmers were especially angered by the call of Peter Mokaba, leader of the ANC's youth wing, to 'Kill the Boer, kill the farmer' (one of the counter-slogans at the rally read: 'I am a Boer and a farmer – come and try me!').

Education

Another area upon which the right had focused its campaign of resistance was in education, especially following the government's announcement in 1990 of its intention to allow white schools to choose for themselves whether they would like to become racially integrated. In April 1990 the Cape Parents' Association rejected this proposal and in June of the same year Afrikaner parents in the Transvaal followed suit through a referendum vote (*Patriot*, 22 June 1990). When the executive committee of the Transvaal Afrikaans Parents' Association (TAO) reacted positively to the proposals, the CP used its influence to persuade the TAO that it would act against the wishes of the majority of white parents in the Transvaal if it approved the open-school models. A month later the TAO, together with the Cape and Northern Cape Parents' Associations, and the over-arching Federation of Parents' Associations (FOSA), rejected racially mixed schools (*Patriot*, 2 November 1990; *Rapport*, 7 October 1990).

The CP mouthpiece, *Patriot*, did its utmost to indoctrinate parents to reject the government's 'open-school' model in its entirety: the paper put forward arguments which emphasized the disadvantages of racially integrated teaching. To counter further what it perceived as a threat to racially separate education, the CP founded the *Volkskomitee vir Christelik-Volkseie Onderwys* (People's Committee for Christian People's Education), which held its first congress in March 1991. The committee decided that the issue of separate education for Afrikaners should be provided for by a future constitution, ironically a position which did not differ much from the NP's position that such education should be available for those who insisted on it. However, the committee distanced itself from the NP by rejecting 'parity in education, open schools and one education system for all' (*Die Burger*, 25 March 1991).

In response to the opening of schools to all races the right wing considered the creation of Afrikaans-only schools based on the principles of *Christelik-Volkseie Onderwys* (CVO) (Christian People's Education). The first of these schools was founded in Pretoria in 1992 with 36 pupils (which had grown to 76 pupils and 18 teachers by 1993), and by mid-1993, 13 such schools had been formed (*Patriot*, 21 May 1993).

Religion
The tension within the DRC, so characteristic of the late 1980s, emerged again in 1990 following a confession by Willie Jonker, a delegate of the DRC, at an interdenominational conference of churches. Jonker asked for forgiveness for the injustices caused by apartheid on behalf of the DRC and the Afrikaner as a whole (*Rapport*, 18 November 1990). His confession was supported by the moderator of the DRC, Pieter Potgieter, but rejected by Treurnicht and Boshoff in their capacities as leaders of the NG Bond within the Church. They rejected the confession on the grounds that they were not prepared 'to confess for the sins of

apartheid unconditionally and that a church body cannot confess on behalf of all of its members' (*Patriot*, 16 November 1990). Right-wing members of the DRC organized a protest meeting in December 1990 and said they would do everything in their power to reverse the decision by the General Synod to support Jonker, but indicated that they did not intend to leave the Church at that stage (*Vrye Weekblad*, 30 November 1990).

In spite of fiery rhetoric, the right wing had relatively little success in its efforts to undermine the unity of the DRC during the early 1990s. In spite of subversive activities by its right-wing members, even the very conservative synod of the western Transvaal region of the DRC decided in June 1991 not to split with the General Synod over its approval of the confession of Willie Jonker one year earlier. Furthermore, only 12 DRC ministers were prepared to support a document published in 1991 entitled *Noodroep: Die Damwal Breek* ('A Call of Distress: the dike is giving way') in which some discontented ministers expressed their concern over the rejection of apartheid by the Church (*Patriot*, 31 May 1991).

Diverse strategies

Many of the other strategies of resistance considered by the right wing throughout the de Klerk era were either impractical or bordered on the absurd. In 1990 the CP threatened to issue its own identity documents intended only for whites, in response to the repeal of the Population Registration Act. In response to what it regarded as one-sided public broadcasting and the misuse of the SABC by the government to indoctrinate whites, the party indicated that it would ask right-wing taxpayers not to pay television licences and to withhold their taxes. Another scheme involved the distribution of thousands of pamphlets exposing the NP's 'crookery' (*Patriot*, 14 June 1991).

Within the ambit of parliament the CP frequently accused the government of being traitors to the Afrikaner nation and had threatened the government with Nuremberg-style trials should it ever come to power (*Die Burger*, 25 September 1990; SABC-TV, 1 February 1991). The CP also regularly employed the tactic of walking out of parliament to show its disgust with the government's reforms. With the last sitting of the tricameral parliament in December 1993, the CP broke all parliamentary traditions by jumping up to sing the national anthem halfway through the proceedings. The CP caucus was joined by CP supporters in the public gallery, one of whom loudly and angrily accused the NP of treason, an accusation which also led to several CP MPs being forced to leave the chamber (*Die Burger*, 23 December 1993).

With the founding of the AVF in 1993 more radical but equally unrealistic proposals were discussed. These included the establishment of a 'government within a government' in the area of the proposed *volkstaat*, consisting of *volksamptenare* instead of *staatsamptenare* (people's servants as opposed to civil servants), and operating in parallel with the South African government: 'Circumstances will leave the [Afrikaner] with no other choice than to appoint elected officials and elected representatives to carry on with the struggle against a communist regime' (deputy leader of the CP, Willie Snyman, *Weekly Mail*, 2–8 July 1993). The AVF also considered holding a referendum among the Afrikaners living within the territory of its proposed *volkstaat*.

'People's mobilization': preparing for the 'Third Freedom War'
Although the possibility of violence has always been regarded as a last-resort option by the right wing, a growing inclination towards violent resistance became evident during the four years leading up to the end of white rule. This was the result of several factors, primarily the realization among the right that it was incapable of stopping the transformation to a democratic dispensation through constitutional means, and secondly, it coincided with the increasing brutalization of South African society, characterized by upwardly spiralling rates of violence and crime and a low-intensity racial and ethnic civil war.

Right-wing activity in this sphere increased substantially during the period 1989–93 and has taken two forms: the threat to resort to violence combined with psychological indoctrination and the organizational mobilization to carry out such a threat, and actual physical violence directed against a variety of targets.

Threats and attempts to justify violence
Following the political reforms under F.W. de Klerk and the transformation of South African politics and society, the CP gradually realized, especially after the 1992 referendum, that it

could no longer reverse the process of transition. Consequently, the party's position gradually become more militant and it undertook to resist the demise of white domination with all means at its disposal. The government took the CP's threats seriously enough for the state president to warn that he would not allow it to wreck the government's reform programme: 'I want to tell the leader of the official opposition to his face: neither the NP, nor the government or myself will allow anybody to set fire to the country' (*Rapport*, 11 February 1990) [translation].

De Klerk's warning and the NP's repeated assurances of the irreversibility of reform predictably caused quite a stir among members of the CP, who perceived this as a unilateral 'changing of the rules' which left the CP with no choice but also to move beyond the traditional parameters of white politics: 'Why, if the government refuses to adhere to the rules of the political game, should we expect right-wing groups to adhere to these?' *Patriot's* English-language supplement asked on 24 August 1990. Explicit threats to resort to violence were employed by the CP in unison with attempts to justify on moral and biblical grounds the use of violence against the state, and it became the foremost tool to prepare its supporters for the 'inevitable' violence which would accompany the quest for self-determination.

The first indication of a shift in the CP's previously docile stance came shortly after de Klerk's February 1990 speech, when Treurnicht uttered the infamous warning that the NP had 'awakened the tiger in the Afrikaner' (*The Argus*, 6 February 1990). CP MPs returned to a special session of parliament in August 1990 with an aggressive and militant disposition, reflecting the changed mood in their constituencies in response to the reforms implemented that year (Wim Booyse, interview 11 April 1991). In April of that year a tense situation in Welkom between black and white residents resulted in Treurnicht blaming the government's reforms for making it necessary for whites to protect themselves: 'People have armed themselves and they have a right to defend themselves. They have their weapons ready and some are threatening to shoot. It is not necessary for me to alert them to the need to be prepared. The government is doing this through its decisions' (*The Argus*, 26 April 1990). Treurnicht also requested his followers who demanded a form of armed response to the government's reforms to wait for a sign: 'To those who talk of weapons and shooting, I say, don't be so hasty, hold your horses, don't jump the gun'. In May 1990 he warned that the NP's intention to hand over power to the ANC would result in the 'Third Freedom Struggle' (*The Argus*, 9 May 1990). The CP also claimed that it would revert to violent resistance if whites are subjected to a black majority:

> If President de Klerk and Nelson Mandela should between them close the avenue of the ballot box for Afrikaners to regain their freedom in their own fatherland, we would regard ourselves as an oppressed people. And if we become the oppressed people, at that stage we will have no choice other than to use basically the same methods that oppressed people normally use to regain their freedom (Andries Beyers, cited in *The Argus*, 24 July 1990).

Koos van der Merwe, reputed to have kicked open a parliamentary door in anger on one occasion, also unambiguously expressed his opinion on violence and a civil war. In August 1990 he suggested that he personally would take up arms if reforms were taken too far (*Monitor*, August 1990). Later that year van der Merwe threatened the state president with a similar fate to that of Ceausescu of Romania, and referred to the overthrow and execution of the former Romanian dictator using it as an example of how de Klerk could be ousted (*Die Burger*, 16 November 1990). He also described how members of the CP were ready to fight with all kinds of weapons, including tanks, jet fighters and submarines (*Rapport*, 18 November 1990). Ironically, while van der Merwe's public statements were threatening during this period, there was no evidence of this in the Koos document, which he was busy compiling at the same time. In this document the attitude taken was that violence would be an extreme last-resort option, for which nobody really had an 'appetite' (1990: 11).

Van der Merwe's threats of a military struggle were echoed by other MPs, including Jan Hoon and Corné Mulder (interviews, 7 February 1991; 11 February 1991). Mulder referred to the 'three million Afrikaners' who could not emigrate like their English-speaking compatriots, and would be forced to fight for their freedom. The description of Afrikaners not being able to flee the country at will became an important part of the CP's imagery of the Afrikaner's commitment to fight to the death to achieve self-determination. Treurnicht repeated this theme when he responded to the White Paper on Land Reform: 'We have not got a boat waiting for us in the harbour to allow us to escape – we cannot and will not flee' (*Vrye Weekblad*, 22 March 1991) [translation]. In October 1992, shortly before the CP decided to join the negotiating process, Treurnicht warned that the time had arrived for the Afrikaner people to prepare for war. He drew an analogy between the position of Afrikaners today and that of Paul Kruger when he declared war on behalf of the Boer Republics against Britain in 1899. Kruger's often-quoted words then were: 'Here I stand. God help me. There is no other way', words which Treurnicht deemed applicable to his position in 1992.

The CP also made a concerted effort to find political and moral justification for violent resistance against what it perceived as an illegal and immoral regime. Apart from its belief that the NP had lost the support of the majority of whites, the CP also believed that should a government act against the interests of its (white) citizens, those citizens have no further obligations to the government and have the right to look after their own interests. According to Treurnicht the government was directly responsible for right-wing violence since its reforms undermined the security of the whites in South Africa, leading them to take matters into their own hands (*Patriot*, 29 June 1990).

The CP furthermore attempted to find biblical justification for a nation's 'right' to resist a government which acted against its interests and freedom. According to Treurnicht, a former minister in the Dutch Reformed Church:

> The Bible does not take the side of tyrants who ignore the rights and freedom of their people and who destroy laws which protect them. The authority of a government is limited by the authority of God.... If a law made by a government contradicts the authority of God or that of the freedom of a nation, it is not only permissible, but also acceptable, to disobey the government (*Die Burger*, 20 August 1990) [translation].

Treurnicht had described his belief in 'justified' opposition to laws which 'contradict the authority of God' in his book written 15 years earlier when he was still a member of the NP, *Credo van 'n Afrikaner*. In this book Treurnicht cited a DRC publication, *Uit Een Bloed* ('From one blood'), to substantiate his claim that laws which were devised to make a nation lose its national identity contradicted the Old Testament and could therefore be regarded as sinful: 'As a *volk* we want to live and let live.... We fight for our survival, because we understand that to commit suicide is as sinful as committing murder' (Treurnicht 1975: 20) [translation]. It is obvious that Treurnicht considered racial integration a sin, to be resisted at any cost. His usage of the words 'fight', 'suicide' and 'murder' (which in this context can be taken to mean national suicide and genocide) are an indication that Treurnicht defined the term 'resistance' comprehensively to encompass civil war.

A further method favoured by the CP to justify violent resistance was to draw comparisons with the struggles for independence of ethnic groups all over the world. Frequent references were made to the instances of secession and civil war in the territory of the former Soviet Union and Yugoslavia, and, in contrast, the peaceful partitioning of Czechoslovakia. *Patriot* closely monitored events in eastern Europe and regularly published articles comparing in glowing terms the secessionist struggles of Estonia, Latvia, Lithuania, Slovenia, Croatia, Slovakia and others, with the 'freedom struggle of the Afrikaner nation'.[5] Quotes from two of these articles illustrate the point:

> The right of nations to use an armed struggle to achieve political freedom is universally acknowledged as moral and justified. For this reason no one is condemning the Baltic states for using violence to oppose Soviet imperialism. Against this background it would be surprising if the Afrikaner is denied the right to achieve his political freedom through violent means if necessary (*Patriot*, 15 February 1991) [translation].

> Why then create another Yugoslavia if the problem can be solved peacefully as was done in Czechoslovakia? (Pieter Mulder, in *Patriot*, 14 May 1993).

'Mobilizing the people'

Until 1993 the CP's actions largely failed to match its militant rhetoric. Its involvement with a paramilitary organization such as the *Brandwag Volksleer* could hardly be equated with the creation of an army capable of helping to achieve white self-determination. The *Brandwag Volksleer* was optimistically labelled as an alternative defence force and was under the supreme command of former Ossewa Brandwag member, Manie Maritz, but even Maritz admitted that it was a purely defensive organization (*Sunday Times*, 29 April 1990). In March 1991 there were indications that the CP was planning the creation of its own *volksleer* (People's Army). The party denied this but admitted that it supported the formation of 'self-protection units' and *tuiswagte* (home guards) by whites (*Die Burger*, 25 March 1991).

By the end of 1992 the proposed people's army had still not been formed, although CP MP Pieter Mulder admitted that there was much support for such a step among right-wing supporters (*Rapport*, 18 October 1992). The idea surfaced again in March 1993 when the CP's chief spokesman on defence, Willie Snyman, suggested that the party would create its own people's defence force should the government go ahead with its plans to integrate the SADF and the military wing of the ANC, Umkhonto we Sizwe (literally 'Spear of the Nation') (*Patriot*, 12 March 1993).

Shortly afterwards, the CP took the first concrete steps to create structures to mobilize its supporters into resistance against 'communism' and to ensure self-determination, by founding the *Vryheidsraad* (Freedom Council). The latter's function was to oversee the mobilization secretariat, the general mobilization council and special-interest councils in areas such as agriculture, education and trade unions at national level. The mobilization structure also involved right-wing supporters at regional and local levels. The members of the *Vryheidsraad* included six CP MPs and four chairmen whose duty it was to oversee the planning of subgroups, while the CP appointed General Koos Bischoff, a recently retired SADF officer, to head the mobilization secretariat (*Rapport*, 21 March 1993; 28 March 1993). With the founding of the AVF in May 1993, the mobilization structure was altered to accommodate the generals (*Patriot*, 14 May 1993).

Apart from Koos Botha, who committed an act of sabotage at a multiracial school in Pretoria in 1991, no high-ranking CP MP had engaged in violence. This changed in April 1993, of course, when a former CP MP and member of the president's council, Clive Derby-Lewis, and his wife, were arrested for complicity in the assassination of Chris Hani, leader of the SACP. The interracial violence which erupted throughout the country as a result, together with the death of the 72-year-old Treurnicht, directly led to the founding of the AVF in May. From this point onwards, the CP's role in the sphere of planning and organizing violent resistance was largely overtaken by the activities of the AVF.

Occasionally the CP leadership still tended to bluster, as for example in September 1993 when it threatened that its supporters would be forced to take offensive/preventative action to protect whites and might have to revert to *strafkommandos* (punishment commandos). These had an analogy in the tactics used by the former Boer Republics to punish cattle theft and other transgressions by black tribes. Later the same month Hartzenberg warned that the installation of the multiparty Transitional Executive Council (TEC) would signal the beginning of civil war, as the opportunities of a peaceful solution to South Africa's problems had been destroyed (*Globe and Mail*, 24 September 1993).

The fact that the AVF was led by several former security force generals as well as by the former head of the SADF, Constand Viljoen, gave new meaning to the prospects and scope of violent resistance among the right. While the AWB had carried the military torch of the right up to this point (mostly with comical results), the entrance of highly experienced military men provided the right with substantial clout. Viljoen initially insisted that the involvement of the generals was not military in nature: 'I am not here to coordinate military action or to train a white army or to do irresponsible things. To me, armed action is always the very, very last resort' (*Financial Mail*, 21 May 1993). His tone changed considerably within a matter of days: 'The Afrikaner people must prepare to defend themselves. A bloody conflict which will require sacrifices is inevitable, but we will gladly sacrifice because our cause is just' (*Patriot*, 4 June 1993).

The AVF focused its own mobilization efforts to obtain the

support of civilian units known as commandos. In May 1993 one of the AVF's generals, Tienie Groenewald, claimed that he could mobilize 500,000 white civilian force members to fight for secession should the need arise (*The Economist*, 15 May 1993). The AVF later estimated that it enjoyed the support of about 100,000 members of the commando system, including the command structures of all but three of the commando units in the area of the proposed *volkstaat* (*Globe and Mail*, 13 August 1993).

The scope of extremist right-wing violence
One of the first public acts of lethal right-wing terror in modern South African times, the slaying of eight blacks on Strijdom Square in Pretoria in November 1988, was regarded at the time as an isolated incident perpetrated by a lone and confused extremist.[6] The relative lull in right-wing violence thereafter gave credibility to this perception. However, in retrospect, Strydom's murderous deeds were the trigger for a drastic increase in the level of right-wing violence from 1989 onwards, culminating in the assassination of Chris Hani. During this period there was an increase of militant right-wing groups to almost 200, and a concomitant proliferation of acts of violence.

The increase both in numbers of extremist right-wing organizations and in the intensity of violence can be explained in three ways: firstly, it was a direct result of the perception among the right that the demise of white *baasskap* (domination) was a foregone conclusion and that parliamentary and non-violent resistance would not prevent this; secondly, increasing right-wing violence was merely one element of an increasingly violent society;[7] thirdly, that the decline of the AWB in 1990 as a cohesive force of right-wing militancy gave rise to a diaspora of right-wing organizations, from one to 57 paramilitary groups in 1991 and to almost 200 in 1993 (interview, Wim Booyse, 11 April 1991; *Time*, 3 May 1993). The decline of the AWB can be attributed to Eugene Terre Blanche's alleged womanizing and alcoholism, his public image as a buffoon and the AWB's perceived lack of militancy.

Extremist right-wing groups were responsible for more than 50 acts of terror during the course of 1990, which represented about 15 per cent of all acts of violence committed during that year (*Vrye Weekblad*, 14 December 1990). This figure increased dramatically over the next two years: between March 1990 and March 1992 there were approximately 95 documented cases of right-wing terrorism (*Time*, 30 March 1992); between 14 December 1991 and 3 January 1992 alone, there were 14 incidents of right-wing sabotage in the Transvaal (*Vrye Weekblad*, 10–16 January 1992). During January 1994 there were 30 acts of sabotage against the ANC in the western Transvaal and Free State, while 41 bombs exploded in the western Transvaal during the first week of February.

Wim Booyse (interview, 11 April 1991) classified the extremist right-wing groups as firstly, the 'brandy and coke set', which consisted of those who talked about violence but did very little in practice; secondly, the transitional group, which had an agenda, objectives and logistics and formed the backbone of the extreme right – these were overtly fascist 'Hizbullah and IRA types' and were characterized by a 'Holy War' mentality; thirdly, the 'counter-revolutionary group', which was the most dangerous and consisted of a number of highly sophisticated strategists and tacticians but kept a low profile (*The Argus*, 23 July 1990).

Being the longest-established paramilitary right-wing group in the country, the AWB regards itself as the supreme guarantor of Afrikaner nationalism. If developments in South Africa ever turned completely against the interests of the Afrikaner, the AWB believes that it would form the buffer between the extermination and survival of the 'Boer people'. For the most part the AWB's militancy has been confined to threats and the military training of its members. Since its founding it has had several armed factions, e.g. Aquila, the *Stormvalke* (Storm Falcons), *Blitsvalke* (Lightning Falcons), the *Witwagte* (White Watch) and the *Brandwag* (The Sentry). In 1990 the AWB launched a campaign to train a new 'Boer Army', whose commanders were instructed to form their own commandos in their respective hometowns. It later became known as the *Wenkommandos* (Victory Commandos), and was under the leadership of 'colonel' Servaas de Wet. De Wet explained that he would fight a civil war by going 'underground': 'It would be a war like you have in Northern Ireland with the IRA' (*Sunday Times*, [UK], 27 June 1993).

Terre Blanche occasionally referred to a 'Boer holy war', and warned in 1990 that the AWB would declare war on the same day that the ANC became part of the government (*Rapport*, 13 May 1990). The creation of the multiparty TEC in November 1993 for practical purposes turned the ANC into part of the government and should accordingly have resulted in the start of an AWB insurrection, but as was the case with so many of other Terre Blanche's ultimatums, it proved to be nothing but an empty threat. However, although declarations of war seemed to be a normal but harmless part of the AWB's day-to-day activities, one of Terre Blanche's threats, uttered in 1990, proved to be valid:

> Hani is warned: the AWB accepts his provocative challenges in the same spirit in which he made them. If the ANC wants to take over our armed forces or wants to maintain law and order in their place, all hell will break loose in the Republic and the Boers will root them out (*Cape Times*, 24 July 1990).

By December 1990 57 suspected right-wing activists had been arrested or detained or were awaiting trial. The government's tougher approach towards right-wing militants and their detention under Section 29 of the Internal Security Act made the AWB even more cautious about getting involved in violence. Following the incident in which three members of the AWB attacked a bus in Natal, killing seven and injuring 26 of its black passengers, Terre Blanche was quick to distance the AWB from the 'Wild West approach', and said the organization did not approve of violence and did not plant bombs indiscriminately (*Cape Times*, 17 July 1990).

Over the following three years the AWB focused on organized public protests which frequently ended up in violence, but each time provided the organization with a moral victory of sorts and with sufficient propaganda to enable it to maintain its already high profile in the media locally and internationally. These included: the attack by 40 AWB members on a group of black children in the Transvaal town of Louis Trichardt in November 1990; the attack on black squatters near the town of Ventersdorp, which led to a running battle between the police and the AWB in May 1991; the attempt by the AWB in August

1991 to disrupt a meeting held by the state president in Ventersdorp, which resulted in three of its members being killed; AWB members rampaged through a black township in April 1993 shortly after Hani's death in Boksburg, provocatively shouting 'your king is dead' and Terre Blanche saying that he would have wanted to kill Hani himself; and the occupation, on the initiative of the AWB, of the World Trade Centre, the seat of the multiparty negotiations, in June 1993.

In November 1993 the AWB and representatives of the highly militant regional IFP leadership in the PWV and eastern Transvaal organized a joint rally in the town of Vereeniging to sign a 'solidarity' pact. The agreement, reached between Terre Blanche and Moisa Twala (but not approved by the IFP's central leadership), stipulated that 'Boer and Zulu would fight together for their freedom and land should they be confronted by a common enemy' (*Rapport*, 20 November 1993). The signing was accompanied by women supporters of the AWB and IFP marching and dancing the *toyi toyi* (a form of dancing associated with mass protest and public rallies) together, and Zulu warriors displaying AWB flags and shouting 'Viva, AWB'. The AWB also admitted that it was providing military training to members of the IFP in the Transvaal (*Cape Times*, 26 November 1993).

Given their similar approach to violence, the Boerestaat Party, under the leadership of Robert van Tonder, and its military wing, the BWB, led by Andrew Ford, formed an alliance with the AWB to create a 'Boer army' early in 1990. This 'army' was organized on commando lines and was similar to those of the former Boer Republics (a commandant in every town and a general for every region). Like Terre Blanche, van Tonder warned that a right-wing revolution would depend on whether the 'quisling' (NP) government intended to hand over power to the ANC, PAC and SACP, and that his organization would resort to violence when the government 'sacrificed the Boer nation's independence and identity' (*Vrye Weekblad*, 27 April 1990).

The extremist group, *Orde Boerevolk*, founded by Piet 'Skiet' Rudolph (the nickname means 'Shoot'), had achieved notoriety by bombing Melrose House (a Pretoria museum dedicated to the Anglo–Boer War), the offices of a black trade union, the offices of the newspaper *Beeld*, and those of the NP. The group's biggest exploit was the theft of firearms, ammunition and equipment from the Air Force headquarters in Pretoria in April 1990. Rudolph and a colleague stole the arms with the help of national servicemen within the SAAF and managed to avoid arrest for several months with the help of friends and a 'fifth column' of right-wing supporters within the security forces. One of these weapons was used three years later to assassinate Chris Hani. While on the run from the police, Rudolph became known as the 'Boere Pimpernel'. He was finally arrested in September 1990, but granted indemnity in 1991 and released from prison.

The Boere-Krisisaksie (BKA), which organized the invasion and blockade of downtown Pretoria by right-wing farmers in 1991, achieved new notoriety in November 1993 when members of the organization raided an SADF arms depot in the northern Transvaal town of Pietersburg. They stole more than three tons of arms and ammunition, including 100,000 rounds of ammunition, 400 hand-grenades and 200 mortars, apparently to arm underground structures of the BKA in the northern and eastern Transvaal. Ten members of the organization were arrested by the police within 24 hours and most of the weapons and ammunition were retrieved (*Rapport*, 7 November 1993).

The Pretoria Boere Kommando group (PBKG), under the leadership of Jan Groenewald, achieved international attention in December 1993 for a highly publicized but totally futile occupation, undertaken in its name, of a historic building dating from the Anglo–Boer War, Fort Schanskop in Pretoria. An estimated 10 to 40 members of the organization, under the direction of their commander, a former SADF officer, Willem Ratte, forcibly occupied the building in a symbolic protest against the first sitting of the new multiparty overseeing body, the Transitional Executive Council (TEC). The occupation lasted 23 hours and only the intervention of the leader of the AVF, Constand Viljoen, prevented a bloody shoot-out between the highly armed right-wingers and the security forces. The siege ended with the arrest of 17 members of the PBKG.

Of the numerous other extremist groups, only a few could boast of having gone past the planning stages on to actual deeds of serious violence. The Order of Death planned the assassination of at least seven members of the cabinet, but two members of its Vaal Triangle cell, Goosen and Lottering, admitted in court that they killed a black taxi driver in order to prove their commitment to the cause (*Sunday Times*, 18 November 1990). The White Liberation Army claimed responsibility for a taxi-rank blast in July 1990 and further threatened to assassinate the minister of law and order, Adriaan Vlok, as well as Chris Hani (*Cape Times*, 10 July 1990). The activities of the World Apartheid Movement (later the World Preservatist Movement), with a foreign component of Belgian and British citizens, was curtailed after the arrest of some of its members following a spate of bombings during the second half of 1990. Members of this organization were suspected of planning to use chemical and biological weapons to kill large numbers of blacks and to assassinate cabinet ministers (*Vrye Weekblad*, 30 November 1990). As has been said, its leader, Koos Vermeulen, had links with international separatist movements such as the Basque Separatist Movement in Spain, the British movement DARE, the Companions of Justice, the New Force Party, the French neo-Nazi movement L'Assault and the Ku Klux Klan in the USA (*Sunday Times*, 9 December 1990). The Boer Republican Army (BRA) expressed a similar admiration for international terror groups, in particular the IRA. It kept a hit list containing the names of all the 'enemies of the Boers', including members of the government, the Broederbond, the ANC, British and American consular staff and the offices of multinationals such as Shell and BP (*Cape Times*, 4 March 1991).

In addition to extremist right-wing groups, white vigilante groups became another potential threat during the early 1990s. These consisted of relatively harmless neighbourhood watches transformed into militant organizations controlled by the right wing, a step that was part of the creation of grass-roots structures which could be utilized, like the commandos and police reservists, in times of civil war. In Boksburg 8000 armed whites formed an organization called *Blanke Veiligheid* (White Security) (*Sunday Times*, 13 May 1990). The Boksburg town council even had plans to incorporate neighbourhood watches over the whole country into one system, controlled by a communications network centred at Jan Smuts airport (*Vrye Weekblad*, 13 July 1990).

Finally, although it is obvious from this discussion that, apart from isolated cases, right-wing violence has not yet gone beyond threat and bluster, it is equally obvious that it has virtually unlimited potential to do so. To illustrate this, in mid-January 1994 the advanced preparations by an underground right-wing organization with links to the AVF, to take over large parts of the Transvaal by force, were revealed to the Afrikaans newspaper, *Rapport* (23 January 1994). These preparations apparently focused around 52 towns in the western Transvaal and included the stockpiling of armoured vehicles and ammunition and detailed plans to kill large numbers of blacks with the help of 'cyanide bullets'. Although the initial reaction was to reject these as mere rumours or as part of calculated efforts by the right to pressure the ANC and NP to make concessions to the Freedom Alliance at the negotiation table, there were growing indications that large-scale right-wing violence was being planned. This was confirmed in a warning issued by the general staff of the SADF to President de Klerk in late-January 1994, that the right wing was planning large-scale violence and would possibly attempt a coup against the government before the April 1994 elections, and that possibly up to 60 per cent of the SADF troops and officers would support the right wing (*Rapport*, 30 January 1994).

The spectre of right-wing violence, initiated as acts of terrorism by small numbers on the extreme right and expanded by the right-wing core into full-scale civil war incorporating elements of the security forces, therefore presents a formidable obstacle to the democratization of South Africa. For the right wing to disrupt the transitional process and perhaps launch a terrorist war against a new South African government, only limited manpower is necessary. As the political scientist David Welsh observed: 'A thwarted, frustrated Right, who are prepared to take up arms, can do untold damage. When you think that the IRA and the Provisional IRA between them probably have no more than about 500 activists, and you look at what they have been able to do, it's very frightening indeed' (*Cape Times*, 20 December 1990).

Conclusion: the Prospects of the Right

The general tendency to view the white right wing in South Africa as a racial phenomenon belies its complex and multi-faceted nature. While it certainly is true that all of its supporters belong to the white racial group and that the attraction of its conservative ideology has enabled it to override the ethnic differences between its Afrikaans- and English-speaking supporters, the existence of the right wing cannot be explained without reference to its ethnic origins and its driving force in Afrikaner nationalism. Neither can the right be understood without reference to its regional and historical base in the northern provinces, or without a mention of its class component.

This book has been guided in many respects by the theoretical framework of Donald Horowitz, which provides a paradigm within which to analyse the inter-ethnic and intra-ethnic nature of right-wing politics. Horowitz hypothesized that there is a psychological dynamic inherent in ethnicity which tends to overwhelm seemingly rational economic and political interests, and that ethnic conflict should be understood in terms of the collective drive by ethnic groups to obtain or maintain social status and power. As applied to the right, this approach facilitates an understanding of issues relating to the roots of Afrikaner nationalism, the subordinate status of materialist issues relative to issues of identity and social status, the policies and objectives of the right wing, and the strategies considered by the right wing to achieve its goals. It also provides an explanation of the underlying motivation for the right wing to create homogeneity in the territory regarded as the Afrikaner or white fatherland. Although such demands often appear to be irrational, they are not unique to the right wing – rather they are the logical response of all minority groups plagued with insecurity and the fear of domination and extinction. In the case of the right, such apparent irrationality reflects the deeper fear for the loss of Afrikaner identity and status, and of domination and genocide.

The apparently irrational constitutional proposals of the right wing illustrate this phenomenon, e.g. the CP's firm belief, as late as 1991, that it could reintroduce the major pillars of grand apartheid against the wishes of approximately 30 million blacks on the verge of liberation, or the AWB's demand for the resurrection of the Boer Republics destroyed in 1902, or Carel Boshoff's plans to create a state for three million highly urbanized Afrikaners in the arid, inhospitable and very rural north-western Cape. Yet, seen in the light of the pervasive, permeative and highly emotional nature of ethnic conflict in general, it is obvious that right-wing Afrikaner nationalism has developed an 'ethnic dynamic' of its own, one in which the forces of industrialization and rational economic and political behaviour play a lesser role.

The origins of the present-day right wing can be traced back to the emergence and mobilization of Afrikaner nationalism during the 1930s and 1940s. The process of ethnic mobilization resulted in an ethnic group with rigid social boundaries strongly reliant on the primordial aspects of Afrikaner ethnicity, such as a common language, religion, history and territory. As the NP began to stray from this narrow path during the mid-1960s, transforming itself into a party which represented broader white interests during the 1970s and 1980s and eventually into a party with an even more inclusive view of South African nationalism in the early 1990s, a new style of right wing evolved to become the spiritual heir of the powerful but destructive ideologies of racial exclusivity and white domination. The right wing therefore did not emerge within an ideological vacuum, but merely represented a continuation of the NP's policies conceived after 1948. The concept of Afrikaner ethnonationalism has been the driving force behind Afrikaner politics for most of the twentieth century and, being based on the preservation of the Afrikaner identity and status through self-determination, it is the single most important element of the right wing's *raison d'être*. If conceptualized in purely ethnic terms without its racist baggage, it is the only part of its ideology which could possibly meet with the internationally accepted norms for the self-determination of peoples. The demand for Afrikaner self-determination received strong reinforcement by way of comparison from the ethnonationalist secessions in eastern Europe following the fall of Soviet hegemony in 1989 and the dissolution of the Soviet Union in 1991 – these are perceived by the right wing as proof of the fact that it is not possible to force competing nationalisms into one state and that its claims are legitimate and compatible with those of nations elsewhere.

The fear of ethnic domination and suppression, a major reason why ethnic groups vie for power, is also applicable to the understanding of the psychological dynamic and roots of right-wing political behaviour, and explains the overwhelming desire by the right wing to achieve self-determination at any price. The fear of domination and suppression go hand in hand with the fear of physical extermination or genocide, which is a prominent feature not only of the right wing but was also ingrained in the collective consciousness of the majority of whites in South Africa; when it comes to self-preservation, there is little difference between a right-wing and a liberal white. Although these fears are largely unfounded, they are a real part of the right-wing psyche, a point acknowledged by the ANC when its president Nelson Mandela repeatedly emphasized that the 'very real fears' of Afrikaners needed to be addressed.

A *right-wing government?*
Although the black majority had received both a say and a veto in the running of the government for the first time with the implementation of the Transitional Executive Council (TEC) in November 1993, South Africa will remain, at least until 29 April 1994, *de facto* and *de jure* largely under white rule. The right wing, being a powerful force within the parameters of white politics, can therefore not be regarded as irrelevant, at least not

until a new non-racial constitution is implemented and the balance of political, economic and military power shifts to the currently disenfranchised majority. This links up with the first – and most unlikely – scenario, in which the right manages to block the transitional process through constitutional means before the non-racial election in 1994. Although the prospect of another whites-only general election or referendum is not forseen, it remains theoretically possible for the right to become the government through a split in the NP to the right.

The NP's failure to secure its core demands on power-sharing and federalism through negotiations and the widespread breakdown of law and order and anarchy could still cause the growing disaffection within the NP's own ranks to turn into open rebellion and provide the CP with a final opportunity to make a grasp for power. Theoretically, the defection of between 45 and 50 disaffected NP MPs to the right would bring a right-wing alliance to power in the existing parliament before April, possibly consisting of the CP, AVF and IFP. Already two NP MPs had joined the IFP and there are indications that a considerable number of MPs, especially those in Natal, could follow suit, while others are considering joining a right-wing/centrist, anti-ANC and anti-NP alliance.

A recent Markinor opinion poll among whites in the Witwatersrand (an area containing almost one-third of all white voters) found that 27 per cent supported the IFP, against 40 per cent who would vote for the NP (*The Economist*, 14 August 1992). In addition, an opinion poll conducted by Africart found that only 32 per cent of Afrikaners preferred F.W. de Klerk as leader of the Afrikaners against the 36.4 per cent who supported the three right-wing leaders, Viljoen, Terre Blanche and Hartzenberg. As Lawrence Schlemmer observed early in 1993: 'Observers are beginning to ask whether or not the governing party and its support structures will hold together long enough to enter the new government of national unity. At times it seems like a race against political odds' (*Prospects*, ii/1, March–April 1993).

While it is not certain whether such a prospective right-wing parliamentary alliance would be able to achieve an overall majority in the House of Assembly, it is certain that even if it does, it would not be able to reverse the settlement reached at the multiparty forum without pushing the country instantly into a bloody civil war.

However, this scenario is extremely remote, especially since the last session of the tricameral parliament occurred in December 1993. This final session represented the last real opportunity for those disaffected with the NP to defect to the right, but in the end all NP MPs voted in favour of the interim constitution (formally titled the Constitution of the Republic of South Africa Act), with only the right wing opposing it. If the Freedom Alliance agree to participate in the elections and their demands for changes to the interim constitution are met, one more sitting of parliament could take place before April 1994. Should the Freedom Alliance not join in and opt for a unilateral secession, anything could still happen, including a mass defection away from the NP to the right, but under such circumstances the existing parliament itself would lose all relevance as the country would be plunged into chaos.

A coup d'état

A slightly more plausible scenario pertains to the prospect of a coup d'état, targeted either against the NP government before the 1994 election, or against an ANC-led power-sharing coalition, after the election but before the command structure of the security forces has been altered. The possibility of a military take-over of the NP government was never a strong possibility in South Africa during the early part of the de Klerk administration: the officer corps in the SADF had a reputation for respecting civilian authority and was too professional to take up arms if it was unhappy with the government.

These perceptions changed early in 1992, exemplified by the NP's defeat in the Potchefstroom by-election as a consequence of the CP's relatively convincing claim that the NP had lost the support of the majority of whites. During the run-up to the March 1992 referendum, dissent within the security forces had intensified. The rumbles of discontent led to speculation by the London-based weekly, *Africa Confidential*, that the referendum was a pre-emptive strike to stave off the possibility of a military coup from increasingly unhappy army and police forces. Other events which strengthened this perception were the many resignations of high-ranking officers for political reasons and the fact that the estimated support for the right wing among the police had grown to between 80 and 95 per cent, and in the SADF to between 70 and 80 per cent (*Vrye Weekblad*, 17–23 January 1992). Other analysts mentioned the distinct possibility of a 'soft coup', i.e. the withdrawal of cooperation with the government by the military, and suggested that this threat has been used repeatedly to get certain reform policies cancelled and has forced the government to accommodate the wishes of the security forces, e.g. by ramming through the 'Further Indemnity Bill' which pardoned politically motivated crimes (Adam and Moodley 1993: 155).

The overwhelming victory of the government's Yes campaign in the March 1992 referendum conclusively destroyed the perception that the NP was reforming without a white mandate, and temporarily laid to rest any thoughts of intervention by wayward elements within the military. However, from the NP government's point of view, the situation *vis-à-vis* the military again deteriorated rapidly thereafter. By the end of 1992 and throughout 1993 rapidly increasing rates of violence and crime, the growing number of attacks directed at white farmers, police and whites in general, gave rise to the perception – even in liberal circles – that the government had lost control of the country and that the growing anarchy had endangered the future of the white community.

The feelings of resentment among civilians and the security establishment were exacerbated by the chaos and racial tension that followed Hani's death in April 1993, and it came as no surprise when a group of former generals, including the former head of the SADF, Constand Viljoen, officially joined the right wing. The SADF general staff recently put this figure at 60 per cent. It is logical that their presence in the right wing could pose a dilemma to the 40,000 white members of the permanent force, of whom probably more than half sympathize with the right. While the claim of one of the right-wing generals, Tienie Groenewald, that he could call on 500,000 white civilian force members to support the right-wing cause, was an exaggeration, the AVF estimate that it had the support of at least 100,000 of the 140,000 members of the white commandos seems plausible.

In August 1993 an ominous development occurred which was the strongest indication yet of a possible link between Viljoen, who still enjoys tremendous respect within the security forces, and the SADF. At about the same time as Viljoen called on his right-wing supporters to join the commandos in August 1993, the SADF began to supply these commando units with assault weapons. In the town of Middelburg in the eastern Cape, each white household received such weapons, not unlike the Israeli and Swiss defence structure in which civilian force members keep their weapons at home. While the SADF claimed that the issuing of weapons to whites was purely defensive, the implication is that it is arming the unofficial military wing of the AVF. Even if a new ANC-dominated government succeeds in ridding the security forces of troublesome officers, it would leave a highly armed civilian force on the loose. What should concern the present government, and a future one as well, is that weapons which are supposedly handed out for 'defensive purposes' are equally effective when used in an offensive capacity. And while it is not likely that the security forces as a whole would defect to the right, it is possible that a few renegade artillery units, supported by a large contingent of commandos, could forcibly occupy parts of the country dominated by whites, in what could be regarded as a series of mini-secessions and white enclaves controlled by the military. This brings us to the third scenario, a secession by the right wing, with the inevitable prospects of a civil war.

Right-wing secession
The strongest argument against the military attempting to seize power can be found in the fact that South Africa has moved so far down the road to a new dispensation that the developments since February 1990 can truly be regarded as irreversible in all respects. Not only is the black community much better armed than before, but the expectations of the majority have been raised to such an extent that even a white military regime employing all the force at its disposal would not succeed in quelling a revolution by the black majority at this stage. This much is obvious even to the hard-liners in the right wing (and in the security forces), which explains why the emphasis has shifted to securing Afrikaner self-determination in a small territory rather than winning control of the whole country. For most of the right wing, self-determination is akin to the creation of an

independent white homeland, which can come about either through a peaceful partitioning or through a violent secession.

The numerous secessions and secessions-within-secessions that racked the territories of the now defunct federations of the Soviet Union, Yugoslavia and Czechoslovakia have led to disastrous consequences in terms of the loss of human lives, the destruction of property and the revival of xenophobic nationalism. The re-emergence of the demand for self-determination worldwide has resulted in 22 new countries being admitted to the UN over the past two years, and if the right wing could have its way, an Afrikaner *volkstaat* would soon constitute a 23rd new UN state.

However, secession is not a popular topic either in South Africa or in the rest of the world, as no government is in favour of voluntarily allowing the dismemberment of its territory and losing a section of its population and economic resources if it can be helped. The ANC used this logic when it indicated unambiguously that it would not tolerate the creation of a sovereign white *volkstaat*. Apart from the political and economic arguments against secession, a right-wing secession would perpetuate white domination in a part of South Africa that the ANC fought to liberate, causing understandable moral resentment against such a possibility.[1]

It is therefore clear that secession, whether by the white right or in conjunction with the IFP in Natal, would be resisted with absolute force by an ANC-dominated government. The prospects of a successful right-wing secession in such a civil war scenario would depend on the degree of military support and the availability of military skills and technology for such an option. It should be remembered that the co-option of the generals into supporting the *volkstaat* cause provided the right with much of the counter-revolutionary skills and technical know-how of the Botha era, as personified by members of the former securocrat establishment – these are the same securocrat ideologists who devised the theory of the 'total onslaught' and who transformed South Africa into the world's eighth nuclear power during the late 1970s.

With some military back-up, technical know-how and the alleged loyalty of the well-trained and equipped forces of the 100,000 members of the commandos which the AVF claimed to enjoy, a secessionist right wing might be able successfully to create and defend a secessionist region in one or more right-wing strongholds and enclaves in the north or eastern Transvaal. For without a properly equipped army, the logistical support of neighbouring states and the moral acquiescence of the international community, the prospect of a secessionist Afrikaner state is extremely poor and would inevitably result, at most, in a rebellion or terrorist war of limited scope.

The alternative to a secessionist civil war would be for the ANC to decide that it would be better off without the disruptive forces of right-wing Afrikaner nationalism. If it managed to contain the scope of a seceding region to manageable proportions, i.e. without disproportionate economic and territorial loss to the remainder of South Africa, a mutually agreed secession cannot be excluded. In terms of conflict regulation or on the maximin principle (i.e. the option with the 'least worst' outcome), such a peaceful Afrikaner secession would be comparable to the partitioning of Czechoslovakia and preferable to the violent disintegration of Yugoslavia. Furthermore, some would argue that the process of forging a South African nationhood would be better served without the reactionary and recalcitrant forces of Afrikaner and perhaps Zulu nationalism.

Accommodating the right wing

Finally, the most likely scenario is one in which a compromise is reached between the demand for a sovereign Afrikaner state and the proposals of the ANC and its power-sharing partners. The demand of the right wing for Afrikaner self-determination has so far been projected and interpreted (with the exception of the AVU and Boshoff) as a demand for complete political independence. In response the NP and the ANC have been firm in their absolute rejection of granting sovereignty to any group/people, while the liberation movement has also indicated that it rejected an ethnically based 'solution' or an autonomous region in which the political boundaries coincide with ethnic or racial settlement.

However, as the country edged closer to the 1994 elections, both sides have indicated a softening in previous absolute positions on the dual issues of sovereignty and an ethnic base for such sovereignty. Viljoen's AVF indicated in September 1993 that the relationship of the proposed *volkstaat* with the central government could vary somewhere between federalism and confederalism. The AVF's insistence on incorporating into its *volkstaat* constitution the 'right to secede' clearly implies an autonomous but not independent region, and is an indication that the AVF has accepted that self-determination does not necessarily imply full sovereignty. The ANC has also appeared to soften. In June 1993 Mandela suggested that the organization might consider granting 'exclusive powers' to Afrikaner nationalists in a regional dispensation if they could point out the boundaries of such a region, and as long as it was a part of a federal, united South Africa. In September 1993 he admitted that the ANC was in the process of negotiating with the right wing, and although the organization could not accommodate 'their demand in the way they have put it' (i.e. complete sovereignty), there was room for compromise to accommodate 'the basic demand of a people wanting a particular region in which to run their own affairs' (*Globe and Mail*, 25 September 1993). Although negotiations broke down in February 1994, there is little doubt that these will be resumed, especially if a resort to violence does not bring about the required result on either side.

Should the multiparty forum or an ANC-led coalition government accept the demands for a federal/autonomous region for Afrikaner nationalists with the principle of non-discriminatory citizenship rights, it would amount to the constitutional recognition of ethnic diversity without racism and discrimination, and would constitute a safety valve for the potentially explosive aspirations of contemporary Afrikaner nationalism. Although the degree of autonomy would have to be negotiated, the minimum requirement from the Afrikaner nationalist point of view would entail the drawing of borders which would ensure an Afrikaner majority within the region. For the remainder, normal federalist principles regulating the interaction between the central government and federal units on matters such as finances, law enforcement, taxation, education and welfare, could be employed, although certain cultural aspects, due to the legacy of apartheid, would be extremely sensitive. For example it would not be acceptable for an Afrikaner federal region to implement any legislation which could be viewed as ethnocentric, for example, as the province of Quebec had done by unilaterally declaring French as its official language and promulgating discriminative legislation forbidding English on outdoor signs in that province.

In such an accommodationist scenario, it could be expected that the right would contest elections not only within its federal region, but also on a national level, and considering its current support, it would not be inconceivable for a right-wing party to obtain the necessary 0.5 per cent of the vote required for a proportional representation in parliament and the 5 per cent required for membership of the executive.

South Africa approaches its first non-racial, democratic general election and the end of 300 years of white domination in April 1994. It remains a deeply divided society, racked with violence; low-key civil war since 1990 has resulted in over 15,000 political deaths. An array of racial, ethnic, ideological, regional and class cleavages presents a formidable obstacle to its prospects for a peaceful transition and the achievement of a harmonious, non-racial, non-ethnic democracy. While the white right wing is merely one component of a much wider challenge posed by the country's pluralism, it is an important one, which, if ignored, threatens to disrupt the entire process of transformation. Although right-wing Afrikaner nationalism and its objective of self-determination are supported by less than two million people out of a total population of 38 million, its ability to disrupt, wreck and destroy goes far beyond its numerical strength and its access to the instruments of destruction – as the destructive and deadly force of scorned ethnonational aspirations in similarly divided societies can bear witness. It is doubtful whether it would be possible forcefully to assimilate this group, or to satisfy their demands through the creation of Afrikaner 'cultural parks', a suggestion once made by the political scientist Marinus Wiechers. Neither would a unilateral dismemberment of South Africa by right-wing separatists be acceptable to the majority of South Africans. Therefore the obvious solution would be to accommodate ethnic aspirations of the right within the parameters of democracy and within one constitution, if not for moral, economic or political reasons, then at least for the purposes of conflict regulation in a deeply divided society such as South Africa.

Notes

Chapter 1

1 For a detailed account of *broedertwis* in the transition from apartheid, see Giliomee (1992).
2 During the early 1990s the right wing founded exclusive Afrikaner schools based on similar principles, but called 'Christian people's education'.
3 Ironically, the 150th commemoration was also hijacked by Afrikaner nationalists, but this time in the form of the right-wing Afrikaner Volkswag; see also Chapter 2, n. 13.
4 Its immigration scheme allowed 60,000 predominantly British immigrants to enter the country during 1947–48.
5 Although the NP had received 52 per cent of the seats in parliament, it had received only 38 per cent of the total number of votes.
6 Even the *verligte* Piet Koornhof objected on occasion to being 'slandered' as a liberal. In January 1993, Koornhof, previously the South African ambassador in Washington, 'shocked' the Afrikaner establishment when he left his wife in favour of a 'coloured' girl less than half his age.
7 At the same time, however, Treurnicht used the Broederbond to delay the implementation of the new sports policy.
8 88 per cent of Afrikaners were urbanized by 1970, with 65 per cent holding white-collar jobs (Lipton 1986: 307).
9 The Information Scandal concerned corruption and the illegal use of state funds by a number of officials in the Department of Information to improve the image of the NP government abroad.
10 The HNP, sensing that it was about to be overtaken by a more powerful right-wing party, did not send any representatives to attend.
11 With regard to the views of students on security issues Gagiano's findings varied considerably: firstly, sympathetic support for the security establishment (still very powerful in 1988) ranged from

212

about 84 per cent of Afrikaners to the 33.5 per cent of English-speaking students; secondly, only 7.7 per cent of Afrikaner and 27 per cent of English-speaking students were prepared to accept an ANC government, while 34 per cent and 30 per cent respectively of both language groups would either emigrate or physically resist such a possibility; thirdly, 10.7 per cent of Afrikaner students favoured partition (the CP's policy), and a further 56 per cent favoured a system incorporating white control or a racial federation (close to the NP philosophy at the time and the CP's today), and only 26.6 per cent of Afrikaner students supported a geographical federation (the DP policy at the time and the NP policy today).

12 The desire of Afrikaners not to lose their sovereignty again is present not only in the ideology of the right wing but also in the strategies of the NP, which has incorporated into its post-1989 reform policies the willingness to share power without 'capitulation'.

13 The *Vierkleur* was used in 1991 by the Boksburg Town Council to show its affinity with the right-wing cause.

14 Ironically, an office-bearer in the AWB, Manie Maritz, was himself an OB activist during the Second World War.

15 While Meyer was merely a passive supporter of the OB during the 1940s, Vorster became actively involved in sabotage and was interned by the UP government during the Second World War.

16 The 'total onslaught' was a doctrine developed during the P.W. Botha era by the security establishment and the Minister of Defence, Magnus Malan. It was a smoke-screen to mobilize whites into supporting authoritarian measures implemented by the state which were intended to curtail civil liberties and to suppress most forms of democratic anti-apartheid protest in the name of anti-communism. It purported to suggest that the country and its strategic resources were being threatened by international communism and its surrogate forces in Africa, such as the Cubans, while the ANC was also viewed as part of the onslaught.

Chapter 2

1 Markinor, Marketing and Media, June 1993.

2 Of the 19 defecting NP MPs under D.F. Malan four were from the OFS and one from the Transvaal (Vatcher 1965: 57).

3 The concept of radical partition as a last-resort option to a situation of anarchy was mentioned again later by Giliomee as one of the possible last-option scenarios for South Africa. Giliomee argued that should a full-scale black–white civil war erupt in South Africa, it could result in mass population shifts and, eventually, partition. He predicted that the line of such a partition could follow the pattern of white settlement before the Great Trek, i.e. the area west of an imaginary line stretching from Upington to Port Elizabeth. The chances of such an outcome would be

strengthened if the settlement reached between the NP government and the black opposition was based on federal principles and resulted in two or three federal units being formed in the western region in which whites and coloureds were in the majority (*The Argus*, 6 April 1991).

4   The two defecting AVU MPs indicated that they might join the AVF, a clear indication that three months after its founding, the AVF sought to develop into an organization with its own identity, rather than just an umrella body for diverse right-wing groups.

5   Interview, H. van de Graaf, news editor of *Die Afrikaner*, 19 July 1991.

6   Economists painted a bleak picture of economic prospects for the *volkstaat*: a very small economy, dependent almost completely on agriculture; very few job opportunities; a labour force which may be totally over-qualified for an agriculturally based economy; and a lack of investment in the manufacturing sector (*Finansies en Tegniek*, 31 August 1990).

7   Nelson Mandela's speech at a graduation ceremony at the University of Cape Town, 30 November 1990.

8   The irony of the 1988 commemoration of the Great Trek was the fact that it occurred against the background of a sharply divided Afrikaner people, while similar celebrations in 1938 (or the 1949 jamboree) had served to strengthen Afrikaner unity.

9   At Ventersdorp in the Transvaal white farmers attacked a squatter camp on the farm Goedgevonden but were forced back by the police using live ammunition.

10 Allegations were made against the Military Intelligence and other elements which regarded Namibian independence as treason to the whites, but attempts to investigate the issue were thwarted by the SADF.

11 It was for long the 'plight' of the white English-speaking community to be 'accused' of being liberal; liberalism was equated with political weakness and lack of patriotism in the mind of the Afrikaner nationalist.

12 Beyers' inclusive definition of Afrikaner ethnicity, i.e. the inclusion of sympathetic English-speakers in the CP's support-base, is reminiscent of the NP's earlier attempts to broaden its own support-base through ethnic engineering, and gives practical substance to Horowitz's argument (1985) that ethnic groups are re-created and re-defined at will, in accordance with the interests of the ruling élite and ethnic engineers.

13 See *Patriot*, 3 November 1989; 12 January 1990; 11 January 1991.

Chapter 3

1   The electoral system distorted the right's true strength, for on a proportional basis it would have received 50 seats instead of 22 for its 30 per cent share of the vote.

2   A survey conducted by M&M in July 1989 indicated that 36 per

cent of respondents would not vote for the NP because of its record on the economy.

3   The Rivonia trialists were the eight members of the ANC, including Nelson Mandela, Govan Mbeki and Walter Sisulu, who were arrested in the suburb of Rivonia in 1963 and sentenced in 1964 to life imprisonment for admitting to sabotage and preparing for guerrilla warfare.

4   Mandela had also been received by P.W. Botha six months earlier. Mandela later indicated that he was particularly impressed that Botha poured the tea himself during their meeting. Mandela's visit to Tuynhuis, the official residence of the State President in Cape Town, to meet with de Klerk, represented the first of many meetings between the two men. In retrospect it became the starting point of a relationship between them which, although sometimes stormy, was founded on mutual respect and a belief in the personal integrity of one another and which greatly facilitated the negotiation process.

5   See Schrire 1991: 139; *The Argus*, 29 November 1991; *Rapport*, 23 February 1992.

6   For the right wing, Winnie Mandela, the ex-wife of Nelson Mandela, is its worst nightmare come true and her words and deeds have so far approximated the preconceived ideas of the right about blacks as a whole, with echoes in other parts of Africa. She has also given many moderate whites an impression of a worst-case scenario for new South Africa, especially as Mrs Mandela stands a good chance of being appointed to a new cabinet. On the other hand, if the CP or AVF participate in the 1994 election and manage to receive 5 per cent of the vote – a very real possibility – they will also have one or two of their MPs appointed to the cabinet – an even 'worse' worst-case scenario for the average South African voter! Winnie Mandela's fall from grace among the left was evident from her failure a few years back to win the leadership of the ANC's Women's League, her resignation from her post as the head of the ANC's Welfare Department and her separation from her husband. However, her standing among the extreme left, the ANC militants, and youth, remained high and she greatly benefited in this respect from the support of other ANC hard-liners such as Peter Mokaba and Chris Hani. She positioned herself clearly to the left of the ANC leadership with her warnings against power-sharing between the ANC and NP and through her accusation that the ANC had gone to bed with the NP for reasons of political expediency. Her tactics paid off, for in December 1993 she defeated Albertina Sisulu to win back the powerful position at the head of the ANC's Women's League.

Chapter 4

1   The 'Koos document' was a considerable political (and financial) windfall to the NP, which sold it at R6 a copy to interested parties.

2   Contrary to his threat, Hoon remained a member of the CP even
    after the party had joined the multiparty forum in 1993.
3   While he was at the Codesa venue, van der Merwe also requested
    and received the autograph of Joe Slovo of the SACP.
4   In contrast to Treurnicht's view that 'reforms were not
    irreversible', the Koos document, representing the minority view
    in the CP, argued that reforms were in fact irreversible: 'The State
    President has had some success with his immoral efforts to make
    his reforms irreversible, i.e. that they become so permanent and
    fundamental that no future government could turn them around
    again' (van der Merwe 1990: 12).
5   See *Patriot*, 6 July 1990; 10 August 1990; 14 December 1990; 18
    January 1991; 15 February 1991; 15 March 1991; 5 July 1991;
    Rapport, 7 June 1992; 14 May 1993; 21 May 1993.
6   The bitter irony of the Strydom case is that he was found sane by
    the court in spite of his ostensibly deranged actions, and released
    from prison after four years as part of a general amnesty to
    'terrorists' of all ideological persuasions.
7   As illustrated by the 15,000 crime-related murders, 3000 political
    deaths and an average per day of 40 murders, 62 rapes and 355
    assaults in 1991 alone (*Prospects*, Vol. 1 No. 4, December 1992).

Conclusion

1   As another example, consider Canada which faces a loss of 25 per
    cent of the population and GDP, and 15 per cent of its territory, if
    Quebec secedes.

Glossary

aksie	action/front
apartheid	separateness
baasskap	domination
bittereinders	lit. bitter-enders; Boers who fought to the bitter end of the Anglo-Boer War
blanke	white
Boer	farmer, citizen of former Boer Republics
Boerestaat	Boer state
Brandwag	lit. fire guard; sentry/sentinel
Broederbond	lit. band of brothers
broedertwis	strife among brothers/Afrikaners
draadsitter	fence-sitter
Federale Volksbeleggings	federal people's investment
geldmagte	money powers/forces
Helpmekaar	lit. 'help each other'
hensoppers	Boers who surrendered prematurely
herstigte	reconstituted (in political context)
hervormde	reformed (in religious context)
laager	protective circle [originally of wagons; now also applied metaphorically to defensive political attitudes]
rooi/swart gevaar	communist/black threat
strafkommando	punishment command
stryd	struggle
tuiswagte	home guard

217

verbond	covenant
vereniging	organization/society
verkramp	conservative, less open to change
verlig	enlightened, moderate
vierkleur	lit. 'four-colour' [flag]
volk	nation/people
volksbeweging	people's movement/front
volksfront	people's front
volkseenheid	people's unity
volkseie	people's own (culture)
volkskapitalisme	people's capitalism
volksleer	people's army
volkstaat	people's state
volkstaters	term applied to the pragmatic wing of the CP
Vryheidsraad	freedom Council
volkswag	people's watch

Note
All long quotes in Afrikaans have been translated into English by the author and are denoted in the book by the word [translation].

Concise Bibliography

Newspapers
Dates of publication of the following South African sources are cited in the text: *Die Afrikaner; The Argus; Beeld; Die Burger; Business Day; Cape Times; Citizen; Daily Dispatch; Eastern Province Herald; Finance Week; Financial Mail; Finansies en Tegniek; Insig; Leadership; Monitor; Natal Mercury; Patriot; Pretoria News; Prospects; Rand Daily Mail; Rapport; Southern Africa Report; The Sowetan; Star; Sunday Star; Sunday Times; Sunday Tribune; Die Vaderland; Vrye Weekblad; Weekly Mail*

Coverage from the following publications is also acknowledged: *Africa Confidential* (UK); *The Daily Telegraph* (UK); *Globe and Mail* (Canada); *The Economist* (UK); *The Guardian* (UK); *International Herald Tribune* (USA); *New Statesman and Society* (UK); *Newsweek* (USA); *The Sunday Times* (UK); *Time* (USA).

Parliamentary and party political sources
Boerestaat Party: '*Nuusbrief*', 1990–91
CP: 'Eighth Transvaal Congress', 1990
——Information pamphlet, February 1989
——'Election News', 1989
——'Maitland by-election News', 1991
——Announcement by Dr. A.P. Treurnicht Regarding the White Paper on Land Reform, 1991
Hansard 1989–92
NP: 'New Action: Five Year Plan of Action', 1989
——'Key Issues – Election' 6 September 1989

Books and periodicals

Adam, H. 'Options for South Africa', *Journal of International Affairs* xl/2 (Winter/Spring 1987)

Adam, H. and Giliomee, H. *Ethnic Power Mobilized: Can South Africa Change?* (New Haven: Yale University Press, 1979)

Adam, H. and Giliomee, H. *The Rise and Crisis of Afrikaner Power* (Cape Town: David Philip, 1979)

Adam, H. and Moodley, K. *South Africa without Apartheid* (Cape Town: Maskew Miller Longman, 1986)

Adam, H. and Moodley, K. *The Negotiated Revolution* (Houghton: Jonathan Ball Publishers, 1993)

Barratt, J. *Conflict and Compromise in South Africa* (Cape Town: David Philip, 1980)

Bekker, S. and Grobbelaar, J. 'The white right wing movement in South Africa: before and after the May 1987 election', in Van Vuuren, D.J. et al (Eds) *South African Election 1987*. (Pinetown: Owen Burgess Publishers, 1987)

Bekker, S., Grobbelaar, J. and Evans, R. 'Vir volk en vaderland/A guide to the white right', *Indicator Project South Africa*. Centre for Social Development Studies, 1989

Berger, P.L. and Godsell, B. (Eds) *A Future South Africa* (Cape Town: Human & Rousseau/Tafelberg, 1988)

Blenk, J. and Von der Ropp, K. *Aussenpolitik*, xxiii/3 (1976)

Booyse, W.J. 'The extremist right: joke or threat?', *South African Foundation Review* (September 1990)

Boshoff, C. 'Power sharing: an Afrikaner point of view', *SABRA: Journal of Racial Affairs* xxxviii/3 (July 1987)

—— 'It is partition or black domination', *Monitor* (April 1990)

Brewer, J. (Ed.) *Can South Africa Survive?* (Bergvlei: Southern Book Publishers, 1989)

Bruwer, P.F. et al *Afrikanerland: 'n Gebiedsaanduiding* (Morgenzon: Oranjewerkers Promosies, 1990)

Charney, C. 'Class conflict and the National Party split', *Journal of Southern African Studies*, x/2 (April 1984)

Crighton, E. and MacIver, M.A. 'The evolution of ethnic conflict', *Comparative Politics* xxiii/2 (January 1991)

Davenport, T.R.H. *South Africa: A Modern History* (Johannesburg: Macmillan South Africa Publishers, 1977)

De Klerk, W. *The Man in his Time: F.W. De Klerk* (Johannesburg: Jonathan Ball Publishers, 1991)

De Klerk, W.A. *The Puritans in Africa: The Story of Afrikanerdom* (London: Rex Collings, 1975)

Deutsch, K.W. *Nationalism and its Alternatives* (New York: Alfred A. Knopf, 1969)

Du Preez, J.M. *Africana Afrikaner: Master Symbols in South African School Text Books* (Alberton: Librarius, 1986)

Du Toit, A. and Giliomee, H. *Afrikaner Political Thought, 1780–1850* (Cape Town: David Philip, 1983)

De Villiers, M. *White Tribe Dreaming* (New York: Viking, 1987)

Elphick, R. and Giliomee, H. (Eds.) *The Shaping of South African Society, 1652–1820* (Cape Town: Longman/Penguin Southern Africa, 1979)

Esterhuyse, W.P. 'The 1987 election: a retreat into the laager?', in Van Vuuren, D.J. et al (Eds) *South African Election 1987* (Pinetown: Owen Burgess Publishers, 1987)

Gagiano, J. 'Ruling group cohesion', in Giliomee, H. and Gagiano, J. (Eds) *The Elusive Search for Peace: South Africa/Israel/Northern Ireland* (Cape Town: Oxford University Press, 1990)

Giliomee, H. 'Broedertwis: Intra-Afrikaner conflicts in the transition from apartheid', *African Affairs* xci (1992)

Giliomee, H. and Schlemmer, L. *Negotiating South Africa's Future* (Johannesburg: Southern Book Publishers, 1989)

—— 'Afrikaner Politics 1977–87: from Afrikaner Nationalist rule to central state hegemony', in Brewer, J. (Ed.) *Can South Africa Survive?* (Bergvlei: Southern Book Publishers, 1989)

Hanf, T. et al *South Africa: The Chances of Peaceful Change* (Bloomington: Indiana University Press, 1981)

Hofmeyer, J. 'How white political opinions have changed: 1977–1990', *Monitor* (April 1990)

Horowitz, D.L. *Ethnic Groups in Conflict* (Berkeley, Los Angeles and London: University of California Press, 1985)

—— *A Democratic South Africa? Constitutional Engineering in a Divided Society* (Cape Town: Oxford University Press, 1991)

Hugo, P. 'Towards darkness and death: racial demonology in South Africa', paper read at the Silver Jubilee Conference of the African Studies Association of the United Kingdom (14–16 September 1988)

The Institute of Criminology, University of Cape Town, 'Back to the laager: the rise of white right wing violence in South

Africa' (1991)

Isaacs, H.R. *Idols of the Tribe* (New York: Harper and Row, 1975)

Kemp, A. *Victory or Violence: The Story of the AWB* (Pretoria: Forma Publishers, 1990)

Kotze, P. and Beyers, C. *Opmars van die AWB* (Morgenzon: Oranjewerkers Promosies, 1988)

Laurie, D. 'Mathematical models for election analysis and their application to white South African politics in the period 1981 to 1987', in Van Vuuren, D.J. et al (Eds) *South African Election 1987* (Pinetown: Owen Burgess Publishers, 1987)

Leach, G. *The Afrikaners: Their Last Great Trek* (Johannesburg: Southern Book Publishers, 1989)

Leatt, J., Kneifel, T. and Nurnberger, K. *Contending Ideologies in South Africa* (Cape Town: David Philip, 1986)

Lemon, A. *Apartheid in Transition* (Worcester: Billing and Sons Ltd, 1987)

Linz, J.J. 'From primordialism to nationalism', in Tiryakian, E.A. and Rogowski, R. *New Nationalisms of the Developed West* (Boston: Allen and Unwin, 1985)

Lipton, M. *Capitalism & Apartheid: South Africa 1910–1986* (Cape Town: David Philip, 1986)

Loubser, J.A. *The Apartheid Bible: A Critical Review of Racial Theology in South Africa* (Cape Town: Maskew Miller Longman, 1987)

Lubbe, W.J.G. *Witman, waar is jou Tuisland?* (Pretoria: Oranjewerkers Promosies, 1983)

M& M Marketing and Opinion Surveys, 1982–91

Maasdorp, G. 'Forms of partition', in Rotberg, R.I. *Conflict and Compromise in South Africa* (Cape Town: David Philip, 1980)

MacCrone, I.D. *Race Attitudes in South Africa* (Johannesburg: Witwatersrand University Press, 1957)

Marais, J.A. 'Die verloening van die Verwoerd-denkbeeld', *SABRA 16de Verwoerd Gedenklesing* (1980)

Manzo, K. and McGowan, P. 'The fears of prominent Afrikaners: is racial reconciliation possible in South Africa?', unpublished paper (July 1989)

Moodie, T.D. *The Rise of Afrikanerdom: Power, Apartheid, and the Afrikaner Civil Religion* (Berkeley, Los Angeles and London: University of California Press, 1975)

Newman, S. 'Does modernization breed ethnic political

Conflict?', *World Politics*, xliii/4 (April 1991)

O'Meara, D. *Volkskapitalisme* (Johannesburg: Ravan Press, 1983)

Pelzer, A.N. *Die Afrikaner Broederbond: Eerste 50 Jaar* (Cape Town: Tafelberg Uitgewers, 1979)

Pienaar, S. *Getuie van Groot Tye* (Cape Town: Tafelberg Uitgewers, 1979)

Pottinger, B. *The Imperial Presidency: P.W. Botha, the First Ten Years* (Johannesburg: Southern Book Publishers, 1988)

Rees, M. and Day, C. *Muldergate* (Johannesburg: Macmillan South Africa Publishers, 1980)

Rhoodie, E. *P.W. Botha: The Last Betrayal* (Melville: S.A. Politics, 1989)

Rhoodie, N.J. et al 'The perceptions of urban whites of socio-political change in South Africa', in van Vuuren, D.J. et al (Eds) *South Africa: A Plural Society in Transition* (Durban: Butterworths, 1985)

Rhoodie, N.J. and Couper, M.P. 'White perceptions of the fundamental issues surrounding the election of 6 May 1987', in Van Vuuren, D.J. et al (Eds) *South African Election 1987* (Pinetown: Owen Burgess Publishers, 1987)

Ridge, S.G.M. 'Chosen people or heirs of paradise; trekkers, settlers, and some implications of myth', in Malan, C. *Race and Literature* (Pinetown: Owen Burgess Publishers, 1987)

Ries, A. and Dommisse, E. *Broedertwis* (Cape Town: Tafelberg, 1983)

Riordan, R. 'Consolidating negative attitudes', *Monitor* (April 1990)

—— 'Interview with Koos van der Merwe', *Monitor* (August 1990)

Rotberg, I.R. and Barratt, J. *Conflict and Compromise in South Africa* (Cape Town: David Philip, 1980)

Rothschild, J. *Ethnicity: A Conceptual Framework* (New York: Columbia University Press, 1981)

SABRA (South African Bureau for Racial Affairs): *'n Nuwe Grondwet vir die RSA: Die Afrikaner se Stand en Tockoms* (Pretoria: SABRA, 1985)

Schlemmer, L. 'The National Party: ideology, aims, role and strategy', in Van Vuuren, D.J. et al (Eds) *South African Election 1987* (Pinetown: Owen Burgess Publishers, 1987)

—— 'South Africa's National Party government', in Berger, P.L.

and Godsell, B. (Eds) *A Future South Africa* (Cape Town: Human & Rousseau/Tafelberg, 1988)

—— 'Cutting it very fine', *Prospects* ii/1 (March/April 1993)

Schoeman, Ben *My Lewe in die Politiek* (Johannesburg: Perskor-Uitgewers, 1978)

Schoeman, B.M. *Van Malan tot Verwoerd* (Cape Town and Pretoria: Human & Rousseau, 1973)

—— *Jaap Marais: Stryd is Lewe* (Pretoria: Aktuele Publikasies, 1980)

—— *Vorster se 1 000 Dae* (Cape Town and Pretoria: Human & Rousseau, 1974)

Schrire, R. *Adapt or Die: The End of White Politics in South Africa* (USA: Ford Foundation/Foreign Policy Association, 1991)

Scruton, R. *A Dictionary of Political Thought* (London: Pan Books, 1982)

Serfontein, J.H.P. *Brotherhood of Power: An Expose of the Secret Afrikaner Broederbond* (London: Rex Collings Limited, 1979)

—— *Die Verkrampte Aanslag* (Cape Town and Pretoria: Human & Rousseau, 1970)

Simpson, G.E. and Yinger, J.M. *Racial and Cultural Minorities: An Analysis of Prejudice and Discrimination* (New York and London: Plenum Press, 1985)

Thompson, L. *The Political Mythology of Apartheid* (New Haven and London: Yale University Press, 1985)

Tiryakian, E. 'Sociological realism: partition for South Africa', *Social Forces* xlvi/2 (1967)

Treurnicht, A.P. *Credo van 'n Afrikaner* (Cape Town: Tafelberg, 1975)

—— 'A race against time', *Leadership* vii/6 (1988)

van der Berghe, P.L. *Race and Racism* (New York: John Wiley & Sons, 1978)

van der Merwe, J.H. et al *Strategie vir 'n Veranderde Situasie*, October 1990 [CP policy document, also known as the Koos document]

van Rensburg, H. *Their Paths Crossed Mine* (South Africa: Central News Agency, 1956)

van Rooyen, J. 'The white rightwing in South African politics. A descriptive study of its roots; an assessment of its strength, and an elucidation of its territorial policies and political strategies: 1969–1992', Ph.D. dissertation, University of Cape

Town (1992)

van Tonder, R. *Boerestaat* (Randburg: Die Boerestaat Party, 1990)

van Vuuren, D.J. et al (Eds) *South African Election 1987* (Pinetown: Owen Burgess Publishers, 1987)

van Zyl Slabbert, F. and Welsh, D. *South Africa's Options: Strategies for Sharing Power* (Cape Town: David Philip, 1979)

Vatcher, W.H. *White Laager* (New York: Frederick A. Praeger Publishers, 1965)

Vereniging van Oranjewerkers: *Oranje Perspektief*, 1987

—— 'n Plan van hoop vir Afrikanervoortbestaan', 1991

—— Grondwet, 1991

Welsh, D. 'The political economy of Afrikaner nationalism', in Leftwich, A. (Ed.) *South Africa: Economic Growth and Political Change* (London: Allison and Busby, 1974)

—— 'The politics of white supremacy', in Thompson, L. and Butler, J. *Change in Contemporary South Africa* (Berkeley and Los Angeles: University of California Press, 1975)

Welsh, D. 'South Africa's ultra-right', *Patterns of Prejudice* xxii/4 (1988); xxiii/1 (1989)

Zille, H. 'The right wing in South African Politics', in Berger, P.L. and Godsell, B. (Eds) *A Future South Africa* (Cape Town: Human & Rousseau/Tafelberg, 1988)

Index

Political parties and other organizations are entered under their full titles, Afrikaans and English. Abbreviations will be found on pp vii–ix.

Names beginning with de, van, etc., are indexed under the preposition.

As far as practicable, sub-headings are in chronological order.

226

Het Volk party, 11
Heyns, Johan, 86
Hofmeyer, Jan, 11
Holomisa, General Bantu, 165
homeland partition *see* Group
  Areas Act; self-
  determination; *volkstaat*
  concept
Hoofstad newspaper, 18, 19, 26
Hoon, Jan, 159, 165, 166, 189
Horowitz, Donald, 3, 35–6, 37, 55,
  117–18, 201
Human Sciences Research Coun-
  cil, 111

Immorality Act (1950), 16, 125
Indian community
  power sharing, 25, 120, 124
  proposed homelands, 158, 159
Influx Control measures, 126
Information Scandal (Mulder-
  gate), 22
Inkatha Freedom Party (IFP)
  support, 64, 105
  Cosag and other parties, 74,
    103, 111, 150, 165
  constitutional negotiations and
    prospects, 110, 170, 197,
    204
  see also Buthelezi, Mangosuthu
Institute for Strategic Analysis
  (INSA), 84
Ireland, Northern, comparison to
  SA, 55
Israel Vision Church (*Gemeente
  van die Verbondsvolk*), 88

Jewish community *see* anti-
  Semitism
Jonker, Willie, 185–6
Jooste, Marius, 174

Kangwane, creation, 66
Kappiekommando, 23, 26
Kaunda, President Kenneth, 135
Kemp, Jan, 44
Kenya
  immigrants to SA, 104

independence movement,
  56, 57
Kerkbode, Die, 18, 87
*Ko-operatiewe Wijnbouwers Veree-
  niging* (Co–operative Vint-
  ners' Society: KWV), 11
Kommandoleer, 91
Koornhof, Piet, 24, 212 n6
Kriegler, Mr Justice, 102
Kriel, Hernus, 99, 124
Kruger, Corlia, 74
Kruger, Jimmy, 26
Kruger, President Paul, 38, 42,
  166, 190
Ku Klux Klan, 96, 199
KwaNdebele, creation, 66
KwaZulu, 66, 110, 111, 126
KWV, 11

Labour Party, 13
Ladybrand by-election (1991),
  143–5
Land Acts (1913/36), 48–9, 67, 90,
  144, 182–4
Langley, Tom, 163
language
  Afrikaans, 4, 9, 13, 37, 60
  English, 105–6
  party policies, 10, 75, 76, 93
L'Assault, 96, 199
Lebanon, comparison to SA, 55
Lebowa, creation, 66
Leibbrandt, Robey, 46–7
Lesotho
  Maseru riot, 144
  SADF attacks, 121
Lightning Falcons (*Blitsvalke*), 195
Local Government Transitional
  Bill (1993), 181–2
Lottering, Cornelius, 97, 198–9
Lusaka accord (1984), 124

Magsaksie Afrikaner Nasionalisme,
  92
Maitland by-election (1991), 143
Malan, D.F., 12, 13, 14, 15, 16, 17,
  45, 139
Malan, Magnus, 99